Differences that matter

Feminist Theory and Postmodernism.

Differences That Matter challenges existing ways of theorising the relationship between feminism and postmodernism which ask 'is or should feminism be modern or postmodern?' Sara Ahmed suggests that postmodernism has been allowed to dictate feminist debates and argues instead that feminism must itself ask questions of postmodernism. In other words, feminist theorists need to speak (back) to postmodernism, rather than simply speak on (their relationship to) it. This 'speaking back' involves a refusal to position postmodernism as a generalisable condition of the world, and uses close readings of postmodern constructions of rights, ethics, 'woman', subjectivity, authorship and film. Moreover, the differences that matter are shown to concern not only the differences between feminism and postmodernism, but also the differences which define the terms themselves. How to do justice to these differences while 'speaking back' is a question central to the ethics of close reading offered in this book.

SARA AHMED is Lecturer at the Institute for Women's Studies at Lancaster University. Following her first degree at the University of Adelaide, she undertook doctoral studies at the Centre for Critical and Cultural Theory, Cardiff University before taking up her present post. She has published widely on feminist and critical theoretical themes, and is editor of the newsletter of the Women's Studies Network (UK) Association, of which she has been an executive committee member since 1996.

Differences That Matter

Feminist Theory and Postmodernism

Sara Ahmed

CAMBRIDGE UNIVERSITY PRESS
Cambridge, New York, Melbourne, Madrid, Cape Town, Singapore,
São Paulo, Delhi, Dubai, Tokyo, Mexico City

Cambridge University Press
The Edinburgh Building, Cambridge CB2 8RU, UK

Published in the United States of America by Cambridge University Press, New York

www.cambridge.org
Information on this title: www.cambridge.org/9780521597616

First published 1998

A catalogue record for this publication is available from the British Library

Library of Congress Cataloguing in Publication data
Ahmed, Sara.
Differences that matter : feminist theory and postmodernism / Sara Ahmed.
    p.   cm.
Includes bibliographical references (p.   ) and index.
ISBN 0 521 59225 9 – ISBN 0 521 59761 7 (pbk.)
1. Feminist theory.   2. Postmodernism.   I. Title.
HQ1190.A35   1998
305.42′01–dc21   98–20051   CIP

ISBN 978-0-521-59225-3 Hardback
ISBN 978-0-521-59761-6 Paperback

For my mother

Contents

Acknowledgements

I would like to thank my aunt Gulzar Bano, who was the first woman who spoke to me about feminism (although we didn't express it in those terms) and whose work, both creative and political, remains an inspiration to me.

My appreciation to my first feminist teachers at university, Rosemary Moore and Penny Boumelha, for all their help and encouragement. Thanks also to Chris Weedon for her support. I would like to acknowledge my enormous debt to all my colleagues at the Institute for Women's Studies at Lancaster University, especially Celia Lury and Beverley Skeggs. I remain very grateful that I have had the good fortune to share coffee and cakes with you all. A very big thanks to Celia Lury and Jackie Stacey for taking the time to read my work and providing me with some engaging feedback. Thanks to Catherine Max for her excellent editorial advice. And thanks to Simon Spooner for a far superior knowledge of the English language.

My appreciation to all of my family whom I have missed very much during the writing of this book, especially my mother, Maureen, my sisters, Tanya and Tamina, and my father, Saeed. Thanks to Don, Jen and Caroline for being there in the past few years.

I have met some wonderful people in Cardiff and Lancaster, with whom I have danced and drank and who have helped remind me of the importance of having a life beyond being an academic (as if I need reminding!). Cheers to you all, especially: Anna, Amanda, Anne, Clare, Fred, Jon, Julie, Imogen, Lorna, Mariam, Matt, Nicole, Sue and Simon O. And a special thanks to Simon.

Introduction: Speaking back

It is difficult to begin writing a book with a sense of anticipation that one's reader may already be feeling a sense of dread. I imagine you scowling, 'not another book on feminism and postmodernism'. And I imagine you yawning, 'hasn't enough been said?' Of course, the fantasies one has of 'the reader' or 'one's reader' are always impossible, always inadequate to their object. But, as someone interested in how feminism and postmodernism can and do speak to each other, I have a sense in which there is a critical reluctance to pursue a debate on or through these terms at all. So, one reader of my work comments, 'my heart did rather sink at the prospect of yet another book on feminism and postmodernism'. This prospect of readers with sinking hearts is, to say the least, alarming. To deal with this doubling of affect (the reader's sinking heart, the writer's alarm) I want to ask: is the difficulty simply the proliferation of books on feminism and postmodernism, or is the difficulty about how the proliferation has taken place and to what effect?

Indeed, at the first academic conference at which I presented my work in 1993 the conference organiser commented on how none of the papers on postmodernism had said anything new or different. She suggested to me that all the papers – which had offered very different positions and were shaped by diverse disciplinary frameworks – were simply re-staging an old debate. I found this judgement surprising and instructive. There was a sense of this 'thing' called 'postmodernism' that had taken over feminist debates (becoming a proper object of feminist dialogue in and of itself) such that any dialogue between feminism and postmodernism could *only* be a re-staging. Immediately then the institutional effects of speaking on postmodernism as a feminist announce themselves. In part, such an act of speaking on, about or to postmodernism is read as a sign of the exhaustion of feminist concerns. So one must ask yet another difficult question: why is there an assumption that the debate between feminism and postmodernism is already staged?

Partly, this difficulty relates to anxieties in Women's Studies about the role of theory that is perceived to be 'male'. As I discuss later, while I do

1

not go along with such a dismissal of (postmodern) theory as 'male', I do think there remains an issue of authorisation that should be a troubling one for feminists. Citing postmodernism does authorise a certain kind of space within the academy that is predicated on hierarchy and exclusion. However, the response to this relegation of space within the academy need not be withdrawal from the debate. On the contrary, I take the issue of authorisation as my impetus: how can we read post-modernism differently *as feminists* and *for feminism*? To speak on post-modernism as feminists does not necessarily involve simply affirming this relegation of academic space. To this extent, our tiredness as actors on the stage may pose trouble (do we have to read this script?), but also could become more troubling (how can we do this differently?).

The critical perception that there has been a proliferation of writing on feminism and postmodernism is linked to the assumption that the act of bringing feminism and postmodernism together can no longer shift the terrain (in other words, that the terms of the debate have taken over its critical purchase). Think, for a moment, of my sub-title, 'feminist theory and postmodernism'. I am self-conscious about how it may appear boring in its bluntness. But, boring or not, the sub-title has significance as a way of entering academic space. The sense in which this book is staging a debate is made clear by the 'and' which stands between the subjects, 'feminist theory' and 'postmodernism', forcing them apart, as it brings them together. The 'and' is not innocent. It carries with it the baggage of the 'two' that is constitutive of the debate within the academy. In other words, the 'and' introduces the debate as a question of critical *relationships* (think how it works without it – 'feminist theory postmodernism'). The gesture of bringing two terms together in this way may appear to be organised by a desire to know or even document their relationship (feminism *and* postmodernism: are they alike? are they different?). Perhaps then, the perception that the debate on feminism and postmodernism can only be a tired re-staging relates to how the debate has been structured around the question of identity or difference. It is hence symptomatic that the relation between feminism and postmodernism has been conceived as *analogous* (Hutcheon 1989: 144). Consequently, with the stress on identity or difference, the question that has framed the debate has been: 'is feminism (like) post-modern(ism)?', or 'should feminism be (like) postmodern(ism)?'

The problem with the question, 'what is the nature of their relation?', is that it assumes that the terms themselves, 'feminism' and 'post-modernism', are not in question or questionable. I would argue that the gesture of bringing the terms together must not allow them to be stabilised as assumed reference points. In order to refuse stabilising the terms as reference points, we need to deal with the institutional politics of definition and naming. What does it mean to designate a text as postmodern? What does it mean to designate a feminist text as postmodern? Such questions may remind us that these two terms, 'feminism' and 'postmodernism', are not simply stabilised by the demand to describe their relationship. That demand takes certain forms over others. It is not so much a demand to know whether postmodernism is feminist (from those who write as postmodernists), but on whether feminism is postmodern (from those who write as feminists). In other words, postmodernism is the assumed reference point in a debate that has largely taken place within feminism and, as a result, has authorised feminism's reflection on itself through either affirmation or disavowal – 'I am (like) you' or 'I am not (like) you.'

Where the debate on postmodernism has taken account of feminism it has been in terms which imply its role in authorising the relationship (see Arac 1986). For example, Craig Owens considers the 'fact' of the absence of women figuring in the postmodern debate (Owens 1985: 61). He also notes that the postmodern debate has been scandalously indifferent to the question of sexual difference (Owens 1985: 59). Despite this, Owens maintains that he will not construe the relation between postmodernism and feminism as being one of antagonism, but will negotiate a course between them (Owens 1985: 59). And indeed, he moves on to argue that the feminist insistence on difference and incommensurability is not only compatible with, but *an instance of*, postmodern thought (Owens 1985: 62). Here, the indifference of postmodernism to the question of sexual difference is noted and at once excluded from the problem of defining the relationship between feminism and postmodernism. The dialogical model of the relationship (a 'course between'), gives way to an asymmetrical power relationship whereby feminism is placed as an instance of, and hence derivative of, the postmodern. Here, feminism is defined in terms of – or in the terms of – postmodernism itself.

We need to ask the following question: under what conditions is feminism included within, and excluded from, postmodernism? Such a question echoes the work of Meaghan Morris. She asks, 'under what conditions women's work *can* "figure" currently in such a debate?' (Morris 1988: 12). Morris observes how although few feminist theorists have positioned themselves *in terms of* the postmodern debate, many of the male theorists 'cited' by postmodern bibliographies also do not position themselves in this way. Given this, she argues, male postmodernist bibliographies function as patriarchal frames (Morris 1988: 13). So while some feminists are typically cited as being influenced by postmodernism (and in this subordinate sense, as being included within it), feminist work is not given the status of originating or charting the field. Here, feminism's inclusion *as* postmodern also defines the terms of its exclusion; feminism is spoken of ('you are part of us'), but does not speak (or, more precisely, is not heard).

The importance of feminists entering the debate on postmodernism may be precisely in order to undo such gestures of authorisation whereby postmodernism comes to define the terms of feminism's existence. Rather than staging the debate by considering feminism's relationship to postmodernism in terms of identity or difference, feminism needs to ask questions of postmodernism: we need to speak (back) *to* postmodernism, rather than simply speaking *on* (our relationship to) it. Instead of assuming identity or difference as expressive of the relation between feminism and postmodernism, this book will ask the polemical question, 'which differences matter, here?' in the very event of speaking back. This agonistic role of speaking back not only opens the stage by interrupting the designation of postmodernism as a reference point, but also re-figures the vitality or animation of the feminist whose speech is no longer authorised from a single place. Your sinking heart and my alarm become not end points that signal the tired gestures of the actors on the stage we inhabit, but moments that move us to look elsewhere within the staging itself.

Questioning postmodernism

Why then assume, in the first instance, that postmodernism is questionable? Does this mean starting with the question, 'what is postmodernism?' I would argue quite the opposite: to begin to question postmodernism as a term that has a set of precise effects is *not* to ask the question, 'what is postmodernism?' Such a question assumes that postmodernism has a referent, that there is something (out there or in here) which we can adequately call postmodernism. So, for example, Scott Lash defines postmodernism as a cultural paradigm specific to, and pervasive of, contemporary society, which describes cultural change, type and stratification (Lash 1990: ix). Fredric Jameson also defines the contemporary state of crisis as constituting a condition of postmodernism, though he constructs postmodernism as a cultural dominant which cannot exhaust the meanings of the contemporary (Jameson 1986: 53). At the same time, there has been much appeal to the indeterminacy of the term 'postmodernism' and the multiplicity of its configurations. Occasionally these two insights are brought together, such that the indeterminacy of the term 'postmodernism' is read as a symptom of the indeterminacy of the thing itself: 'the very semantic deferral associated with this complex morpheme [postmodernism] is a perfect enactment of that which it is involved in signifying' (Whitehouse 1989: 2). On the one hand, postmodernism is read as indeterminate and as potentially signifying *anything* (that is, as lacking in boundaries *per se*), while on the other, it is stabilised as a reference point for the contemporary re-figuring of modernity, whether that re-figuring is traced in cultural, political, intellectual or epistemological terms (Burgin 1986: 49).

Such constructions of postmodernism as a reference point for 'the contemporary' take for granted the discursive apparatus of 'postmodernism' itself, that is, its status as a signifier. This taking-for-granted of 'postmodernism' through assuming its referentiality is connected to the opening up of its potential to signify anything (its unboundedness). Ferguson and Wicke, for example, discuss postmodernism as a name for 'the way we live now', at the same time as they consider its status as a 'porous capacious' signifier, ready 'to leap over borders and confound boundaries' (Ferguson and Wicke 1994: 1–2). The effects of this doubling are extremely problematic. The link between indeterminacy and reference mean that the referential function of postmodernism is generalised without limits. Postmodernism refers to unboundedness (or the unboundedness of contemporary sociality): it refers to its own impossibility as referent and hence comes to mean *potentially anything*.

The way in which postmodernism comes to mean potentially anything returns us to the problematic of the 'now' within Ferguson and Wicke's narrative ('the way we live *now*'). Such a concept of postmodernism as the 'now' inscribes postmodernism as in the present and so *present to itself*. Postmodernism, as the now which is outside the temporality of passing (time), here constitutes the fantasy of an arrival, a fantasy which slips from 'now' to 'here' (postmodernism as the here of the now). We might also want to consider the 'we' within Ferguson and Wicke's narrative: who is the 'we' that inhabits postmodernism ('the way *we* live now')? The fantasy of a generalisable and unbounded postmodernism translates quickly into a fantasy of an *inclusive* postmodernism: a postmodernism that speaks to and for all of us. I would argue, in contrast, that this postmodern 'we' is constituted through acts of exclusion and othering – that the apparent 'unboundedness' of the postmodern both constitutes and conceals its boundaries. We could hence ask the following question: who is the 'not-we' of postmodernism that lets this 'we' take place, or take its place?

Is there, for example, a relation between the 'we' of postmodernism and the West? In post-colonial theory, the use of 'postmodernism' as a term for all contemporary re-writings of the script of modernity has been read as a form of imperialist mapping. As Helen Tiffin suggests, the posing of analogies between post-colonial fictions and American and European 'postmodern' fictions, on the simple grounds of coincidence in non-realist narrative forms, obscures or conceals the differential political and historical context of such writing in such a manner that post-colonialism is understood only in relation to transformations in Western culture (Tiffin 1988: 171–4). Tiffin elaborates, 'the so-called "crisis" of European authority continues to reinforce European cultural and political domination, as potential relativisation of its epistemology and ontology acts through such labelling once again to make the rest of the world a peripheral term in Europe's self-questioning' (Tiffin 1988: 171).[1] The interpretation of other forms of re-writing from marginal spaces and subjects as a sign of a postmodern crisis in identity here re-incorporates the fractured histories of those others into a Western identity (where, in some sense, the West re-figures its identity through the crisis posed by the other). The West calls the other to speak, but hears the speech as a sign of a crisis that already belongs to the West. An inclusive or generalisable postmodernism – a postmodernism which knows no limits (or does not know its limits) – hence becomes a form of symbolic violence.[2]

The potential of the name 'postmodernism' to incorporate others through the language of crisis represents what is at stake in the assumption that postmodernism has no limits (whereby the loss of limits becomes a sign for 'the way we live now'). Such an unbounded postmodernism has a hegemonic function – it is a way of bringing differential and contradictory phenomena back to a single reference point or meaning. Here, every-thing, in the event of being named as postmodern, becomes just any-thing like any other-thing.[3] Posing questions to postmodernism such that it cannot speak for others means giving up the assumption that it has a direct referential relation to 'the way we live now': it means giving up the assumption that postmodernism is a generalisable condition. To avoid the hegemonic function of a generalisable postmodernism, we also need to pay attention to the instability of the term without designating that instability as a symptom of what postmodernism already is. Tracing the movements of the signifier 'postmodernism' means precisely refusing to see postmodernism as boundless.

One way in which postmodernism comes to be bound as a particular way of intervening in the world (rather than as a generalisable condition of the world) is to think of postmodernism, not as something that simply exists as such, but as something which is constructed through the very writings which assume its existence. Such an approach is taken up by Steven Connor in *Postmodernist Culture*. He argues against an analysis which questions 'what is postmodernism?' and calls instead for an analysis of what the discourse of postmodernism is doing. Connor asks, 'how and why does the discourse of postmodernism flourish?' (Connor 1989: 10). This shift enables postmodernism to be examined as a discursive space which *does something*, rather than simply meaning or expressing something.

Connor does not examine exactly what this shift may imply in terms of a specific politics of interpretation. In some sense, his text still presupposes the value of postmodernism by sliding from what it does as a discursive space to its location in the academy as a power structure which produces knowledges (Connor 1989: 10–11). By doing so, he defines the effects of postmodernism as an *expression* of the institutional power of the academy. However, thinking of postmodernism as produced within institutional limits is precisely to understand the contested nature of its knowledges and boundaries. In *Ludic Feminism and After*, a book which takes a stand against postmodernism and 'postmodern feminism', Teresa Ebert cites one of the readers of her work: 'Ebert is, I fear swimming against the tide' (Ebert 1996: xi). Here, postmodernism and 'postmodern feminism' are figured as dangerous tides (a force of nature, no less!), against which critics of postmodernism are lone, even lonely, swimmers. However, I do not think this is a useful representation of the status of postmodernism and 'postmodern feminism'. We cannot assume that postmodernism has a fixed role and identity within the institutional apparatus of the academy (as an orthodoxy or a consensus). Indeed, having experienced the effects of postmodernism in very different academic departments (in one case, it was excluded as a danger to reading, in another it was taken as a sign of reading), I can immediately see that its institutional status is always contested. Postmodernism then does not constitute *an* institution or *a* discourse, but is constituted through both institutional and discursive limits.

Postmodernism may be constructed and stabilised by particular texts that cite themselves as being either postmodern or about postmodernism. However, it also exceeds any such inscriptions. It brings into play broader inter-textual practices involving, for example, ways of reading, ways of constructing bibliographies on postmodernism, and ways of teaching on postmodernism. This means that texts that do not explicitly cite themselves as postmodern will be read and taught as part of a postmodern critical tradition (the work of Jacques Derrida comes to mind). Postmodernism *does* something as a textual formation whose meaning is yet to be decided, but which remains determined by its very citation in an inter-textual field of reference. Reading postmodernism as an inter-textual space for the negotiation of meanings and values will enable us to trace how postmodernism is stabilised in the specificity of its inscriptions (in theoretical and cultural texts), and yet is open to renewal, transformation and *dis-placement* in the gap between those inscriptions, the name of postmodernism, and the inter-textual horizon within which that name circulates.

The question, 'what is postmodernism doing?', might lead us to another question, 'where is postmodernism?' At one level, this question seems to assume that postmodernism has a location that is stable and fixed (postmodernism is here or there). However, this question may invite us to consider how postmodernism is produced in differential and potentially antagonistic sites both within and beyond the academy. The question, 'where is postmodernism?', requires a more direct confrontation with the issue of disciplinarity. To some extent, postmodernism is more easily reduced to an object or referent when the boundaries of disciplines are taken for granted – so, for example, if we restrict our readings of postmodernism within a given discipline (literature, sociology, philosophy, law etc.), then postmodernism is more clearly locatable in a set of questions, texts and authors (= a canonical postmodernism) which can then come to stand for, or stand in for, what postmodernism actually is. However, by thinking more reflexively about how postmodernism is produced within disciplinary formations, we can then work across disciplines, to consider the multiple sites of its production and dissemination.

This book takes the risk of moving across such disciplinary boundaries, not as a way of refusing a canonical postmodernism (such a refusal would be impossible), but as a way of understanding the limits of its production. The risk, of course, in reading texts from different disciplinary formations as examples of postmodernism, is that we might assume we are reading 'the same thing'. However, it is also important that we do not reify disciplines: the citing of postmodernism across disciplines might not involve 'the same thing', but those citations have an intimate relationality or connection. In *Differences That Matter*, I will read texts that have come to be read, taught and known as postmodern, closely and critically, without then attempting to produce a theory of postmodernism as simply, 'the same thing'. Rather, the book will raise the question of how the writings of postmodernism might relate to each other in terms of the constitution of their objects, rather than assuming that such connections are determined by the singularity of the name, 'postmodernism'.

Reading postmodernism

A concern with what postmodernism is doing requires a commitment to *close reading*. Close readings may serve to demonstrate how postmodern texts establish their own limits and boundaries, as well as how this process of de-limitation does not (and cannot) fix postmodernism into an object. Close readings may suspend general judgement on postmodernism *per se* (as part of an ethical and political commitment not to read postmodernism as generalisable in the first place). However, the possibility of judgement is not negated by closer reading: indeed, getting closer to the text also involves a form of distanciation (without which closeness would constitute the violence of merger). Moving from proximity to distance, a closer reading of postmodern texts makes judgements through engagement. This approach to closer readings is hence bound up with ethics, with the meta-discursive question of what makes some readings more just than others.

To exemplify such a practice of closer reading we can consider Jean-François Lyotard's *The Postmodern Condition*. This text has come to have the status of one of the primary articulations of postmodern theory. Such an authority takes the form of the *authorisation of definitions*: Lyotard's text is often cited for the purposes of defining the postmodern. Indeed, the repetition of catchphrases lifted from *The Postmodern Condition*, 'postmodernism is a crisis of legitimation', or 'postmodernism *is* the end of meta narratives', is readily apparent in recent discourses on postmodernism. Given this process of dissemination which quite clearly has moved through and beyond the actual text in question, the name 'Lyotard' has become a part of the cultural, political and economic dynamic called 'postmodernism' that his text originated to report on, or describe, at the request of the Conseil des Universités of the government of Quebec. The circulation of phrases from Lyotard's text has become, in itself, an event within the world of politics, to which we might suppose that the text, in its 'reflection' on this world, maintains a relation of exteriority. The absence of such a position of exteriority in the descriptions offered by Lyotard can be seen as symptomatic of the problem of defining the postmodern itself, the ways in which such definitions have a purchase and authority which are productive rather than merely descriptive.

Given the material effects that the circulation of *The Postmodern Condition* has produced through its authorisation of a certain concept or definition of the postmodern that has disseminated throughout public discourses and bodies of knowledge, then it can be read, not merely as a position on, but an instance of, the so-called postmodern. As such, a close and rigorous reading of the text may help us to engage the discursive space of postmodernism as *doing* something rather than merely expressing something. So how do the definitions offered by the text construct their own object? In *The Postmodern Condition* the term *modern* is used, 'to designate any science that legitimates itself with reference to a meta-discourse of this kind making an explicit appeal to some grand narrative, such as the dialectics of Spirit, the hermeneutics of meaning, the emancipation of the rational or working subject, or the creation of wealth' (Lyotard 1989: xxiii). The term *postmodern* is used to designate an incredulity towards meta-narratives which is simultaneously a product of, and presupposed by, progress in the sciences (Lyotard 1989: xxiv). Here, 'the narrative function is losing its functors, its great hero, its great dangers, its great voyages, its great goal. It is being dispersed in clouds of narrative language elements' (Lyotard 1989: xxiv). *The Postmodern Condition* can be read as constructing the relation between modern and postmodern in terms of the contrast between a belief in structure, totality and identity, and a belief in difference, dispersal and heterogeneity. Although the text is describing shifts in knowledge which we may define *as* postmodern, those shifts are actually organised into particular forms by the text itself. Hence, we could think of postmodernism as involving particular ways of constructing the values of difference, dispersal and heterogeneity (through or against a reading of modernity), rather than seeing postmodernism as expressive of those concepts or values *per se*.

So while we can think of *The Postmodern Condition* as a commissioned report on knowledge, we can also think of it as a text which employs *its own methods*. One method of analysis which is employed by Lyotard is his use of narrative pragmatics. Early on in *The Postmodern Condition*, Lyotard defines narrative pragmatics by an event of exclusion: that is, he distinguishes a pragmatic analysis of the narrative function from one which focuses on extrinsic details such as the institutional assignment of subject positions (Lyotard 1989: 20). His analysis of the narratives of the Cashinahua people suggests that the pragmatics of those narratives are 'intrinsic'. Details such as the assignment of the role of the narrator 'to certain categories on the basis of age, sex, or family or professional group' are hence excluded from his model of the pragmatics of the transmission of narratives (Lyotard 1989: 20).

However, this passage on the pragmatics of the transmission of the Cashinahua's narratives complicates the distinction that Lyotard explicitly makes. Lyotard links the authority of the narrator or storyteller to the prior post of being a listener: 'the narrator's *only* claim to competence for telling the story is the fact that he has heard it himself. The current narratee gains potential access to the same story *simply* by listening' (Lyotard 1989: 20, emphasis mine). Lyotard comes to this position by focusing on the naming function of the narrative. The story is introduced with the name of its hero, and ends with the name of the narrator. This identifies the hero with the narrator and implies a possible interchange: 'in fact, he is necessarily such a hero because he bears a name, declined at the end of his narration, and that name was given to him in conformity with the canonic narrative legitimating the assignment of patronym among the Cashinahua' (Lyotard 1989: 21).

But while the naming process is intrinsic to the narrative and organises the positions of the subjects of the narrative, this passage opens up points of excess and contextualisation. The assignment of the patronym (naming from the father) brings into play the narrative's constitution within a broader social structure organised around the authority of the father. In this sense, the positions of the narrator and the hero are not fluid, open or determined 'simply' by the pragmatics of the narrative's transmission, but are over-determined by the social divisions of power which assign the proper name (as transcendental signifier) to the male. This closure or delimitation simultaneously takes place in narrative (the assignment of the patronymic name) and beyond narrative (in the gendering of subject positions within institutions). The transmission of the narrative takes place then within a social context which *becomes* intrinsic to its effect. This blurs the distinction between the intrinsic and extrinsic which Lyotard uses to exclude an analysis of social structures (age, sex, family, professional group). Such contradictions enable us to expose the text's reliance on a separation of linguistic exchange from broader structures of social differentiation in his model of narrative pragmatics. The authority of the storyteller becomes inseparable from (even if it remains irreducible to) the authority of the father and the passing of the father's name.

This autonomisation of the narrative function from the social organisation of power has quite clear ideological implications. It neutralises the political effects of discourse and implies the fluidity of narrative in the form of the *interchangeability* of positions of discursive authority. It conceals then the over-determination of posts in language games by prior and relatively stable social assignments such as represented by the groups the text itself differentiates: age, sex, family, professional group. The pragmatics of a narrative's transmission are therefore inseparable from the divisions of power that give certain subjects or social groups the authority to speak. Such authority cannot be seen as intrinsic to narratives, but as *complicating the very separation of (pragmatic) narratives from institutions.*

The method of analysis employed by *The Postmodern Condition* hence involves the construction of the values of difference and fluidity (narrative pragmatics) against structure and regulation (institutions). What is clear through my reading of Lyotard's postmodernism as having a method, is that such texts invest postmodernism with particular meanings and values in the event of describing it. So while certain concepts and values are normally taken as reference points for postmodernism (postmodernism *is* difference, fluidity, indeterminacy), we can now read them as in construction, as being organised into particular narratives and methods. It is not the case that any emphasis on difference or heterogeneity can simply be named as an instance of a generalisable postmodernism. Rather, postmodernism involves particular ways of organising or ordering such concepts and values in the process of constructing itself as an object.

These ways of ordering values such as difference have precise political effects – they are not innocent or neutral. The assumption of difference and heterogeneity masks the role of structures of authorisation in which postmodernism is itself (ironically) implicated. However, the identification of postmodernism and concepts and values such as 'difference' is unstable, precisely because 'difference' does not exist as a pure, undifferentiated category. Lyotard's method which defines and values difference against structure and totality hence breaks down. This breaking down is the site of critical potential: for example, it can help us shift our understanding of the relation between narrative pragmatics and institutions. Indeed, if the oppositions that are constructed by the text to secure the narrative on postmodernism break down, then this suggests that the object of postmodernism (or postmodernism *as* object) is not fixed by the text. That is, the undoing of the fixed terms of the constructions implicit in the methodology (narrative pragmatics/difference – institutions/totality), is an undoing of the very designation of 'postmodernism' itself as a pure category which can be distinguished from its other, the modern. In this sense, while postmodernism constructs itself as an object, that object remains an impossible one.

And feminism

I have suggested that questioning postmodernism involves challenging both its assumed referentiality and indeterminacy. Such a questioning of postmodernism means an ethics of closer reading: my approach involves getting closer to postmodernism in order to trace the particularity of its inscriptions. I have argued against reading postmodernism as a generalisable and inclusive condition, demonstrating the violence against others which is at stake in such a reading. Giving up postmodernism's generalisability means precisely resisting the process whereby it comes to speak for (or as) others in the event of naming the place they inhabit. What implications does my approach to questioning through closer reading have for feminism?

The problem with positioning feminism inside or outside of postmodernism has already been considered in terms of how postmodernism has constructed and authorised the relationship. Here, feminism's inclusion within postmodernism, perhaps as a symptom of the crisis of identity already posed by postmodernism, also defines the terms of an exclusion, where feminist voices are not heard. However, the issue is internal to feminism and has been a conflict within feminism, and not just between feminism and postmodernism. Feminists have also positioned feminism within a generalised postmodernism. For example, Susan Hekman argued that both feminism and postmodernism challenge the 'anthropocentric' definition of knowledge, although feminism is still *historically* and *theoretically* a modernist movement, relying on the discourse of emancipation (Hekman 1990: 2). She argues that feminism 'has much to gain' by an alliance with postmodernism against modernism given the centrality within feminism of the attack on (gendered) dichotomies. Hekman's project is to construct an argument for a postmodern approach *to* feminism, chronicling the similarities between the two, and showing how postmodernism can help solve the question of 'the woman's nature', and showing how feminism can contribute to postmodernism by adding the (lacking) dimension of gender (Hekman 1990: 3).

Hekman's approach implies that feminism needs postmodernism in order to be able to deal with the epistemological issue of 'woman's nature' – a position which perhaps can be understood in relation to her conception of feminist theory as being 'rooted' in modernism (Hekman 1990: 152). Hekman hence does not consider the complex, multi-faceted history of feminist epistemology which has dealt with the issue of woman's nature through a critical reading of modernity, in particular, of the Cartesian subject and its founding dichotomy mind (reason)/body (see chapter 4). One could also mention the feminist critique of the discourses of abstract rights and individualism, which serves to further reinforce that the relation between feminism and modernity has always been, at the very least, one of critical ambivalence. In this way, Hekman's call for feminism to become postmodern forecloses feminism's own internal and critical relation to the modern at the level of practice as well as theory (see chapter 1). The act of naming feminism as postmodern refers feminism back to postmodernism in such a way that the complexity of feminism's histories is already over-looked.

Furthermore, Hekman's suggestion that feminism can add to post-modernism the dimension of gender is problematic. Does post-modernism lack gender – or such an agenda? While postmodernism might lack substantive reference to gender, this does not mean that it lacks gender. One of the most powerful feminist critiques of modern philosophical discourse is precisely the critique of the possibility of such neutrality. Indeed, the way in which particular theories are structured by an apparent gender neutrality is well documented by feminist theorists, outside the issue of postmodernism. In, 'Feminism, Philosophy and Riddles Without Answers', Moira Gatens argues that sexism in philo-sophy is not incidental, or accidental, but *structural* (Gatens 1991: 187). As such, philosophy is *not* a neutral framework which is *then* filled with sexism, and which can be retained in its entirety while correcting any sexist bias (Gatens 1991: 186). The history of feminist philosophy has entailed an analysis of the way in which the seeming sex-neutrality of philosophical discourse entails the function or dynamic of a masculine power, and has articulated the possibility of women being visible in philosophy precisely through a critique of the notion of neutrality (Gatens 1991: 193).

It follows, then, that a feminist questioning of postmodernism which undoes its role as authorising feminist discourse must begin by under-mining the assumption that it lacks gender. In other words, a closer reading of particular inscriptions of postmodernism must involve an examination of how it operates *as a gendered modality of enunciation*. A lack of explicit reference to gender must be understood then as *structural* rather than incidental (as, in itself, a form of gendering). However, such a way of reading postmodernism is not exhaustive: to read post-modernism as gendered is not to read it as *having* a gender (post-modernism is male), but to look at the gendered effects of its particular inscriptions. To read postmodernism as gendered is not the only point of entry for an examination of its particular effects. The meaning and effects of that gendering are unstable and contingent on other forms of inscription.

So, for example, my analysis of *The Postmodern Condition* suggested that postmodernism was constructed by the text as a particular method for destabilising the modern. The text does not deal with the question of gender. I would argue that the very nature of the methodology used by *The Postmodern Condition* makes such an absence structural rather than incidental to the text. My reading shows that the productive effects of this narrative of the postmodern exceed the discreteness of this very term, embedding it within a complex scheme of value differentiation. This scheme relies on a set of problematic hierarchies between difference and structure, as well as local and general, which are implicit in the opposition set up between narrative pragmatics and institutions. Given this, it is symptomatic that 'gender' is an absent term in *The Postmodern Condition*. To introduce gender, as a positive term of analysis, into this narrative of the postmodern, would be to engage in a major shift of its terms. A feminist reading of the text may stress that its seeming gender neutrality is a mark of the privilege of the masculine, with its emphasis on the atomisation of the social, the mobility of the subject, and the determination of knowledge purely through the transformation of local boundaries.

What follows from such a critique of postmodernism as gendered rather than neutral is an understanding of feminism's role in the debate as *transformative*. Adding gender to the explicit terms of postmodernism (precisely by reading its gendering in specific formations), means transforming it: it means destabilising the terms of reference whereby it constitutes itself as an object. The transformative potential of feminism – its inability to simply inhabit other discourses which marginalise questions of gender – signals the potential of the debate to move us elsewhere, beyond the stage where there are simply two subjects in place. Speaking of the difference of feminism, as a difference that matters, undoes the critical trajectory whereby feminism either mirrors or distorts the face of postmodernism itself.

Speaking in this way of the critical difference of feminism is not to essentialise feminism, or to turn feminism into a discrete subject. An analysis of the difference *of* feminism does not suspend an understanding of the difference *in* feminism. Writing as a feminist does not necessarily assume that the meaning of feminism is fixed in time and space. This identification has effects that are discernible – but it does not stabilise feminism into a discrete subject position. In this book, speaking to postmodernism as a feminist works to destabilise both terms, pointing to the differences that matter which are located within (and not just between) the terms.

Part of the critical difference of feminism is its foregrounding of the social relation of gender. But 'gender' itself cannot be situated as a proper object which guarantees the feminist trajectory. Much of my concern in this book is precisely with how gender can only be understood in relation to other formations of power. Thinking of gender as an articulated rather than isolated category means giving up the assumption that feminism itself is inclusive, or simply speaks on behalf of all women. Sexual difference cannot be ontologised as *the* difference that matters: sexual difference exists in a complex set of inter-connections with other differences. This book's refusal to stabilise feminism and postmodernism as the proper subjects of a critical debate will also open the question of an-other subject, that of the post-colonial. Here, the question of the post-colonial may suggest that there are other women whose faces are not reflected in the mirror of Western feminism, who might speak back again; indeed, who might speak back to those who have already spoken back. If feminism refuses to remain authorised and hence fixed by its designation as postmodern, then feminism itself becomes subject to reiteration beyond the terms of any such debate. Feminism itself becomes open to destabilisation precisely by not being fixed as either (belonging to) modern or postmodern.

And theory

Of course, there is another term. So far, I have drawn your attention to three that have slid across my pages: 'feminist', 'and', 'postmodernism'. The fourth term in my sub-title, so far missing from my analysis, is 'theory'. How does this term impact on my project?

My use of the term, feminist theory, is quite strategic. The object of the book is not 'theory' *per se* and much of the book concerns itself with feminism in practice. The reason 'theory' is explicitly named by the title is precisely to undo the assumption that the debate between feminism and postmodernism is a debate about which 'theory' feminism needs to advance its political practice. I want to argue against the view that feminism is a practice that lacks theory and henceforth requires author-isation by theories themselves (such as Marxism, liberalism or post-modernism). Such a construction refuses to recognise that feminism has always posed theoretical and critical challenges *in its very practicable demands* (Ahmed 1995; Ahmed 1996a).

It is certainly the case that feminist theory does not often get recognised as 'theory'. In one department I've worked in, research is organised into various categories, including race and ethnicity, gender and 'theory'. There were no feminists included in the 'theory' category. Such an implicit construction of 'theory' often gets conflated with those working with post-structuralism or postmodernism (though if they are working with these and feminism then they get put in the 'gender' category!). I think we must be very careful not to repeat the mechanisms of exclusion that dominate the reproduction of 'theory' in academic life. In the context of ethnography, for example, Margery Wolf comments, 'one can find feminist social scientists who are indignant and at the same time wryly amused to hear the critiques they have levelled for years now being translated into postmodernist terminology and taken *very* ser- iously' (Wolf 1992: 6–7). As Wolf suggests, feminism is often not read as theory, and the *translation* of feminism into postmodernism may define the terms of both feminism's entry into, and disappearance from, theoretical dialogues.

Partly, my ethics of closer reading is a way of questioning the status of canonical texts – the texts that come to be named as, '(high) theory'. We need to read such theories precisely *as* texts, if we are to question rather than assume their 'status' as (high) theory. The separation of 'theory' from other kinds of writing can often involve a linear and progressive narrative (perhaps from Saussure to Derrida via Lacan and Foucault), which is organised around proper names. Such a use of proper names functions to establish and police a boundary between what is (proper) theory and what is not. In my experiences on 'theory' courses, the first demand is that one must 'know the master': in other words, 'doing theory' becomes a process of gaining knowledge *about* certain canonical texts, rather than opening out the possibility of different interpretations of those texts.

The possibility of other interpretations is predicated on a re-thinking of the purpose of reading. For me, the purpose of reading is to be critical and to question. It is my belief that a reading which works against, rather than through, a text's own construction of itself (how the text 'asks to be read') can actually 'do' more. The disobedient reader is not in this sense a failed reader who is asking questions that the text itself has rendered obsolete. Rather it is a reader who interrupts the text with questions that demand a re-thinking of how it works, of how and why it works as it does, for whom. Being critical (which can involve very simple tactics of hesitating, pausing etc.) does not necessarily involve a depen- dence on the assumption that there is a 'meaning' or 'truth' which can be uncovered. Being critical is precisely being open to the (structuring) effects of the text in such a way that those effects become questionable rather than simply traced in the event of reading. Close and critical readings of theoretical texts make clear how theory itself is a form of praxis: theory involves a way of ordering the world which has material effects, in the sense that it both constitutes and intervenes in that world.

Critical readings need to pay attention to the authorisation of certain theoretical texts within the academy. Considering the institutional production of theory moves from the question of 'who is the author?', to 'who authorises theories?' As it has already been suggested, the theore- tical dialogue between feminism and postmodernism has been authorised by 'postmodernism': it is when feminism is read in terms of postmodernism that it becomes named as 'theory'. If we think of this book as staging a theoretical dialogue between at least two subjects ('feminism' and 'postmodernism') then we need to address not the question, 'who spoke first?', but the question, 'whose speech is authorised as proper speech, that is, as originating the terms?' Dialogue is not simply about 'who speaks', but about whose speech *gets heard as authorising the dialogue* or, in this context, whose speech gets heard and authorised as 'theory'. This book seeks to undo the gesture whereby postmodernism is authorised as the 'theory' which can 'help' feminism resolve its practical dilemmas – an authorisation which necessarily involves *not hearing* the voices of many feminist scholars. Clearly then, a critical reading of authorised theoretical texts is in itself a political act which may transform ways of knowing within the academy.

Given this, a feminist response to the relation between theory and authorisation need not be a suspicion of theory as such, but rather a sustained reflection of the institutional politics of 'doing theory', and a sensitive articulation of the complexities of the relation between theory and practice. I would argue that the question we need to ask is not, 'should feminism use theory?', as feminism (as with any other political discourse) always does use theory: it is always going to involve ways of ordering the world. For me, the question is rather: 'is this theoretical framework explicit or not?' Feminism needs to make explicit its theoretical frameworks and it needs to do so precisely in order to re-conceptualise the relation between theory and practice. That is, feminism needs to debate which are the *better* ways of understanding how gender relations operate, and how those relations can be challenged most effectively. Explicit theorising is precisely about thinking through the necessity and possibility of social change. It is about justifying the decisions we make, the language we use, how we read, how we speak to each other, and the very forms of our political organisation. I 'do theory', not because I lack any immediate concern for 'the political', but because my concern for the political forces me to question the knowledges and formations of feminism itself – to question rather than assume what the identification 'feminist' will mobilise at all levels of political struggle. Theory does not suspend political conviction – it makes sense of it.

This book will not only read postmodernism as a feminist in order to make explicit the impact of feminist theorising, it will also constitute a statement about the necessity of feminist epistemology. I do not mean by this that feminism can be defined as a set of knowledges. On the contrary, it is because there is no essential meaning to the word 'feminism' (the instability of the term is precisely its potential to move 'us' to different places) and because there is no direct, unmediated relationship

between 'women's experiences' and feminist knowledges, that we need
to think through the question of epistemology. We need to think through
the question of how we may come to make knowledge statements as
feminists and we need to develop criteria (which will never be fully
agreed upon, or which could never be taken for granted) for establishing
what might be a 'better account' (we cannot assume that we'll know the
difference). Interestingly, Jane Flax in 'The End of Innocence' dismisses
the whole notion of a feminist epistemology and the assumption that
feminism requires a theory of justification. She implies that feminist
justificatory strategies (loosely defined as strategies which validate the
conclusions of feminist research), could only work as a form of violence
which would either imagine neutrality or try to persuade people into a
consensus. She also suggests that such justificatory strategies would not
work because 'it is simply not necessarily the case (especially in politics)
that appeals to truth move people to action, much less to justice' (Flax
1992: 458).

Flax mis-defines the need for justification with the need for an
absolute and regulative concept of truth. As Nancy Fraser has argued,
the need for justification exists precisely because truth no longer exists
as an automatic ground or reference point for any position (Fraser 1989:
181). The notion that feminism can do without epistemology overlooks
the importance of theoretical interrogations of all categories of thought
for the very formulation of feminist strategy. Such a notion overlooks
the importance of strategies of argumentation to support, not simply
truth positions (but inclusive of them, in their radical contingency), but
the very values implicit in a feminist model of justice. It is because
values and truth statements do not strictly correspond to any pre-given
real, that we need to find justification for our positions on the basis of
how they may explain and contest gender divisions. The 'we' through
which I signal the force of a feminist community of knowers and actors
does not suspend difference, division and conflict. If anything, the 'we'
is a performative utterance that *creates* a community through an articulation of the differences which necessitate the critical debate in the first
place.

Differences that matter

Close reading provides the methodological framework for this book.
Each chapter provides close and critical readings of texts that have been
read as expressive of postmodernism in different disciplinary contexts.
What binds the chapters together is not then an object in any proper
sense, but the way in which each chapter stages a reading of a particular

set of texts in order to make a judgement on how those texts constitute their objects. The judgements that are made will not become solidified into an absolute pronouncement of 'what's wrong with postmodernism', though neither will they be left as discrete positions or end points. Rather, they will be re-worked as sites of critical potential for feminism: by locating problems, say, in how postmodern texts have dealt with the question of ethics, I will then provide an alternative way of dealing with such a question. Throughout, I will move from a particular judgement to a more general reflection on the differences that might matter for feminism. The close readings of particular postmodern texts hence enable me to delineate a trans/formative feminist position.

However, as I have already suggested, there is a danger and a risk in tracing 'postmodernism' across such diverse contexts of signification or disciplines. That danger may lie precisely in the assumption that we *can* talk about postmodernism across different levels of signification (the levels which disciplines may constitute as 'their objects'), such as the experiential, the metaphysical, the political, the cultural, the social and the psychic. I would argue that such a 'crossing over' is not only the danger of this book, but also the condition of its possibility. We must be careful not to reify these levels, to assume that they have an existence which is, so to speak, independent. The relation between these levels of signification is undecidable, but determined. For example, if we take 'the body', we need to refuse any assumption of the body as a material given that operates at one level, in order to understand 'the body' as *a trace of the collision between different levels*: this body feels, it is mine (psychic), this body is read and interpreted (textual), this body is touched by others (social), this body is written as 'the body' (theoretical/philosophical), and so on. The writing of postmodernism inevitably crosses over boundaries – both disciplinary and otherwise – as those boundaries are themselves already unstable.

Although reading postmodernism across different contexts of signification is not only possible but necessary, there still remains a dangerous implication that I am using postmodernism as a thread that unravels through these contexts. However, each reading I offer of a 'postmodern text' will trace that text in its particularity, getting closer to it, before the danger and risk of a more general judgement is taken. I will hence *not* read each text symptomatically – as if there was a general post-modernism that contaminates each text. Despite this, I hope that *Differences That Matter* will still be read as a risky and dangerous book – a book that dares to make judgements despite – or even because of – the differences that already inflect the/its terms. As already suggested, each chapter will not simply end there – with different judgements about different postmodern texts. Rather, the chapters will move from the readings of differences that matter, towards re-thinking how feminism may deal with each set of questions. In other words, the close readings of postmodern texts will be transformative readings: a feminist 'speaking back' to postmodernism which will move from proximity to distance.

This book begins, not simply by entering the postmodern debate as a feminist, but by considering how feminism itself has been read as being split between a modern impulse at the level of practice and a post-modern impulse at the level of theory. In order to challenge this model of feminism, chapter 1 examines how feminism destabilises modern conceptions of abstract human rights at the level of practice in its differential utterances of 'women's rights'. Such a destabilisation has theoretical implications that can be clearly differentiated from post-modern critiques of the concepts of 'rights'. My concern here with the dialectics of theory and practice is intended to displace the model of feminism which sees its origin in modernity and its future in post-modernity. I interrupt this discourse of 'belonging' in which feminism is assumed to have a proper object and trajectory which begins and ends outside itself.

Having begun with the forms of feminist practice, the book then turns its attention more directly to postmodernism. Chapter 2 examines how postmodernism becomes written as an ethics of otherness and differ-ence, looking in particular at the work of Jean-François Lyotard and Emmanuel Levinas. My reading questions the very possibility of cele-brating otherness and difference in abstraction from the constitution of both in embedded and structured settings. The feminist ethics posited, in contrast, refuses the gesture of celebrating 'the other' as an impossible figure, but begins with the necessity of re-dressing the relations of violence which bind a particular other to a given place. In chapter 3, I discuss how postmodernism comes to be figured as 'woman' given its apparent alignment with difference and otherness. I provide close read-ings of Jacques Derrida's *Spurs: Nietzsche's Styles* and Gilles Deleuze and Félix Guattari's *A Thousand Plateaus*, examining how 'woman' is emptied out as a signifier in order precisely to be filled by a re-constructed 'postmodern' masculine subject. This chapter poses the question of how feminism can theorise the instability of 'woman' as a signifier without losing sight of the over-determined relation between 'woman' and women as historically constituted and embodied subjects.

In chapters 4 and 5, I discuss how postmodernism becomes con-structed as the 'death of the subject' and 'the death of the author', looking closely at the work of Jean Baudrillard, Arthur Kroker, Roland Barthes and Michel Foucault. In chapter 4, I suggest that the postmodern narrative of the subject's death collapses a theory of textuality into a theory of indetermination. I examine how a feminist theory of the subject as constituted through identificatory practices may be developed through a critical engagement with both psychoanalysis and postmodern narratives of the subject. In chapter 5, I consider how the postmodern narrativisation of the author's death can close the text to the difficult questions raised by the gendering of the authorial signature. I discuss what it might mean to pose the difference of women's writing without assuming the authorial signature as an ontological given. The final section of the chapter qualifies my claims about the difference of women's writing by discussing the relation between authorised writing and auto/ethno/graphies of empire.

In the final two chapters of the book, I consider how postmodernism becomes read or seen as a particular kind of literary text or film. I ask: what is at stake in the designating of such texts as postmodern? In both chapters, I examine how postmodernism involves ways of reading and seeing that construct the text in the event of describing it. In chapter 6, I examine the meta-fictional narratives of Robert Coover and how these narratives have determinate and gendered effects despite (or even because of) the use of self-reflexivity. In chapter 7, I discuss the films of David Lynch and Peter Greenaway, examining how the 'implosion of the image' relates to the figuring of 'the woman'. In both chapters, I examine how the naming of such texts as postmodern involves the elision of issues of violence (the texts, in the event of being read or seen as postmodern, are often assumed to have over-come the problems of violence in their very over-coming of representation). The difference of a feminist interpretation may be precisely the refusal of such a fantasy of over-coming, which enables violence to be fetishised as the play of narrative against itself.

Thinking through the relation between postmodernism and feminist theory is here thinking through differences that matter. The question, 'which differences matter here?', is one that animates my readings of particular postmodern texts. However, a concern with differences that matter is not just a concern with differences between feminism and postmodernism. There are differences that matter that already inflect both terms. How to do justice to *these* differences in the very event of 'speaking back' to postmodernism as a feminist is a question that will be central to the ethics of reading offered in this book.

1   Rights

In what space does feminism belong? It is this kind of question concerning belonging – concerning the proper space of feminism – that has led to a representation of feminism as straddled between the contradictory demands of practice and theory. On the one hand, feminism has been identified as inherently modern – as a politics committed to emancipation, agency and rights. But on the other hand, feminism has been seen to be pulled towards the postmodern, to the very critique of the onto-theological nature of such beliefs. Here feminism, as a set of theoretical perspectives, has increasingly been identified as postmodern or, as discussed in the introduction, as derivative of postmodernism. This division between modern and postmodern elements in feminism is hence mapped on to a division between practice and theory. Regina Gagnier, for example, argues that feminism cannot undermine its basis in a realist epistemology nor its normative ground in humanism, given that it presupposes that the oppression of women exists and that its project is to make the world better for women (Gagnier 1990: 24). But, at the same time, she argues that feminism is pushed towards a postmodern ethics and politics via its very emphasis on the culturally over-determined constitution of the gendered subject (Gagnier 1990: 24). Likewise, Jean Grimshaw argues that feminism needs:

to engage with those theories which deconstruct the distinction between the 'individual' and the 'social', which recognise the power of desire and fantasy and the problems of supposing any 'original' unity in the self, while at the same time preserving its concern with lived experience and the practical and material struggles of women to achieve more autonomy and control over their lives. (Grimshaw 1988: 105)

Here, feminism's need to engage with 'deconstructive theories' is asserted. However, the use of the phrase, 'at the same time', also suggests that such an engagement must take place in the context of a concern with lived experience and practical struggle – a 'taking place' which is hence constituted as a potential limit to the engagement. These two elements of feminism – the deconstructive or postmodern and the realist or modern – are hence separated as the differential realms of theoretical engagement and practical struggle.

But is there such an inherent contradiction between the demands of feminist practice (as struggle) and feminist theory (as engagement)? Does this, as Susan Hekman would argue, represent a split between a modern origin and a postmodern future (Hekman 1990: 2–3)? In the first instance, one must question rather than assume such a contradiction between the demands of practice and theory. Understanding feminism in terms of an inherent disjunction between practice and theory is problematic on two counts. Firstly, it undermines the importance of theory to the formulation of political and strategic decisions. Secondly, it implies that theoretical engagement is uninformed by the problems and contingencies of practical politics. Rather than assuming such a disjunction, we can consider how the very demands made by feminism in practice have, in themselves, theoretical implications. Otherwise, as I discussed in my introduction, there is a danger in assuming that feminism is a practice that lacks theory, and hence that feminism requires authorisation through theories that are assumed to originate outside of feminism itself.

In this chapter, I will challenge such a representation of a necessary disjunction between feminist practice and theory, and with it, between modern and postmodern elements of feminism, by considering the issue of rights. Rights can certainly be understood as a centre-piece of modernity, with the initial French civil code, the Declaration of the Rights of Man, representing the first attempt at a modern constitution based directly on the sovereignty of the people (Carty 1990: 1). Does feminism's use of rights discourse mean that feminist practice inhabits the modern in contradistinction to recent shifts in feminist theorising? Is feminism inevitably modern given the use of rights discourse? Does the questioning of rights in some feminist theorising mean that feminism has shifted from the modern to the postmodern? In attempting to deal with these difficult questions, I will raise the possibility that the feminist challenge to the modern discourse of rights may spring, not from feminism's theoretical engagement with postmodernism, but from the way in which feminism uses rights discourse in practice. The question then becomes, not whether feminism uses rights *per se*, but how feminism uses rights discourse in such a way that those rights become subject to a critical displacement.

Dealing with the politics of rights discourse must, in the first place, deal with the question of 'the law' and of modern jurisprudence, through which rights are both instituted as givens and enforced as obligations. My analysis will hence raise a number of issues. Firstly, I will examine the relationship between law and embodiment. Such an examination will proceed through a close reading of how postmodern jurisprudence constructs the law in relation to bodies. While Douzinas and Warrington place postmodernism alongside feminist and Black critiques as giving 'a voice to the echoes of what has been almost silenced down the long corridors of the time of law' (Douzinas and Warrington 1991: xii), my reading will focus on the way in which postmodernism frames a critique of 'the body of the law' that does not deal with the structural relation between law and particular bodies. Secondly, I will examine the relation between legal citation and rights. While pointing out how deconstruction importantly enables a critique of foundationalism through an emphasis on citationality, I will also problematise this approach by looking at the pragmatic relationship between citationality and embodiment posed by feminist critiques of rights discourse. I examine how feminism has an ambivalent and critical relation to the discourse of abstract rights at the level of practice, addressing three examples which embrace a diversity of both political and legal contexts: the use of rights discourse in the UN conference for women in Beijing (1995); models of reproductive rights in the abortion debate; and, within Britain, feminist responses to the Child Support Act (1991). This chapter considers then, not only how feminism at the level of practice may challenge the modern definition of rights, but also how such a critical feminism resists incorporation into the postmodern due to the pragmatic concern with how law and rights differentiate bodies in historically specific contexts. So while I will question the model of feminism which sees it as 'rooted' in modernity given its use of discourses such as rights (Jardine 1993: 434), I will not then seek to place feminism within a generalised postmodernity.

Law and embodiment

How does postmodern legal theory involve a shift in an understanding of law? Such a term – postmodern legal theory – assumes that post-modernism has produced a coherent body of knowledge within legal theory and hence takes the term 'postmodernism' itself as being unproblematic. Such a taking for granted of the term 'postmodernism' is clearly evident in the context of legal theory, where postmodernism has largely been constructed through the language of application. That is, postmodernism *in* law has been defined as the application of post-modern theory *to* a reading of law. This language of application assumes the stability of postmodernism in the first place. However, such a stability is produced through the application and does not pre-exist it.

Take, for example, Costas Douzinas and Ronnie Warrington's model of what postmodernism in law involves: 'A sensitivity to different forms of speaking and writing; an attention to the repressed and oppressed dialectics and idioms that are always within but apparently excluded from complex texts; an intention to unsettle apparently closed systems and empires of meaning' (Douzinas and Warrington 1991: x). If we take 'the law' to refer to the body of rules that are customary in a community and recognised as prohibiting certain actions and enforcing the imposition of penalties, then postmodernism in law examines how the writing of such rules does not lead to the closure of meaning, but to the opening out of uncertainty, ambiguity and conflict. To this extent, postmodernism in law suggests that the law is irreducible to 'a body of rules': that the law involves the *symbolic coding* of obligations and prohibitions (the commands, 'you must' and 'you must not') which are without foundation in a given society or community. Postmodernism is hence constructed as a way of reading the law *as a text*. In this section, I will discuss postmodernism as the very event of reading the law through postmodernism: that is, as produced through the very designation of postmodern legal theory as a field of writing and knowledge.

In the first instance, such a field of writing constitutes a return to the fathers of law. Texts that have defined themselves as postmodern readings of law have engaged in a critique of foundationalism through a close reading of some of the authorising and canonical accounts of law's origin – whether in the form of classical mythology, Enlightenment philosophy or modern analytical jurisprudence (Carty 1990; Douzinas and Warrington 1991). Carty argues that such a canon begins with the paradox of what is the source of law: of how the law can be the source of itself (Carty 1990: 3). Jurisprudence attempts to deal with this paradox, through narratives of self-legitimation which find the source of law through law itself. Postmodernism in law constructs itself against these meta-narratives. As Gary Minda puts it, in his survey of postmodern legal movements, 'For postmoderns, law cannot be an autonomous, self-generating activity because there are no fixed foundations in which one can ground legal justification once and for all' (Minda 1995: 246). The critique of foundationalism in jurisprudence constitutes a return to the letter of the law, to the very grammar of how law is written as originary.

Significantly, this return has not involved an emphasis on the relation between law and embodiment which has distinguished the feminist concern with the paternal writing of law's origins. I want to argue that this absence is structural rather than incidental. This becomes clear if we examine how 'the body' appears as a signifier in Douzinas and

Warrington's *Postmodern Jurisprudence*. The bulk of their narrative con-
sists of a critique of the law through a critique of the idea of *a body of the
law*. Indeed, bodies may occupy the very terrain of the 'non-legal': that
which is excluded from the body of the law. They suggest that traditional
jurisprudence:

> sets itself the task of determining what is proper to law and of keeping outside
> law's empire the non-legal, the extraneous, law's other. It has spent unlimited
> effort and energy demarcating the boundaries that enclose law within its
> sovereign terrain, giving it its internal purity, and its external power and right to
> hold court over the other realms. For jurisprudence the corpus of law is literally
> a body: it must either digest or transform the non-legal into legality, or it must
> reject it, keep it out as excess and contamination. (Douzinas and Warrington
> 1991: 25)

Here, the return of law's other to the law is the constitutive passage of
the law, defining the pragmatic procedure of policing boundaries which
inevitably, in its very demarcation of an 'outside', is doomed to fail.
What particularly interests me in this passage is the construction of the
body upon which it depends. Law is *literally* a body in so far as it is *like* a
body – involved in acts of consumption and expulsion. Through
analogy, the desired (and impossible) integrity of the law becomes the
desired (and impossible) integrity of the body. But whose body? The
gesture of this passage relies on an inscription of an undifferentiated
body, a body that *does* simply consume and expel, even if it problematises that body through a critique of the conceptual apparatus of
organicism and traditional jurisprudence. The analogy sustained
between *this* body and the law entails its own set of assumptions and
legislations about who (or what) is the subject of the law. For bodies are
never simply and literally bodies: they are always inscribed within a
system of value differentiation; they are gendered and racially marked;
they have weight, height, age; they may be healthy or unhealthy; they
may be able-bodied or disabled. This postmodern critique of traditional
jurisprudence hence challenges the notion of law as a body only by
keeping in place the undifferentiated nature of that body, working to
destabilise the integrity of that body through destabilising the relationship between what is inside and outside it.

The implications of this assumption of an undifferentiated body can
be traced in Douzinas and Warrington's critique of traditional jurisprudence. In one article, their critique of foundationalism proceeds through
a close reading of an authorising tale of law's origins deriving from
classical mythology: Sophocles' *Antigone*. The conflict here is between
Antigone's desire to bury her brother and the King's decree which
forbids the burial of the traitor. Douzinas and Warrington read this tale

as originary: 'it refers to the leap, both original and final, in which man founded himself by finding himself before the "other" who put to him the first, continuing and last, ethical command which constitutes the philosophical foundation of law as laid down in *Antigone*' (Douzinas and Warrington 1994: 190). By reading the text, in which there is a dramatic conflict between divine and human law, as a crisis in origins (of the command, 'you must') the question of sexual difference is made derivative. The conflict between man and woman is subsumed under the irreconcilable conflict between human and divine which constitutes the crisis of law's force: 'We can conclude that at the mythical moment of its foundation the law is split into divine and the human . . . Antigone teaches that the *nomos* rises on the ground of the polemical symbiosis of female and male, singular and universal, justice and the law' (Douzinas and Warrington 1994: 222). Here, the general critique of legal foundationalism – in which law finds its origin in the split between the divine and the human – takes place through the rendering of sexual difference as secondary, as merely one form of difference in a chain of differences which derive from the originary difference: divine/human.

However, we must be careful here not to privilege sexual difference as 'the difference' that marks the crisis. The already differentiated nature of 'the body of the law' is irreducible to the gendered body, but represents the law's own situated-ness in a complex sociality. The indeterminacy of the law's letter suggests how law is immersed in social relations, such as the paternal relation, which govern and regulate embodied subjectivity. At the same time, posing the question of the gendered body and its relation to law opens up the *limits* of the postmodern critique of *the body of the law*. Here, feminism becomes a limit point of the postmodern narrative – which is not to say that feminism opposes the postmodern critique of legal foundationalism, but rather that the concerns of feminism with the relation between law and particular embodiments helps to define the limits of that general critique.

One of the most interesting texts to deal with the question of the law in relation to the gendering of embodiment is Zillah Eisenstein's *The Female Body and the Law*. She argues here that the law is phallocratic, that is, it reflects the dominance of the phallus as a symbol of the male body in a social order that privileges the bearer of the penis (Eisenstein 1988: 4). Eisenstein introduces the pregnant body in order to decentre the privilege of the male body (Eisenstein 1988: 1), and to remind us of a potential difference between females and males that makes sameness, as the standard for equality, inadequate (Eisenstein 1988: 2). Eisenstein recognises that the pregnant body is not simply an essence that we can

recover from the weight of phallocratic discourse (given its very immersion in the ideology of motherhood). The pregnant body is simultaneously real (as a biological entity) and ideal (as a social construct) and
therefore exists in between these realms (Eisenstein 1988: 224). Given
this, for Eisenstein, a feminist politics of the law must stay in between
these realms: in between sex and gender, difference and sameness,
between liberalism and the phallus on the one hand, and deconstruction
and feminism on the other (Eisenstein 1988: 224).

One of the problems with Eisenstein's thesis concerns her use of the
term 'phallocentrism' to describe the relationship between language and
embodiment. In her argument, phallocentrism undoubtedly involves the
construction of the body through language and institutions. It is a
symbol of the male body that gains its meaning from the already
privileged nature of that body. In this sense, the phallus symbolises the
penis as a privileged mark of sexual difference. But here privilege comes
both before *and* after the phallus: it is both already inscribed on the male
body, and a consequence of the symbolising of that body in a specific
economy. One consequence of the ambiguity over the role of the phallus
in either naming or constructing privilege may be an over-hasty totalisation. That is, her use of the term 'phallocentrism' implies that privilege
is a total and singular system, free from the contradictions and opaqueness that a relation of power would surely generate in the production of
antagonistic subject positions. It also repeats, rather than deals with, the
question of how privilege may mark the body. Is it enough to say the
phallus symbolises the penis in a society of male privilege? Surely we
need to work out the dynamics of that process whereby certain signs
come to have a privileged status.[1] Such a complication of the relation
between language, bodies and power may finally question the use of an
all-embracing term 'phallocratic' in the context of legal studies. The
idea that law *reflects* a pre-existing discursive or power regime neglects
the extent to which each site within the social itself is potentially
productive rather than simply reflective, involved in the negotiation of
contradictions and power relations at a complex and particularised level.

The same ambiguity concerning the relation between bodies and
language occurs in the metaphorisation of the pregnant body. The
demarcation of sex from gender, the pregnant body as biological and the
pregnant body as social, implies that the pregnant body could (at least
potentially) exist outside of its interpellation into a semiotic system,
whether or not that existence is construed in terms of an essence. I use
metaphorisation quite deliberately. Eisenstein is clearly using the pregnant body to *figure* a certain politics of representation and difference.
'The pregnant body' is hence inscribed within the evaluative demands of

her own narrative of law. In this sense, the division of sex/gender within the pregnant body is itself discursive, governed by law. Ironically then, the terms of Eisenstein's own argument work to reveal the non-availability of a sex which is before or beyond the law. Such a non-availability suggests that the gendering of bodies takes place through the law. If this is the case, then the temporality of law as a process (the constituting of legality) implies the existence of a determinate or structural relation *and* a gap between law and embodiment. That is, if the gendering of bodies takes place through a legal process, then gender is both determinate on legality, as it is indeterminate given the non-availability of law as an object in itself.

At one level, Eisenstein's analysis relies on an organic relation between the law and the body, by defining the body of the law as male. The existence of a gap between law and embodiment, and the particularity of the bodies that law may consequently figure and de-figure, is hence excluded from the terms of her analysis. However, at another level, Eisenstein's act of metaphorising the pregnant body serves to reveal the non-availability of a gender which is before the law, or which is the law. The pregnant body's status is not that of the 'real', but is a figure, and as such is constituted and regulated by symbolic law. Given that the pregnant body is only available as a figure (only entering the text through the constitution of law itself), Eisenstein's work enables us to recognise that gender is contested through the law, implying an open structural process in which law itself genders bodies in particular (but not fully determined) ways.

In this sense, a feminist critique of law as a gendering practice may involve a recognition of the gap between law and embodiment, that is, a gap which would problematise any equation between law and the male body. An understanding of the fractured and difficult relationship between law and embodiment enables us to theorise how law involves the shaping and differentiating of bodies and, as such, how bodies are themselves not fully determined within or by the law. Not only does this undermine any equation between law and the male body, suggesting that law is gendering rather than gendered, but it may also suggest that law's relation to embodiment cannot be reduced to gender: the bodies that law differentiates in the process of constituting itself as an object, are always subject to other differences. This approach to law and embodiment interrupts the general postmodern critique of legal foundationalism – and of the (impossible) demarcation of what is inside and outside law – by recognising how what is constructed as 'within' law is already differentiated and that such a difference makes a difference to the policing function of jurisprudence.

Rights and citationality

Significantly, there is very little postmodern literature on 'rights'. Such an absence reflects an implicit understanding of rights: that the discourse of rights belongs to modernity with its emancipatory meta-narratives (such that the 'post-ing' of modernity constitutes the 'post-ing' of rights). So, for example, Anthony Carty's *Post-Modern Law: Enlightenment, Revolution and the Death of Man* assumes the disappearance of Rights as an aspect of Man's own disappearance (Carty 1990: 5). Indeed, there is no suggestion that rights could be understood beyond the Rights of Man: they are assumed to belong to an Enlightenment whose death we should celebrate (Carty 1990: 4). In his consideration of rights and the death of Man, Carty defines postmodernism through deconstruction. He writes: 'Post-modern thought sets a limit to the Enlightenment episode perhaps most precisely by being "deconstructive"'(Carty 1990: 4). A reading of Derrida on law may hence provide us with an insight into the relation between postmodern legal theory and rights which goes beyond any simplistic equation between rights, modernity and death.

In 'Force of Law: The "Mystical Foundation of Authority"', Derrida argues that a deconstructive approach to law proceeds:

by destabilising, complicating, or bringing out the paradoxes of values like those of the proper and of property in all their registers of the subject, and so of the responsible subject, of the subject of law (*droit*) and the subject of morality, of the juridical or moral person, of intentionality, etc., and of all that follows from these, such a deconstructive line of questioning is through and through a problematisation of law and justice. A problematisation of foundations of law, morality and politics. (Derrida 1992: 8)

The law is deconstructable either because it is founded or constructed on interpretable and transformable textual strata or because its ultimate foundation is by definition unfounded (in so far as the act which finds law cannot have in itself foundation if it is to be construed as legislative or creative, as the origin or beginning of law itself) (Derrida 1992: 14).

Derrida specifically defines aporias where the deconstructive possibilities of law may settle. Of significance to my concerns is what he defines as the '*épokhè* of the rule'. Here, Derrida begins with the common axiom that one must be free and responsible for one's actions in order to be just or unjust (Derrida 1992: 22). But at the same time, this freedom or decision of the just must follow a law, prescription or rule, having the power to be of a calculable or programmable order (Derrida 1992: 23). In respect to questions of legal practice then, 'to be just, the decision of a judge . . . must not only follow a rule of law or general law but must also assume it, approve it, confirm its value, by a reinstituting act of interpretation, as if ultimately nothing previously existed of the law, as if the judge himself invented the law in every case' (Derrida 1992: 23). Therefore, for a decision to be just and responsible it must 'in its proper moment' both be regulated and without regulation, 'it must conserve the law and also destroy it or suspend it enough to have to reinvent it in each case, rejustify it, at least reinvent it in the affirmation and the new and free confirmation of its principle' (Derrida 1992: 23).

What I think is useful about this deconstructive attention to an aporia in the concept of just action is the way in which it simultaneously attends to law's relation to the past as a faith in precedent, with its newness in the form of its imagined otherness to the past it confirms. What follows from this irreducible doubling of the legislative moment is a securing of the performative or citational aspect of the law. The act of citing the law as the invoking of the past which gives foundation to the present decision constantly re-opens the past, interprets it, decides upon it. The inventive aspect is precisely history's refusal to stay in the past as an ontologically distinct foundation, separate from the authority of who speaks the law, or whose speech is authorised by the law. For deconstruction, law's ability to found (or find) itself is troubled by the very citational act this demand puts in place. If law is always performed, spoken and enlisted as proper (to law), then what is other to law does not simply return, but was already there in the act or the gesture, the moment, when a demand of and for law takes place. The demand for a decision necessarily goes through a passage of the undecidable: a passage which exceeds the very opposition between calculable programmes and the incalculable. The undecidable as a trace or 'ghost' becomes lodged in every decision, cutting it open, as the irreducible demand of the other, the demand that we must decide about what is impossible (Derrida 1992: 24).

What may such an emphasis on law as citation have to say about rights? Perhaps we could return here to the letter of the law: to the liberal legal scholar Ronald Dworkin's attempt to account for the role of the judge. In 'Hard Cases', Dworkin argues that adjudication must be subordinated to legislation: that judges must adjudicate upon that which has been already legislated by a democratically elected (= accountable and representative) political party. He suggests that any attempt to invent laws and establish them retroactively would constitute an injustice against a defendant. As a result, he argues that adjudication itself must be *unoriginal* even if the decision is original. This unoriginality is linked to his position that adjudication should be governed by principle and not policy. That is, judicial decisions must enforce existing political rights and must, in this sense, evoke an institutional history. He concludes: 'so the supposed tension between judicial originality and institutional history is dissolved: judges make fresh judgements about the rights of parties who come before them, but these political rights reflect, rather than oppose, political decisions of the past' (Dworkin 1975: 1063).

So, here, Dworkin resolves the paradox of the need for unoriginal adjudication and original judgement through a theory of rights as already decided; the judge's decision is a fresh decision, but a fresh decision about rights which are already decided. The decision by the judge *can* only confirm the principles which have already been agreed through political history. This model of rights, as a guarantee of principle, positions rights as prior to the potential conflict involved in decision-making. The writing of rights as having an institutional history which the judge must affirm hence places rights before that history, as a sign of its originary justice. What a deconstructive reading suggests, is that rights must be re-invented in every decision, reaffirmed through being cited and decided upon. Rights cannot be the guarantee of 'the before' or the already decided (as either 'natural' or 'political' rights), but take place through being cut open, through the re-invention of their form. The relation posited here between rights and citationality suggests that rights are constituted through the decision and in that act of (re)constitution are subject to re-iteration and displacement. Rights in this sense always come after an event which marks them out as belonging here or there: their citation is their re-invention, and that re-invention establishes and enforces the boundaries of the rights which are assumed as universals.

What are the implications of the model of rights as citationality for feminism? Drucilla Cornell suggests that feminism should supplement a theory of the alterity or otherness of the law with a notion of gender as a system. Her work exceeds a purely deconstructive reading, retreating to the philosophy of Luhmann to theorise the way in which the relation of gender stabilises the boundary between inside and outside that the law is involved in policing. What Cornell argues is that feminism needs a theory of the system in order to explain the interaction between the semantics of desire and gender hierarchy within the social order (Cornell 1992: 76). Her work implies the inadequacy of a deconstructive strategy to account for the stability of social relations and the legal system (in particular to explain why feminist legal forms have been so difficult to achieve). In other words, deconstruction needs to be supplemented: as a theory of lack (in Cornell's terms), it is also lacking. As my reading suggests, however, the deconstructive emphasis on the undecidable comes through the determinate oscillation between the calculable (and in this sense the systematic) and the incalculable (that which resists systematisation). What deconstruction lacks then (at least within the context of legal theory) is not so much a theory of systematisation. Rather, I would argue that deconstruction as a strategy for reading law is not *sufficient* for a feminist politics of the law because it is not a pragmatism: it does not detail the specific content of laws and their effects according to regimes such as gender.

But to argue that deconstruction is not a pragmatism, and that deconstruction therefore cannot define the parameters of feminist legal theory, is not to inscribe the absence of pragmatism in deconstruction as unproblematic *in itself*. I think the issue of pragmatism raises a set of problems that are central to a deconstructive jurisprudence and, concurrently, to the inscription of a jurisprudence which we can call postmodern. It is interesting, for example, that Derrida himself coins a term, 'programmatology', for the meeting of a pragmatist and deconstructive (grammatological) approach. He argues that such a meeting will define an approach that both takes into account the potential for randomness inscribed by the iterability of the sign, while also recognising 'the situation of the marks', that is, 'the place of senders and addressees, of framing and of the sociohistorical circumscription, and so forth' (Derrida 1984: 27). However, the notion of a 'meeting' of deconstruction and pragmatics points to a *double deficiency of both as strategies for reading law*. The absence of a socio-historical, contextualised and contingent analysis cannot then be simply positioned as incidental to a deconstructive strategy: it structures and limits how that strategy might operate at the level of intervention.[2] Indeed, Derrida's invention of a new word for the meeting of deconstruction and pragmatism ironically performs the necessity of exceeding the boundaries of deconstruction for a reading of the marks of law. In other words, 'programmatology' may perform the role of the radical supplement (Derrida 1976: 144–5). The necessity of the term itself reveals that deconstruction is incomplete, in need of supplementation. The absence of pragmatics and, in this, the absence of an attention to the way in which law performs within historically specific contexts such as gender, is structural to a deconstructive reading of law. Pragmatism cannot be simply added to deconstruction: it would involve its radical transformation.

An attention to the historically situated nature of law's mark makes a difference: a difference that is not pure and self-evident, but becomes present precisely through the readings and writings of the law that place law within the social field. A feminist concern with rights as citationality – as subject to repetition and displacement through the legal demand –

hence operates within the pragmatic field in which rights embody particular subject positions. In other words, a constitutive question for a feminism in dialogue with postmodernism and deconstruction becomes: what difference does the citation of rights make in the constitution of gendered subjectivity? This question is the limit point of Carty's postmodern reading of deconstruction on law in which rights as death can evoke only the impossibility of Man.

Embodied rights

The development of a feminist approach to rights may be shaped by an assumption that law and legality is a gendering process: that rights themselves, as citational acts, mark out boundaries which are clearly gendered. Feminism has located how the concept of abstract rights intrinsic to classical liberalism and traditional jurisprudence is necessarily exclusionary, revealing that the construction of a universal, intrinsic right has entailed processes of selection and exclusion (that universal suffrage equals male suffrage). If the concept of rights has to be extended to include women's rights, then its status as universal or self-evident is called into question. Rather than rights being intrinsic (in the form of self-property/ self-ownership), they become at once historically produced and defined along exclusive and partial criteria. Furthermore, rights become productive of the very process of group differentiation, whereby the legitimate subject of rights (the subject who is proper, and has property) is always already the subject of a demarcated, stratified social group which is exclusive of others. Within a classical liberal framework, 'rights' defined 'men' as a group (or 'fraternity') which excluded women, through the very act of constituting that group as a universal. To refuse the universalism of this rights discourse would be precisely to make visible its role in the differentiation and hierarchisation of social groups.

The focus on the group or the collective is indeed central to a feminist discourse of rights. Such a feminist discourse may stress the way in which rights differentiate one group from another, and so determine the relative mobility of subjects. As Iris Marion Young has stressed, 'rights are not fruitfully conceived as possessions. Rights are relationships not things, they are institutionally defined rules specifying what people can do in relation to one another. Rights refer to doing rather than having, to social relationships that enable or constrain action' (Young 1990: 23). Rights are a product of a discursive and institutionally mediated process, functioning as signs which are exchanged and which overdetermine subject mobility.

The linkage of rights with the demarcation of social groups, and hence the reproduction of power differentials, is clearly at odds with any idealised project whereby rights are expanded to include all subjects, regardless of whatever differences between them are proclaimed. That is, if rights are part of our pre-existing discursive economy (suggesting that we cannot simply 'give them up', but must work critically through them, if theory is to engage the social), and if they function to divide resources in the forms of property and power, then rights can be seen as necessarily entailing conflict. Rights evoke interests, and the conflict of interests is instructive of the dynamic and divisive contingency of the social itself. The focus on rights as necessarily exclusionary, as necessarily marking out an other, means that feminism cannot simply reify rights as essential, or represent women's rights as intrinsically 'right' and exhaustible, as if the conjoining of 'women' and 'right' would lead to an absolute and closed programme for action (otherness hence dividing the name 'women', opening out the possibility of differences, as well as dividing the concept of 'right').

This model of a feminist discourse of rights is at odds with the one offered by Patricia J. Williams in *The Alchemy of Race and Rights: Diary of a Law Professor*, although I am very sympathetic with her more general project of critiquing the privatisation of rights (Williams 1991: 102). Williams constructs a narrative whereby 'rights' are set up as a kind of victim, of 'a constricted referential universe', in which they are constrained by the maintenance of a body of private laws epitomised by contract (Williams 1991: 159). The problem with this approach to rights is that it neutralises the very importance of the exclusive nature of rights claims, which, as I have argued, function to stabilise relations of power in the form of the delineation of social groups and hierarchies. It disregards the significance of the extent to which any positive definition of rights is necessarily exclusive, negatively marking out an other which is expelled from its boundaries (which is not to deny that there are more and less exclusive definitions of rights). As a result, women's rights do not precede their articulation in specific contexts: the event of citing women's rights marks out boundaries which can only be concealed by assuming that such rights are self-evident. The feminist critique of how the concept of abstract human rights defines the terms of women's exclusion from the public sphere, as it conceals that exclusion, here becomes an internal critique. Citing women's rights also constitutes, rather than re-presents, a political subject. So while citing 'women's rights' serves to demonstrate the boundaries that established 'human rights', that act also serves to establish its own boundaries.

The importance of recognising the exclusions which are authorised through rights discourse is clear if we consider the use of 'women's rights' within the context of international feminism. It is the limitations of rights discourse *in practice* that demonstrates the importance of a feminist critique of a universalist model of rights. The issue of universalism was central to some of the 'trouble' that was evident at the UN conference for women held in Beijing in 1995 – a conference that gave an imaginary form/forum to the (impossible) object of international feminism. On one level, it was a 'trouble' that enabled the disappearance of feminist issues from the reporting of the conference. Much of the media attention was spent discussing the conflict between the USA and China – with concern expressed within the USA about China's 'appalling' human rights record (a concern that led to the question: should Hilary Clinton speak at the conference?) (Robinson 1995). Likewise, the Chinese Foreign Ministry were reported to have complained about such criticisms, suggesting that they were a way of attacking 'traditional values' (Hutchins and Munnion 1995). Here, 'women' appeared and disappeared as an object in an exchange about who was entitled to speak of 'human rights'.

Furthermore, the concern about China's 'brutality' was clearly expressed by some Western feminists. For example, Suzanne Moore writes, 'many other people have expressed reservations about the Beijing conference, the chief one being that it is held in Beijing. China is hardly known for its commitment to free speech or to women's rights' (Moore 1995). Here, China is evoked as 'the other' in order to construct the rights of the West – after all, to focus on the abuses in an-other culture is one way of authorising one's own culture (and one's *entitlement* to speak of such rights abuses). We need to reflect upon how the setting up of an international feminist agenda could involve the authorising of the power of Western feminists to define the terms. The use of 'rights discourse' within the conference agenda hence marked out division and antagonism rather than a universal: who has the 'right' to authorise what constitutes 'women's rights' as 'human rights'?

In order for a more mutual engagement within international feminism to take place without such an authorisation, the starting point must be the recognition of the incommensurability of feminist constructions of 'women's rights'. This incommensurability is set up by Nana Rawlings, the 'first lady' of Ghana, as a problem with Western feminism during her attendance at Beijing: 'I'm fed up of attending international conferences where delegates bang on and on about female circumcision. We know that it is a problem and we are trying to deal with it. We don't need anybody to come and tell us that. I say let's first tackle the problem of unfair trading between the developed and developing world' (cited in

Johnson 1995). Here, the implication is that Western feminism has projected its own concern with issues of reproductive health on to 'its others' precisely because of what it cannot see, that is, *its failure to see the international division of labour as a feminist issue*. Here, the event of citing 'women's rights' through making decisions about what that right demands, marks out the boundaries of 'women' – and of what it means to be oppressed as women. As a result, the event of citing women's rights marks out what is assumed as the proper object of feminism.

It does not follow from this argument that female genital mutilation is not a feminist issue, or that Western feminists should not be unconcerned by this practice. Rather, a more mutual engagement would require that one 'gives up' the power to authorise what are the 'proper objects' of feminist dialogue precisely by giving up one's power to authorise what constitutes women's rights.[3] Such a refusal of authorisation presupposes a recognition that 'women's rights' is a sign which is up for grabs – open to being re-defined – rather than belonging to an already existing political and legal subject. In other words, feminists need to make visible the boundaries which constitute 'women's rights' rather than assume their universality. It is the demands of feminism *in practice*, in the context of international political relations, that reveal the necessity of such a substantive critique of universalist rights discourse.

Indeed, the very undecidability of what constitutes a right has implications for feminist practice. The feminist debate on abortion in the West, for example, has centred around the question of whether or not to frame the pro-choice position in terms of women's reproductive rights. The very conflict over abortion can be re-defined as a conflict over what is essential, that is, over what constitutes a subject with proprietal rights (Johnson 1987: 193–4). As a result, the abortion conflict is characterised by competing rights claims, based either on the notion of the rights/autonomy of the mother, or on the rights/autonomy of the foetus. The conflict, dealt with as a rights conflict, becomes centred upon whether the foetus constitutes a subject with proprietal rights. A feminist approach may argue that the sociality of the subject, its constitution within and through the social itself, means that the foetus, attached to the body of a social subject, does not constitute a subject with proprietal rights.

Alternatively, a feminist approach could base itself on the undecidability of where the body of the woman ends. The question of the foetus becomes then a question of the integrity of the mother (is it inside or outside the body, is it an aspect of, or external to, her proper self, the rightful domain of her property?). The impossibility of answering this question without neglecting the instability of the boundaries of the mother's body does not simply negate the autonomy of the mother. More precisely, it establishes that autonomy (of the mother or the foetus) cannot be the grounds for the viability of abortion, as the lack of bodily integrity (and hence the instability of the boundaries of the social subject) leaves us without a proper subject to actualise its rights in a freedom of will and action. Indeed, thinking through pregnant embodiment[4] may serve to question the model of the autonomous and integral subject central to the discourse of abstract rights. To treat the foetus as a subject with rights is to efface the mother's body. Such a dis-embodying of the mother *and* foetus is described by Rosalind Petchesky in her reading of the pro-life film, *The Silent Scream*. As she suggests:

the free-floating fetus merely extends to gestation the Hobbesian view of born human beings as disconnected, solitary individuals, paradoxically helpless and autonomous at the same time. It is this abstract individualism, effacing the pregnant woman and the fetus's dependence on her, that gives the fetul image its symbolic transparency, so that we can read in it ourselves, our lost babies, our mythic past. (Petchesky 1990: xi)

Furthermore, an attention to the mother's *feelings* may also serve to destabilise the separation between mother and foetus implicit in the discourse of foetal rights. The pain and anxiety that surround abortion suggest an affective relation between mother and foetus, in which the foetus becomes an aspect of the mother's self-representation as an embodied, emotional and contingent subject. The impossibility of deciding where the subject begins or ends in pregnant embodiment helps shift the debate on abortion from the realm of the individuated subject who 'owns' rights and towards an understanding of the political subject as contingent and relational, as always embedded in relationships with others who cannot be relegated to the outside.

By showing how the problematic of pregnancy declares the non-availability of a notion of autonomy grounded on the integrity or rights of the subject, a feminist approach also shifts the debate on abortion from the question of abstract rights to the question of power relations. As Catherine MacKinnon and Mary Poovey have both pointed out, in light of their interrogation of *Roe v. Wade* (1973), the feminist use of the discourse of individual, abstract rights in representing their position in favour of women's choice, can prove counter-productive. In this particular case, individual rights are framed in terms of 'privacy' (the right to non-interference from public bodies). This concept of the private is precisely that which conceals the political nature of the gendered subject's access to resources, such as information and guidance on contraception, as well as abortion procedures (MacKinnon 1992: 358–62). As Poovey argues, the notion of individual rights framed around the ideology of privacy, 'may actually exacerbate sexual oppression because it protects domestic and marital relations from scrutiny and from intervention by government and social agencies' (Poovey 1992: 240). A feminist approach may actually involve the disruption of the discourse of individual rights. It shifts the debate from one of autonomy to one of power relations precisely by recognising how privatised rights involve the policing of women's bodily boundaries.

'Rights' is not simply a sign which is always under dispute in its citation in political debates. It is also a signifier which is used by feminist action groups in the event of making their demands. This signifier can often involve naming or self-reference, as with the British feminist action group: Rights of Women (ROW). A cursory glance at a *ROW Bulletin* would suggest that this word 'rights' is used pragmatically, as the sign which most effectively carries the weight of a political demand, being part of the pre-existing discursive economy of radical politics. ROW, that is, does not offer, in itself, a theory of rights. To demand such a theory would be to miss the point concerning the necessities of action within feminism: rights occupy the practical or strategic realm of a demand on others. But the strategic aspect of rights does not mean that their employment lacks implications for theory. Rather, the level of theory becomes at once a question of competing strategic organisations of the real. In order to examine how 'rights' is used by feminist action groups such as ROW, I want to examine responses to the Child Support Act in Britain (1991).

The Child Support Act shifts responsibility for the maintenance of children from the state to the absent parent, setting up an agency to enforce collection. How has feminist opposition to the act involved the mobilising of rights discourse? An article in ROW's Spring 1993 *Bulletin* (*ROWB*) draws attention to the structural effects of the Child Support Act on gender relations by evoking competing conceptions of rights. The article begins by commenting on the *procedure* used to pass this act – it was introduced by statutory instrument and was hence not opened to parliamentary debate (*ROWB* 1993: 2). The article moves from a literal description of the act to an interpretation of its effects. It claims that the act is *about* the welfare of the Treasury – and not women or children (*ROWB* 1993: 2). In this sense, the *ROW Bulletin* looks beyond the literal for an implicit agenda. The article comments specifically on the way in which the act relies on gender-neutral terms (such as the absent parent) to conceal or obscure the way in which its structural effects on men and women are different (*ROWB* 1993: 4). The most important of these effects is not defined as the erosion of women's rights, but as the construction of women's dependence on men through the removal of an automatic entitlement to Income Support (*ROWB* 1993: 3). The second important effect is the way it normalises the family and heterosexuality – so that women who choose to have children on their own, or lesbian mothers, are made invisible and illegitimate (*ROWB* 1993: 3). The *ROW Bulletin* hence focuses on the normative constraints initiated by particular legislative inscriptions of the social. The concept of women's rights is hence not evoked in terms of the integral rights of an abstract individual. Rather, the concept of rights is used to convey the organisation of subject mobility by various legal definitions of entitlement. It remains here a productive and critical gesture which is attentive to the normalising effect of dominant conceptions of right.

The Child Support Act provides us with an important example of the way in which rights claims fit into a model for feminist action. The literature on the act provided by Legal Action for Women, another British feminist action group, may also be of significance. They define the act as an enshrinement of parental duty, which empowers the secretary of state to assess and collect maintenance payments. The act's stated purpose is 'to establish the rights of children to maintenance from both parents' (Legal Action for Women 1992: 44). Its implicit effect is 'to establish the right of government to refuse to maintain children and their carers, and to end rights of children to maintenance from the state, therefore destroying the absolute right of subjects to Income Support' (Legal Action for Women 1992: 44). Here, the word 'rights' is employed in antagonistic positions implying that, as a signifier, its contexts of utterance are unstable. In this sense, rights can become vehicles for conflicting inscriptions of the social.

But, you might ask, can there be wrong rights? My attempt to differentiate between rights claims suggests an alternative question: whose rights wrong whose rights? This alternative question not only sees rights as relational, but also as involving an antagonism of interests. It demands an ability to differentiate between rights claims *according to the subject and bodies they cite and hence put into place.* In the case of the government's model (that is, the government's justification or legitimation of the Child Support Act), 'who gains' is 'the taxpayer' or 'the public purse'. Both these constructions of 'who gains' evoke an undifferentiated subject or community. The creation of an imaginary consensus to found the legitimacy of the rights claim gives that claim an absolute foundation as an abstract, transparent and self-evident vehicle of Truth – a process which relies on dis-embodying rights, abstracting them from the shape of any particular subject or body. In this sense, the government's model of rights participates in a metaphysics that conceals the uncertainty, instability and division that marks the social relation itself.

The feminist model of rights asks the question 'who gains' in order to restore the opaqueness and conflict concealed by the metaphysics of the governmental right. The 'who' of this model is particularised rather than universal, differentiated along the terms of gender, sexuality, class and race. Specific consequences are defined as follows: the Child Support Act will destroy single mothers'/children's independence from men by denying them Income Support; it will discourage women from escaping from violent relationships; it will open the way for greater levels of government surveillance; it will increase the poverty trap for single mothers by removing supplementary benefits such as free prescriptions, dental care and milk vouchers; and it will 'reimpose a Dickensian discipline, by reversing the movement of all kinds of people to follow their preferred family relationships, lifestyle and sexual orientation, despite limited incomes' (Legal Action for Women 1992: 47). Here, the metaphysics of government right is disrupted in the process of dividing the imaginary consensus into stratified relations of power and conflict. This entails a process whereby the rights claims of the then Conservative government are shown to be illegitimate, invalid and in this limited sense, 'wrong'.

Does it follow, then, that the critical feminist model of rights is 'right'? This is not necessarily the case, as the very particularity of the feminist interpretation may suggest that it would not claim to saturate the discourse of rights, so that an all-inclusive right is made available. The focus on the erosion of women's rights defines the constitution of the right claim itself within the terrain of politics whereby mobility is over-determined in the form of relations of power. The right to state support that organises the radical and feminist position functions as a critical rejection of the relation of dependence for women on men within the family unit that the withdrawal of such a right would consolidate. The absence or presence of a right claim in forging social relations hence over-determines the mobility of particular social groups within ideological formations such as the nuclear family. The implication of rights in a relation of power suggests that the employment of rights functions as a citational act, which stabilises its subject in the event of a delineation (in this case, by re-presenting 'women'). But as citation, the feminist politics of rights does not fully control its subject (women), leading to possibilities of disruption and otherness, whereby women would cease to be adequately named by the rights that specific programmes put in place. In the context of the Child Support Act, and feminist interventions into family law, the rejection of the dominant conception of right which reifies the nuclear family opens out the possibility of women's subjectivities being inscribed otherwise, in alternative social arrangements and relationships. Such alternatives could not be fully defined by any programme for action – they remain open in the sense that subjects may find themselves in places other than their legal demands.

A feminist politics inscribes a different and differentiated subject in its employment of 'rights': a subject which it both cites (as 'women') and whose instability or lack of integrity it presupposes in the very act or gesture of citing. Feminism's use of rights discourse entails an embodiment of the very concept of right. Rights here do not simply re-present women as a body and so fix her body and police her boundaries. Rather, the notion of embodied rights calls into question the possibility of not having a body (and hence the inevitability of contingency and particularity) as it describes the process whereby bodies become cited and hence constituted through legal demands. This process does not take the bodies of women for granted, or obliterate differences between women, or differences between feminisms. The focus on embodiment as a process, at once temporal and historical, both institutionally delimited as well as performatively inventive, is my call for feminism to deal with the question of how gender systematises itself through law, as it imagines an alternative inscription of women's bodies in the process of re-inventing women as subjects *after* the law.

My concern in this chapter has been to undo the critical gesture whereby feminist theory and practice are divided as modern and postmodern. I have demonstrated how feminism, at the level of practice, has an ambivalent and critical relation to rights. However, I have also differentiated a feminist intervention on rights and modernity from a general postmodern critique. Rights are not simply overcome (as in Carty's model of postmodernism) through theoretical engagement, or simply held in place at the level of practical struggle. Rather feminism's struggle to transform power relations in historically specific contexts involves a challenge to, and destabilisation of, both modern and postmodern conceptions of rights. Rights themselves are differentiated and embodied through the political and legal demands made by feminist action groups.

Such demands have theoretical implications which resist being designated as either modern or postmodern. Feminism, as a form of practical theorising, can be understood as a trans/formative politics in its very refusal to belong either here or there. So while this chapter has not been about postmodernism *per se*, it has raised important questions about how we might designate postmodernism as a space (where one can be either inside or outside). The refusal of feminism to be designated as either inside or outside constitutes a movement in the term, 'post-modernism', itself. The dis-belonging of feminism may point then to a conceptual horizon where modernism and postmodernism themselves cease to be understood as places one can simply inhabit. Feminism, as a transformative politics, may transform the very conditions in which it is possible to speak of postmodernism as on one side of the law or the other.

2　Ethics

What is at stake in the production of a 'postmodern ethics'? This is a difficult question that demands a cautious analysis. Postmodern ethics does not exist prior to its articulation in specific texts. The designation of 'postmodern ethics' as a field or position involves a form of writing which fills both 'postmodernism' and 'ethics' with meaning in the event of conjoining the terms. The importance of asking how postmodernism writes itself as an ethics is clear if we think through some of the claims made on its behalf. Some of these claims assume that postmodernism, in the first instance, involves the erasure of the ethical or the substitution of ethics by aesthetics (Bauman 1993: 2). Consider the sub-title of one book: 'Postmodernism and the Rediscovery of Value' (Squires 1993). The term 'rediscovery' is powerful and suggestive. It evokes a narrative: the ethical was discovered, but that discovery was negated or forgotten in postmodernism and, as a result, after the postmodern, one can only rediscover what has already been lost. Such a narrative of departure and return is clear in the introduction to the book: 'the contributors to this collection share, from admittedly distinct perspectives, a common concern to accept and retain some of the gains made by the critical mores of postmodernism, but also to recognise and surpass the problems in these attempts to suppress value' (Squires 1993: 5). Here postmodernism becomes defined as an intentional suppression of value and evaluation. Such a narrative of postmodernism's relation to the ethical (in which there is a trajectory from loss to potential rediscovery) is problematic. Indeed, one could argue that this narrative is symptomatic of a modern episteme: the conflation of postmodernism with the demise of the ethical organises that demise around the challenge posed to the categories of universality and rationality. Postmodernism is here the temporary forgetting of the ethical demand in so far as it names itself (ambiguously) as a 'posting' of modernity.

Indeed, much of the recent commentary on postmodernism and ethics has argued that postmodernism comes to 'value' precisely that which has been read as missing in modernity: that is, difference, heterogeneity and otherness (Bauman 1993). Postmodernism has been seen as 'on the side of the other', or conflatable with the very value of 'difference', precisely in so far as it challenges the reduction of the Other to the Same and unleashes the radical heterogeneity which is suppressed by the modern conception of the universal.

However, in this chapter, I want to avoid making any general pronouncements on how postmodernism deals with the ethical which presupposes that the essential debate is between universality versus difference and sameness versus otherness. Such a construction of the ethical debate is highly reductive and assumes the stability of modern/ postmodern by taking certain ethical and epistemic categories as reference points or markers, rather than as that which is being contested. In this chapter, I will discuss examples of postmodern re-thinkings of ethics – Lyotard's rejection of universality, as well as procedural models for dealing with ethical disputes (as forms of consensus), and Levinas's re-construction of the ethical relation in terms of the radical alterity of the other. I will also deal with the question of how a feminist intervention in ethics may challenge both of these approaches. I will attempt to theorise such a challenge in terms of feminism's particular attention to the embodied nature of the ethical subject, and will also consider how feminism may re-figure its ethical relation to 'other women'.

A postmodern ethics of difference and dissensus

In Chris Norris's work, Lyotard's re-thinking of ethics in terms of the incommensurability of language games (*The Postmodern Condition*) or phrase regimes (*The Differend*) is taken as representative of the failure of postmodernism in philosophy, criticism and cultural theory to offer 'a cure for modernity and its manifold discontents' (Norris 1993: 166–7, 186). Indeed, through his reading of Lyotard's philosophical texts alongside shifts in political discourses which posit and celebrate 'new times', Norris argues in very strong terms, that postmodernism is 'a symptom of the present malaise' (Norris 1993: 186). He suggests that postmodernism in general, and Lyotard's work in particular, fails to provide any critical challenge to the rise of new forms of conservative thinking precisely in so far as it assumes that the concepts of critique and judgement are residual signs of an outdated modernity. To this extent, arguments concerning the impossibility of universal judgement support and (ironically) *legitimate* the political status quo. Postmodernism becomes here a *symptom* of the contemporary in its very failure to address the normative, ethical and political necessity of making judgements. Rather than assume such texts are symptoms, I think we need a closer examination of how the impossibility of 'universal judgement' is theorised. We cannot assume that there is a singular political effect implicit to a substantive critique of universalism. Instead, we need to ask: how does the construction of postmodernism in Lyotard's work organise itself through a critique of universalism in ethics, and what particular form and effects does that critique have?

In *The Postmodern Condition* the question of ethics is introduced through a discussion of the crisis in legitimation. As discussed in my introduction, Lyotard argues that modern meta-narratives operate through a universalising of legitimation: they legitimate themselves through reference to universal laws, truths or values (meta-narratives and meta-prescriptions). In contrast, he sets up postmodern legitimation as that which is local or context-immanent, springing from within linguistic practices and communicational interaction (Lyotard 1989: 41). The contrast between modern and postmodern forms of legitimation works to suggest that any attempt to universalise legitimation functions as a form of terrorism which refuses the radical difference and heterogeneity of language games or phrase regimes (see also Lyotard 1988).

In the first instance, the consideration of forms of legitimation of rules and principles operates through a contrast between the social and the scientific. A postmodern form of legitimation is described as analogous to the role of paralogy in scientific activity (Lyotard 1989: xxv). Here, science is not determined by anything other than the transforming boundaries of its own production – it is transformed only by the introduction of new and antagonistic claims. Lyotard's model of legitimation by paralogy becomes the basis for a new ethics which aims for the production of dissension rather than consensus. Such dissension is locally determined and unpredictable: it resists appropriation and control by the performative criteria of use-value or utility. A respect for paralogy would involve a recognition of the ethical principle that, 'a universal rule of judgement between heterogeneous games is lacking in general' (Lyotard 1988: xi).

At one level the turn to paralogy involves a critique of the use of meta-prescriptions to govern the conflict between such heterogeneous games. However, in the case of scientific pragmatics, Lyotard argues that the turn to meta-prescriptions is feasible as such meta-prescriptions would petition players to accept different or new statements (Lyotard 1989: 65). Here, this form of legitimation is valued in terms of the effects it will produce. However, he then qualifies the analogy he has set up between the social and the scientific by arguing that the turn to meta-prescriptions in the social is not feasible. He writes:

Social pragmatics does not have the 'simplicity' of scientific pragmatics. It is a monster formed by the interweaving of various networks of heteromorphous classes of utterances (denotative, prescriptive, performative, technical, evaluative, etc.). There is no reason to think that it would be possible to determine metaprescriptions common to all these language games or that a revisable consensus like the one in force at a given moment in the scientific community could embrace the totality of metaprescriptions regulating the totality of statements circulating in the social collectivity. (Lyotard 1989: 65)

His argument against sustaining the analogy between the social and the scientific – that the social is not a totality – assumes that meta-prescriptions can only practically function in the context of a totality. But, in his discussion of science, meta-prescriptions are those prescriptions which define what 'moves must be' in order to be admissible (Lyotard 1989: 65) and which, through paralogy, are open to revision. As such, meta-prescriptions within scientific pragmatics do not function in the context of a totality. Given this, the pragmatic fact of the non-totality of the social is irrelevant to the potential effects of meta-prescriptions as a partial regulation of the production of rules. The idea of meta-prescriptions within the social does not have to begin with the assumption 'that it is possible for all speakers to come to agreement on which rules or metaprescriptions are universally valid for language games' (Lyotard 1989: 65). The criteria of universality does not have to be assumed for the meta-prescriptions to have effectivity. Lyotard's setting of paralogy (local dissent) against meta-prescriptions (universal consent) is hence problematic. It relies on the assumption that meta-prescriptions can only function if we universalise their effectivity and hence sets up a false opposition between immanent and universal forms of legitimation. It is through this equation of meta-prescriptions and universality that *The Postmodern Condition* is able to privilege the para-logic as the only form of ethical legitimation.

Furthermore, the setting up of difference and heterogeneity against meta-prescriptions and universality is reductive. To privilege difference against totality is to keep the opposition in place. Valuing difference and heterogeneity through a critique of totality works to reify difference by assuming it can exist as a pure, undifferentiated category. The implications of this reification can be traced in *The Differend*. Here, Lyotard discusses the Cashinahua narratives as examples of 'small' and self-legitimating narratives which cannot be reconciled into the universal story of man. He argues that a wrong occurs when the Cashinahua are judged in relation to that story; a judgement which violates their incommensurability or their otherness (Lyotard 1988: 156). But Lyotard's own text still works as a narrative that positions or enlists the

Cashinahua in a certain way, involving in some sense the 'translation' of the Cashinahua into an example in an argument.

My point here would not be to accuse Lyotard of 'wronging' the Cashinahua community according to the ethics of the differend he has delineated (to accuse him in this sense of being a failed postmodernist). Rather, I want to argue that this conception of an ethical practice as being a respect for the differend is an impossible one. The very *demands* of narrative and argument mean that incommensurability is *already* violated, even in the event of 'taking' incommensurability as an ethical ideal. Accepting that violence against difference is irreducible may alter how we relate narrative to ethics. We would no longer work with an opposition between narratives which totalise, which refuse heterogeneity (modern) or narratives which resist that totalisation by celebrating what is heterogeneous (postmodern). What we have instead is an economy, an understanding of the difference between narratives as a matter of degree.

Lyotard's argument does not simply involve the critique of universality (the idea that there are rules which are universally valid for all language games), but also the assumption that consensus is in itself unethical (other than when it can contribute, paradoxically, to dissensus or paralogy). I would share his critique of some philosophies of consensus, including those of Jürgen Habermas, which assume that conflict is a sign of irrationality and can be transcended or eliminated. To this extent, *The Postmodern Condition* provides an important account of why consensus should not become a proper object of ethical dialogue. However, one could also argue that 'consensus' cannot simply be transcended by a (postmodern) ethics of paralogy. That is, Lyotard requires some notion of consensus for his own ethics to be feasible: a consensus over the effect that he desires (the production and maintenance of paralogy). His setting up of paralogy against consensus cannot pragmatically or practically work, as players need to consent to paralogy for it to be possible. They need to consent to, and have institutional reinforcement for, the elimination of terrorism, which Lyotard defines as the threat to eliminate a player from a game (Lyotard 1989: 63). The impossibility of overcoming consensus complicates his privileging of paralogy as the basis of a postmodern ethics.

The impossibility of overcoming consensus suggests that there are still decisions to be made about how to deal with ethical conflicts and disputes that must transcend local or mini narratives. The need for some regulative structure, some procedure for sorting out criteria that can 'adjudicate' between competing or conflicting language games (as the demand for evaluation which is irreducible to a given set of values), has been interpreted by some critics as demanding the retention of some notion of rationality. For example, Christopher Norris argues that we should not reject forms of enlightenment critique that involve some appeal to the manifest disparity between things-as-they-are and things-as-they-might-be, according to the standards of enlightenment critical reason (Norris 1990: 37). But that critical reason is not given the status in Norris's argument, of one set of values and one form of persuasion (or one standard of legitimacy), but as the adjudicating criteria *between* values. In contrast, Iris Marion Young stresses how the opposition between reason and the realm of desire (affectivity/the body), as a logic of identity which denies and represses difference, has been intrinsic to a history of violent exclusions (Young 1987: 59–60). Through the very definition of a rational subject, certain 'concrete' subjects become excluded from the realm of citizenship. Those who have been seen to 'lack' rationality, such as women, become the other against which norms of moral and political responsibility are defined. Such a substantive critique of rationality calls for, not the giving up of the value of reason *per se*, but a giving up of its status as a criteria *in itself* for adjudicating between competing values. If reason is re-conceptualised as a value rather than as the normative basis of evaluation, then the evaluative process itself could include affective and bodily dimensions of meaning.

Although Lyotard offers an important critique of the assumption of rationality, he falsely equates the impossibility of rationality with the impossibility of (provisional) consensus. The adjudicating criteria, or meta-prescriptions (what, in relation to scientific meta-prescriptions, Lyotard has called a contextual and revisable consensus) themselves have the status of 'values' which can be open to revision through processes of dialogue and argumentation. Self-reflexivity about the status of criteria as 'values' would not necessarily lead to an infinite regress, where no decision can be made. Decisions do not require absolute principles to govern or legislate them. Rather, self-reflexivity about the status of criteria as values would prevent any criteria from becoming solidified into an absolute principle.

In *The Postmodern Condition* a critique of universality leads to a refusal of a procedural model for dealing with cases of ethical conflict within the social: such procedures are assumed to require universal standards of validity (as an un-revisable consensus). However, I would argue that the critique of universality is precisely that which renders the necessity of thinking through procedural issues. If there are no universal foundations for dealing with ethical conflicts, then 'we' need to establish criteria for making judgements. Here, there is a 'we'. There is a link made between the criteria used for judgement and a subject position: the question of ethics also becomes a question of 'who is speaking here?' Such a question draws our attention to the implication of ethics in relations of power. Indeed, one could argue that without any procedures for regulating social and ethical conflict, those who are already most powerful would profit from paralogy. To this extent, Lyotard's conflation of universalism, meta-prescriptions and consensus avoids dealing with power relations as they operate positively to constitute subjects and their access to linguistic and technological competence.[1] A recognition of power as productive may suggest that paralogy, as the unregulated creation of dissension, could covertly serve the dominant power interest. A free agonistics of conversation without a self-reflexive space for agreement over values which could regulate the distribution of (verbal and non-verbal) resources, would be unfree and over-determined by pre-existing and relatively stable structures of power and authority. As John McGowan argues, the model of freedom which organises Lyotard's ethics is a negative one, which defines freedom in terms of a detachment from (any notion of) the social totality (McGowan 1991: 181–8).

The production of difference is impossible outside some form of regulative structure, in which there is a revisable consensus over its own status as value. Without such forms of regulation, a belief in the value of difference would translate into the power of some to define the terms for others. As such, the value of difference entails its own complication and relative undoing, a point which deconstructs the hierarchy difference/consensus and suggests a third term which mediates a space between them. I would suggest that this term cannot be contained by a demand for theoretical purity, as it entails the pragmatic and inexhaustible meeting of the ethical demands and conflicts that saturate daily life and inform the embodiment of the social subject.

A feminist critique of universalism

My reading so far has suggested that Lyotard's critique of concepts of totality, universality, consensus and rationality in both *The Postmodern Condition* and *The Differend* has its limits. In this section, I want to re-think those limits by posing the question of the relation between ethics and gender. My analysis will involve an examination of how different feminisms have dealt with ethical issues. I will demonstrate how the question of gender and ethics does not produce 'a feminist ethics' but, in contrast, destabilises feminism and questions the possibility of any ethical inclusiveness.

Significantly, the category of feminist ethics is often conflated with the category of female or feminine ethics, derived in particular from object-relations psychoanalysis. This conflation can be seen as problematic: it suggests that ethical practice is unilaterally determined by a given gender norm. Such a conflation sees a feminist ethics as an automatic translation from women's experiences. But this question of the relation between female and feminist ethics is a significant one, and the positive influence of Carol Gilligan's *In a Different Voice* in determining a shift from traditional approaches to ethics should be recognised. It is perhaps too easy to dismiss Gilligan's work as essentialist, although neither should this issue be simply ignored.[2] After all, Gilligan's work questions the parameters of Kohlberg's model of moral development by suggesting that it relies on a male standard of what is ethical, defined as an orientation towards justice and individual rights. Gilligan's research (involving semi-structured interviews with women) suggests that an alternative female voice is discernible, a voice that emerges through an ethics of care and connection. Although that voice is characterised by 'theme' rather than 'gender', it is nevertheless traced primarily within 'women's voices' (Gilligan 1982: 2). Gilligan's work suggests that the idea of a universal moral theory neglects the process of gender differentiation and, consequently, the located and embodied nature of subjectivity.

A feminist critique of universalism may begin with a critique of the subject of universal ethical theory. Such a subject or 'the ideal observer' is masculine, rational and disembodied. The ideal observer is *abstracted* from the contingencies of the social, including the bodily realm, in order to fulfil the criteria of universality, which involves treating *like situations alike*. As Lynne Arnault argues, such abstractions are impossible, as people's social identity or location necessarily affects their understanding of the world, and hence any evaluative procedure (Arnault 1990: 195). 'Moral agents' are socially constructed, embodied members of historically shifting groups.

The implications of this critique of 'the ideal observer' are debated in Seyla Benhabib's work (Benhabib 1987; 1992). Benhabib examines how Kohlberg's moral theory distinguishes between generalised and concrete others. The former requires us to view each and every individual as a rational being entitled to the same rights and duties we would want to ascribe to ourselves, while the latter requires us to view the individual as having a concrete history, identity and affective-emotional constitution (Benhabib 1987: 87). Benhabib concludes that the generalisation and abstraction of the other leads to a denial of difference (Benhabib 1987: 89). Here, the critique of an ethical norm leads to an alternative ethics attentive to difference, otherness as well as the connected, relational nature of the subject.

The ideal observer who positions others as general rather than concrete is gendered in a variety of ways. This gendering takes place through the replication of a social value attached to masculinity, the capacity to separate oneself from one's situation. But it also participates in the Cartesian separation of the faculty of reason from the extrinsic details of body, affectivity and sociality – all values associated (negatively) with the feminine. The deployment of this masculine ideal may exclude from ethical consideration the very value of femininity with its constitutive basis in a notion of affective connection with others. In this sense, a feminist critique of a universalist ethical paradigm may actually align itself with the values associated with the 'feminine', not as that which women simply are, but as that which is made invisible by the universalist criteria implicit in the ideal observer. A feminist ethics may help here to expose how ethics involves fluid and contingent relationships between subjects and bodies (rather than an abstract self). Such an ethics may employ values such as 'care' and 'connection' precisely to dislodge the universalist language of past ethical paradigms in order that women can become visible as subjects of and in ethics.

Beyond the exclusion of the 'value' of the feminine, the masculine ideal of abstract moral autonomy structurally hinders members of subordinated groups from participating on a par with members of dominant groups in communicative interaction. The very criterion of an abstract individual as moral agent, as well as the concept that ethical problems or situations can be identical, disguises the way ethical problems entail the meeting of (at least) *one with another* – whose otherness demands dialogue. If ethics involves confrontations with 'others', then it is also necessarily implicated in *relationships of power*. In ethical situations, subjects may themselves be constrained and determined by the asymmetry of power embedded in the very means of discursive interaction. The pre-existing relation of dominance between women and men means that the ideal of an abstract individual as moral agent may serve to reproduce this relation of dominance, not only because women's actualised subjectivity may be incommensurable with it, but because it fails to recognise women's relative immobility in framing the terms of moral discussion.

The development of a specifically feminist approach to ethics involves an understanding of how gender differences are contested and replicated both in specific social values and within general ethical theories. A feminist approach to ethics does not derive simply from women's experiences, or the values implicated in the production of femininity as a set of psychological or moral traits. However, that is not to say that a feminist ethics is fully detached from the social production of femininity.

For the values that orientate 'femininity' are precisely those that help dislodge the universalism of prior moral theories. In its emphasis on affective connection with others, and the implication of value in embodiment and relationships, 'femininity' can become re-inscribed as a site of critical refusal: a refusal to replicate the subject of ethical theory. This critical refusal is at once an ethical demand: a demand for procedures which recognise the embodied nature of ethical subjects and the asymmetrical relations of power which frame their access to moral discourse.

It is here that a feminist approach may challenge Lyotard's model of postmodern or paralogic ethics. The critique of rationality and universalism involves a recognition of the situatedness of ethics in relations of power and hence the importance of developing procedures to challenge the reproduction of hierarchical forms of interaction. Such an approach does not abstract 'difference' from its embeddedness in social relations. There is no easy slippage here from ethics to difference despite the substantial critique of universalism that is implicated in the recognition of the relation between ethics and gender. Indeed, we could re-read *The Postmodern Condition* by examining how the abstraction of difference as a value involves *a re-writing of masculinity beyond the universal*: a masculinity predicated on its very flight from the de-limitations of social structure.

However, the concern with the ethical that shapes a feminist understanding of the relation between masculinity and universalism is not 'exterior' to feminist political practice. How do we make ethical decisions as feminists given the absence of universalism and the link between universalism and the exclusion of women from moral discourse? What are the implications of this critique for the ethics of feminism itself? Interestingly, it is the assumption of universalism that may enable the elision of how the question of ethics is internal to feminism. Alison Assiter's *Enlightened Women*, for example, argues that there is a universal basis to ethical decisions. She argues that, as feminists, we should take up 'the standpoint of communities of individuals which are more committed to emancipatory values' (Assiter 1996: 91). But, I would argue, who defines what are 'emancipatory values'? Is this term fixed and given, or is it open to being defined in different ways? Who, within a given community, authorises the definition of 'values'? To what extent then are definitions of 'value' implicated in power relations?

The reliance on 'emancipatory values' as a self-evident category poses some problems in Assiter's reading of Gayatri Spivak. Here, she argues against Spivak's position that it is uncertain whether the liberal colonial disallowing of suttee (widow self-immolation) was emancipatory for women (Assiter 1996: 84). In other words, Assiter argues that the disallowing of suttee was emancipatory for women as, 'a value is more emancipatory than another if it has the effect of removing a person or group of people from subjugation' (Assiter 1996: 84). But is it clear that the disallowing of suttee was simply emancipatory even in this sense? The work of Spivak, amongst others, would complicate this account, precisely by reading the colonial decision as the liberation of Indian women from Indian men by white men. In other words, the debate around suttee can be seen as the conflict over who had the right to speak for Indian women. Modern values around 'emancipation' feed into colonial values around 'civilising the natives' (saving them from themselves). It is here that Spivak's gesture makes sense as an account of the ambivalence of the disallowing of suttee – the subaltern woman does not speak (Spivak 1988).

We cannot, then, lose sight of who is defining 'emancipatory values' for whom, if we are to recognise the mediation of ethics by politics. To argue against the self-evident nature of the category of 'emancipatory values' is not to bracket the realm of ethics as simply indeterminate. On the contrary, it is to argue that 'we' need to *make decisions* about what values are more emancipatory than others, as well as what may constitute 'emancipation'. These decisions are always partial and imperfect; they are (and should be) open to being contested. Any such decisions also need to be informed by a recognition of the divisions within, as well as between, communities that may determine 'who' shapes the criteria used.

A critique of universalism for feminism, in contrast to the postmodern critique offered by Lyotard, calls us to self-reflexively consider the criteria used for the determination of value as such. For feminism, this self-reflexivity is a demand to consider how to find ethical means for dealing with power differences between women. A critique of the detached, masculine subject is not simply about making women present as embodied moral subjects. Rather, it is about recognising that women have differing access to moral discourse and that 'universalism' can give some women access to that discourse at the expense of others.

The way in which a critique of universalism enables attention to the power differences between women and the development of a more ethical feminism is clear if we consider Terry Eagleton's call for feminism to admit to its need for universalism. He argues that feminism, despite its occasional emphasis on the impossibility of 'truth', needs (given its political demands) to 'make judgements'. He goes on to suggest that the 'necessary and proper universalism of the judgement that the oppression of women in any form is always morally wrong, and that no appeal to cultural tradition can constitute a defence of such conduct, runs into headlong conflict with a cultural relativism' (Eagleton 1990: 385).

The examples used by Eagleton to demonstrate how cultural relativism contradicts the moral and political demands of feminism – footbinding and clitoridectomy – introduce issues of international politics. These are examples of cultural traditions which are implicitly positioned by Eagleton as being oppressive to women in cultures other than those of late capitalist Western democracies. It is through the use of these examples as illustrative of a paradox for feminism that Eagleton makes clear that the feminism that he is speaking of (and for) is Western feminism. It is assumed to be a Western feminism whose contamination by postmodernism would lead to an inability to make judgements about issues of women's oppression *elsewhere* in *other* cultural traditions. There is clearly violence in this gesture, a violence that points to the inadequacy of the assumption that ethics and politics is simply a struggle between cultural relativism (the 'postmodern' Western feminist) and universalism (the 'modern' Western feminist). One immediately needs to re-think the politics of the gesture whereby Eagleton speaks of Western feminism's political forms by alluding to examples from 'beyond' the West. How is that 'beyond' inscribed other than as an object/example to illustrate the needs of a subject implicitly assumed to be the Western feminist? What else does this do but confirm Western identity as predicated on the violent exclusion of the other?

Such processes of othering are discussed by Chandra Mohanty in relation to Western feminism. She analyses how feminist attempts to account for the universality of gender oppression have led to the production of the category of 'the third world woman' within feminist analysis. Mohanty discusses the way in which Western feminism has used universal categories to understand gender relations: categories which have actually been derived from their own experiential frameworks. Such feminist approaches often proceed through producing 'third world women' as objects of knowledge: 'An analysis of "sexual difference" in the form of a cross-culturally singular, monolithic notion of patriarchy or male dominance leads to the construction of a similarly reductive or homogeneous notion of what I call the "third world difference"' (Mohanty 1991: 53). Here, the third world woman is interpreted in terms of a Western understanding of gender oppression: the representation of her as a victim of a universal patriarchy positions the Western feminist subject as an authority, while taking the West as a reference point for understanding different forms of power relations. In this way, Mohanty argues that Western feminism's universalist models reinforce a colonial relation.

But what Mohanty concludes through this informed analysis is not that Western feminists should become cultural relativists. On the contrary, the focus of her article is, to some extent like Eagleton's, on the need to make decisions about issues of value across different cultural formations – and such differences are irreducible to the division between inside (West) and outside (third world), as they are internal and constitutive of any given cultural formation. Rather than simply assuming that cultural traditions elsewhere function as signs of women's universal oppression, we need an ethics which is sensitive to the located and complex nature of particular cultural traditions and practices. A sensitive and contextualised approach to cultural specificity and difference would lead the Western feminist away from an ethics of *universal judgement* (which Mohanty rightly sees as a self-affirming politics) and towards an ethics where judgements are made possible only through *specific engagement*.

Furthermore, in this process of engagement, Western feminists may be able to hear the voices of women resisting those 'other' cultural traditions. Rather than speaking for those 'other' women by identifying other cultural traditions as signs of a universal patriarchy, Western feminists could unlearn the violence of 'universalism' (where the West becomes conflated with the universal) and learn to speak to, and hear, different women. Ethics could become a relation or passage made possible by a (necessarily unequal, but nevertheless surprising) dialogue between different women. Ethical decisions become strategic decisions which are bound by a set of normative constraints: decisions which are inventive, partial and temporary, rather than founded in an assumed universality.

Clearly, then, Eagleton's gesture which calls for (Western) feminism to 'admit to' its need for universalism misses the point about the hegemonic effect of universalist assumptions. It also fails to recognise that the act of giving up universalism (and, returning to my discussion in chapter 1, giving up universalist conceptions of what constitutes 'women's rights') may enable a different kind of ethical relation between gendered subjects differently and unequally positioned by the international division of labour which is based on a more mutual engagement. The critique of universalism may call feminists to think through the procedures they set up for dealing with such conflicts of value: to work towards a more mutual encounter by acknowledging the power differentials that make absolute mutuality or correspondence an impossibility.

In this section, I have argued that a feminist critique of universalism emerges through its concern with the gendered and embodied nature of the ethical subject. Such a concern involves an emphasis on the importance of developing ethical procedures which recognise the relationality of that subject (connection), and the domains of affectivity (such as care) which are excluded from the model of the ideal observer. This critique of universalism pushes at the limits of Lyotard's postmodern paralogy which, in its reification of difference, assumes that any attempt to regulate ethical relations constitutes the terror of consensus and totality. However, the critique of universalism through an emphasis on gender does not produce an integral ethical community of women. Posing gender as a difference leads to an ethics in which gender no longer becomes *the difference*. Ethics becomes an issue that is internal to feminism itself, involving a recognition of the difference and otherness within feminist communities and self-reflexivity about the criteria used to make value judgements. The need to make decisions about values given the absence of universalism leads to an ethics based on engagement with an other that one cannot simply represent. It is this question of otherness in relation to postmodern and feminist re-writings of the ethical that I now want to address.

Otherness

To the extent that we become obligated to think through how to engage with an unrepresentable otherness, then the domain of the ethical is immediately shifted. This shift is made clear by Rosalyn Diprose in *The Bodies of Women: Ethics, Embodiment and Sexual Difference*. She points out that the term 'ethics' derives from the Greek word *ethos*, meaning character and dwelling. For Diprose, such a derivation suggests that ethics 'is about being positioned by, and taking a position in relation to, others', or about the '*study and practice of that which constitutes one's habitat*' (Diprose 1994: 18–19). The discrepancy between her model and universal ethical paradigms is explained as more than a simple question of etymology. The structural difference relates to what is assumed to be the relation between character and dwelling: 'An ethics based on universal rational principles assumes that our "being" is a discrete entity separate from the world . . . An ethics based on the problematic of place, on the other hand, claims that our "being" and the "world" are constituted by the relation "in"' (Diprose 1994: 19). What differentiates Diprose's ethics from universalist paradigms is precisely the argument that one's character or ethos is inseparable from one's habitat: that being is inherently 'worldly'. The consideration of ethical relations in terms of the engagement with otherness depends upon the critique of the autonomous self-present subject and a recognition of the inter-subjectivity of being-in-the-world.

Significantly, postmodernism has written itself as an ethics through a readmission of the proximity of the Other. As Zygmunt Bauman argues:

If postmodernity is a retreat from the blind alleys into which radically pursued ambitions of modernity have led, a postmodern ethics would be one that readmits the Other as a neighbour, as the close-to-hand-*and*-mind, into the hard core of the moral self, back from the wasteland of calculated interests to which it has been exiled; an ethics that restores the autonomous moral significance of proximity; an ethics that recasts the Other as the crucial character in the process through which the moral self comes into its own. (Bauman 1993: 84)

The proximity of the Other in such writings of a postmodern ethics is not simply spatial; that proximity or nearness reflects the relation of being as being-for-the-Other. The Other constitutes the very force of the ethical demand. Bauman's construction of such a postmodern ethics relies primarily on the work of Emmanuel Levinas. Bauman writes, 'Levinas's is *the* postmodern ethics' (Bauman 1993: 84, emphasis mine). But we must be careful about how we read the inclusion of Levinas in the domain of 'postmodern ethics'. Such a reading of Levinas as postmodern has involved a framing of his texts by writers such as Zygmunt Bauman and Simon Critchley. I would argue that Levinas's work does not invite the possibility of a philosophy of otherness *per se*, precisely in so far as the Other – as the Infinite – resists thematisation, but is also already thematised. In other words, while Levinas's re-visiting of philosophies which have prioritised the ontological may involve a critique of how otherness has been 'domesticated', his texts also assume the impossibility of 'rescuing' the other from this entrapment in the obligation to thought or 'thinking' (the impossibility of 'siding' with the Other through the philosophical). This relates not only to the Other as always ungraspable, but also to the *necessity* of thematisation in relation to the Other – a thematisation which is differentiated from 'knowledge' which begins and ends with itself, but which is necessarily reductive at the same time (Levinas 1991: 158). But despite the question of where Levinas's texts begin and end in relation to postmodernity – an impossible and over-determined question – his texts have nevertheless authorised a discourse on ethics and alterity. Such an authorisation has at times been played out in terms of how *not* to return to Levinas or how, through a faulty reading, to do justice to his texts (Derrida 1991; Critchley 1991). But even the event of ingratitude – of not returning to Levinas but to the Other – becomes a gift for Levinas, a writing of the text for Levinas. Hence, within postmodern ethics, Levinas has become a proper name – with a difference.

In *Time and its Other*, Levinas shifts the terrain of philosophy from ontology to ethics. Ethics is not understood in terms of the normative realm of morality, but the primordial ethical experience embodied in the face-to-face encounter with the Other. One has an endless obligation to the Other. But the Other is not present to the subject in the form of a being with rights. The Other is present only in its unpresentability; the Other is radically alterior to the subject and cannot be subsumed to it:

To be sure, the other (*l'Autre*) that is announced does not possess this existing as the subject possesses it; its hold over my existing is mysterious. It is not unknown but unknowable . . . The relationship with the other is not an idyllic and harmonious relationship of communion, or a sympathy through which we put ourselves in the other's place . . . The other's entire being is constituted by its exteriority, or rather its alterity. (Levinas 1987: 75–6)

The ethical relation to the Other takes the form of the face-to-face encounter. The face at once 'gives and conceals' the Other; it both constitutes the Other's proximity (its nearness which resists incorporation into the side-by-side), and yet already withdraws the Other into the mystery of the future. This relation is an event that cannot be assumed by the subject, that cannot simply have a place within the subject's being. Rather the radical alterity of the Other presents itself to the subject in terms of the impossibility of being (in-the-present) as such. Such an ethics is, in the first instance, a contestation of a philosophy of the subject: a philosophy that begins and ends with the virility of the intentional subject ('*the power to be able*') (Levinas 1987: 82).

Levinas suggests that the relation with the Other (the 'intersubjective space') is radically asymmetrical: 'The Other is, for example, the weak, the poor, "the widow and the orphan", whereas I am the rich and powerful' (Levinas 1987: 83). It is here, for me, that the question of the ethical construction of the Other within the narrative becomes uncertain. The Other is not reducible to these figures; to make such a reduction is to turn the Other into a being whose place can be assigned. These figures do not have a referent in a real being – the force of figuration here is precisely the *undoing* of the possibility of reference as such. So what is the status of this figuration in the text? These figures come to signify that the Other is marginal, that the Other does not possess the mastery of speech and signification. This serves to make clear that the Other's relationship to the Same is one of negation: 'the Other is what I myself am not' (Levinas 1987: 83). The marginality of the Other – its poverty, deprivation or destitution – is hence intrinsic or essential to Otherness. The Other is what I am not *because* of 'his' alterity: this because-ness is 'formal'.

In *Totality and Infinity* the priority of alterity over the figures through which it is expressed is clear:

These differences between the Other and me do not depend on different 'properties' that would be inherent in the 'I', on the one hand, and on the other hand, the Other, nor on different psychological dispositions which their minds would take on from the encounter. They are due to the I–Other *conjuncture*, to the inevitable *orientation* of being 'starting from oneself' toward 'the other'. (Levinas 1979: 215)

This orientation is given priority 'over the terms that are placed in it' (Levinas 1979: 215). It is here that Levinas's gesture is open to complication. The orientation towards the Other is valued precisely through being rendered irreducible to the concrete particularity of an-other who is visible only through the figures who stalk his text. This irreducibility, on the one hand, demonstrates the endless and Infinite obligation I have to the Other. It takes place by refusing to psychologise the Other as a being with characteristics I am will-ing to respect. But in the gesture of refusing psychologism, Levinas also erases the question of how a particular other may become a force in the ethical relation, rather than a term *through which otherness mediates its force*. In this sense, the figuring of the other as the dispossessed does not deal with the material embodiment of those who are dispossessed from moral discourse. The use of such figuration slides over the question of the relation between particular others who are dispossessed, and the Other as radically other who cannot belong within these figures. Is it possible, I would ask, to trace the force of the particular other, as potentially other to the Other, as potentially interrupting the writing whereby we caress the voluptu-ousness of the Other, without retreating to a psychologist model which reduces the other to an-other Being?

In Levinas, the deployment of figures for the Other which is in principle unfigurable serves to separate the Other from the 'worldliness' of the encounter with an-other despite his explicit refusal of any such abstraction. Although the face-to-face is an encounter with a particular Other (the face is 'expressive'), that encounter itself is ethical only in so far as that particularity cannot be named. In this sense, while Levinas's ethics refuses a model of the generalised other whose rights we can automatically know, it nevertheless generalises the other *precisely through a discourse on its unknowability*. This generalisation works by deploying figures of the particular other which erase that particularity (the weak, the poor, the widow and the orphan).

The implications of the erasure of the particular through figuration is evident in Levinas's writing on sexual difference. It is of significance that Jacques Derrida and Simon Critchley both challenge Levinas here and evoke figures of 'the woman reader'[3] in order to respond ungratefully – and hence more justly – to Levinas's texts (a just reading does not simply return to Levinas, but is a gift to the other who cannot be subsumed by Levinas's texts). Derrida argues that Levinas prioritises ethical difference over sexual difference: 'It is not woman or the feminine that he has rendered secondary, derivative, or subordinate, but sexual difference. Once sexual difference is subordinated, it is always the case that the wholly other, who is *not yet marked* is *already* found to be marked by masculinity' (Derrida 1991: 40). To some extent, this challenge suggests that a philosophy of ethical difference itself is im-possible: the self–other relation is not unmarked and that its very constitution as unmarked *conceals the mark of privilege* (in this case the masculine). Indeed, in *Totality and Infinity* the concern is with fecundity and the relation of lover (he) and Beloved (she) – the ethical relation is here expressed through the caress as a form of trans-substantiation. The trans-substantiation engenders a beyond – the ethical relation of the lovers produces 'the child' (Levinas 1979: 266). The engendering of the beyond, however, returns us to paternity: it is the father's relation to 'the child' that embodies the strangeness of the other with whom I am most intimate (Levinas 1979: 266). The erasure of the mother (from Beloved to child) – in whose body an-other comes into being – demonstrates how the 'I' is marked as masculine as it is assumed to be unmarked by (sexual) difference. Indeed, my critique of the erasure of the particular other in Levinas is of resonance here: the self–other relation is an impossibility that is *already marked*, and that marking engenders a difference.

However, I would take issue with how Derrida inscribes 'sexual difference' in his (mis)reading of Levinas's texts. Here, sexual difference becomes present in order to name what has been missed out in, or elided by, Levinas's texts. But in doing so, sexual difference comes to stand for difference itself (the 'difference' that is made secondary through the prioritising of ethical difference as first-philosophy). This repeats the gesture at work in Levinas's text when he writes: 'the difference between the sexes is general – appeared to me as a difference contrasting strongly with other differences, not merely as a quality different from all others, but as the very quality of difference' (Levinas 1987: 36). Derrida, in making sexual difference 'the difference' that challenges Levinas, repeats this prioritising of sexual difference over and above other kinds of difference that may 'derive' from ethics (a process which enables him to assume the figure of 'the woman reader'). I would argue that a feminist reading of this dialogue must not repeat the very same gesture – to recognise the violence when sexual difference comes to stand for difference *per se*: a process that makes other differences themselves derivative (other differences matter). The importance of such a refusal to repeat the gesture through which philosophy comes to mourn the (dead) body of the woman, is to begin with the possibility that differences themselves already mark the other to whom I am endlessly obligated (rather than seeing the other as a mark of a difference – including sexual difference – which obligates me).

How might a feminist ethics of otherness proceed differently? To begin with, a feminist approach may address the particularity of an-Other by assuming that *a* philosophy of otherness is impossible as such. Such a particularity may not simply be figured. This is particularly clear in Spivak's reflection on her translation of Mahasweta Devi in *Imaginary Maps*. Here, Spivak formulates a model of ethical singularity, not of the other *per se*, but of the subaltern woman, who remains other to the various privileged categories of otherness (migrant/exile/diasporic/post-colonial) within Western knowledges. Such a singularity takes the form of a mutual engagement and hence involves both accountability and responsibility.

Spivak clearly argues for the necessity of translation and against 'cultural relativism'. Translation (and reading as translation) is a figure for engagement. It involves proximity to the other. An ethical reading may be a reading which gets close to the text, which caresses its forms with love. It refuses to judge the text from afar and to fix the text as a discernible object in space and time. But that closeness or proximity, which avoids the distanciation of universalism, does not involve the merging of one with the other. The idea of translation simply as proximity to the other implies that in engagement (or mutuality) the subject and the other merge, becoming one. While the line between the translator and text becomes unstable in proximity, it also constitutes the limits of translation: of that which cannot simply move across. An ethical translation or reading moves between distance and proximity, complicating any simple relation between ethics and time/space which is central to the violence of universalism. Indeed, the necessity of making decisions and judgements as one reads, and the impossibility that those decisions and judgements can be founded in the 'truth' or 'real' of any text, suggests that a more just reading may move close and leap away with a risky zeal. But by getting close enough, this translation admits to its own precariousness and violence. Here, issues of reading and translation can be understood in terms of the engagement with the other.

Indeed, in the context of Spivak's work, this engagement is not the rendering present of the subaltern woman. Rather, there is something which does not get across, something which is necessarily secret. Hence ethics (and the ethics of translation) becomes for Spivak, 'the experience of the impossible' (Spivak 1995: xxv). The impossibility of ethics is negotiated through a singular encounter with the subaltern woman. A meeting. A secret meeting which is also a gift in that it resists the structure of an exchange. The meeting does not have a proper object which moves from one to the other. Rather, the meeting is yet to be determined as such. It is a meeting between the translator who wants to do justice to the subaltern woman's texts and the subaltern woman whose position in the encounter is not that of the native informant whose truth is assured in being spoken for. Significantly, the engagement with the impossibility of ethics takes place through the meeting between women – between women as embodied subjects – who are differentially positioned in an international division of labour. One has a speech which is authorised – an Indian feminist who works partly in America – one whose speech is being authorised for the reader of English through the other's translation. I see this encounter as working at the level of the personal, affective realm of embodied subjects. It is through their meeting that a gift is offered, a gift which caresses the hand of the reader, of myself as reader, as I touch the pages. Through the fractured and divided embodiment of the subaltern women, the impossibility and necessity of an ethical encounter becomes imagined.

In the afterword, the secret encounter – the encounter which necessarily reveals and conceals – becomes the scene of global justice. Spivak writes: 'I have, perhaps foolishly, attempted to open the structure of an impossible social justice glimpsed through secret encounters with singular figures; to bear witness to the specificity of language, theme, and history as well as to supplement hegemonic notions of a hybrid global culture with the experience of the impossible global justice' (Spivak 1995: 197). Here, the ethical relation is traced as an encounter between the singular subaltern woman and the global – between the particularity of her embodiment and the international division of labour in which she is positioned as producer and native informant. Global justice – impossible but named – becomes imagined through the staging of this encounter. The particularity of the subaltern woman who is irreducible to the model of other or to the otherness of the other, is glimpsed only partly by witnessing the hegemonic forms which render her speech marginal. The encounter which is an engagement is both mutual and impossible: it is not fixed as an exchange; it is her future (her as the future) which surprises us.

Here, the particularity of an-other to which we must be obligated is at once a recognition of how the other is marked and constituted in a broader sociality. It is this relation between the particular and the general which interests me. The particularity of the relation to the subaltern woman is write-able only through an understanding of her situatedness within the gendered and international division of labour and speech. As such '*her* otherness' is irreducible to Otherness: she is given priority over any such abstraction and negation, refusing to become the scene over which the dominant self commands and fails to speak. Clearly, the particularity of the subaltern woman shifts the writing of the other in Levinas's work. In *Otherwise than Being* the question of 'the social' as 'other than a neighbour, but also another neighbour' is introduced or named as a 'a third party' (Levinas 1991: 157–61). The third party is a *permanent entry* into the intimacy of the face-to-face and is hence not detachable (the social is not detachable as such). But at the same time, the concept of 'thirdness' implies that the relation with the other is, at some level, a relation of 'two' who are in proximity. But in the ethical relation to the subaltern woman, sociality is irreducible to third-ness – it is already traceable in the body of *this* other who commands me. The sociality already marks the body of an-other to whom I am obligated.

The impossibility of ethics – and the undecidable secret which is at once concealed and revealed by ethics – can only be traced, then, through the particularity of bodies which are, in their particularity, already bound up in an international and gendered division of labour. Any demand for responsibility towards an-other is hence already a demand to challenge the relationships of force and authorisation which bind an-other to a certain place (the subaltern woman does not speak). In other words, a concern with the particular other (who is spoken for) is also a demand for a consideration of what ethical procedures (how to read, act, speak, listen etc.) would enable a more mutual and responsible engagement. The unlearning of 'speaking for' is here the basis of an ethical engagement and requires an understanding of the relation between the particular other and the gendered and international division of labour.

How this project differs from a postmodern valuing of otherness is clear if we analyse Derrida's interpretation of Levinas's mode of the other as radically alterior for a discourse of justice. Derrida places distributive justice on the side of that which is sacrificed by a Levinasian notion of the absolute asymmetry of the other (Derrida 1992: 22). However, for feminism, the pragmatic question of distribution already determines the relation between who is positioned as symmetrical to, and radically alterior to, the subject. The ethical relation cannot be abstracted from the particularity of embodied subjects who are authorised to speak differently and unequally. Transformation and the re-imagining of ethics begins then from the subject's uncertain and messy embodiment. How one lives out the body is a question of access to authorisation, of who gets authorised to speak, of whose names are authorised through the logic of property (authorship). In this sense, the embodiment of subjects leads us to the question of distributive justice; it leads us to the question of the resources (in the form of both economic and cultural capital) that inscribe certain subjects as disembodied (as being able to speak over time and space, as being able to speak for the universal). It demands what can be seen as necessarily collective political action[4] which would challenge the authorisation of certain bodies as proper subjects. This authorisation constitutes as real and universal the boundaries of the subject as Western/Man. In this sense, issues of power and authorisation (which can partly be theorised in terms of distribution) become integral to the ethical.

The ethical demand of the particular other is to formulate procedures which can challenge the distribution of economic and cultural capital within moral discourse itself. But it is the engagement with this other who cannot be figured as the Other which also prevents these procedures from being solidified into the Law, or a Truth which would subsume the particular other into a universal. Such procedures do not and cannot guarantee ethics. The re-dressing of relations of force and authorisation must begin with secret encounters with singular figures if we are to avoid (the violence of) speaking for the subaltern woman, or the violence of claiming that ethics resides positively in a universal or in a set of procedures for making judgements.

That postmodern ethics becomes figurable *through the Other* is a sign, then, of its withdrawal from the material realm of embodied subjectivity, a realm in which subjectivity is constituted through a gendered and international division of labour that already demands that the Other must speak, as it speaks for her. In some sense, these postmodern ethical writings call the Other to speak from the centre: they command the stage in which the Other's speech is desired as the possibility of (his) dispossession. At the same time, the flight from an-other through an ethics of Otherness becomes a masculine retreat from the material constraints which constitute the force of ethical demand. It enables the assumption that an ethics which obligates itself to the Other can avoid the necessity of challenging the unequal distribution of resources through collective political action from the very beginning, from the face-to-face. In contrast, the feminist ethics posited here is not the forging of 'new' relations to the Other as an impossible figure, but the re-dressing of the constitutive violence which binds her to a given place. Such re-dressing comes in the form of secret and singular encounters which cannot hold her in this place.

By posing issues of gender, and through this, differences that are not named by gender, this feminist writing stalks the horizon of post-

modernity and poses trouble for those who claim that, within postmodernism, otherness and difference are welcomed back after their
'casting out' in modernity. By questioning the very possibility of cele-
brating otherness and difference in abstraction from the constitution of
both in embedded and structured settings (the gendered and international division of labour), this chapter questions the very designation
of 'postmodern ethics' as an object. The borders around that object are
as unstable as the categories of difference and otherness which the
object has been assumed to contain (at least in these renderings). The
collapsing of the object is here the site of a new critical potential: a
potential which is at once feminism's gift to the postmodern, the loving
caress.

3   Woman

How has the relationship between postmodernism and woman come to be determined? Just as postmodernism has been read as the welcoming back of 'the other' from the violence of identity thinking, so too it has been read as the feminisation of the philosophical. As is clear from my reading of Levinas's work, the ethics of difference is partially figured through the feminine. But what does this figuration reveal for a philosophy we might call, however inadequately, postmodernism? Is this a sign that the deconstruction of identity predicated upon the negation and expulsion of difference is, at once, the deconstruction of masculinity predicated upon the negation and expulsion of the feminine? Is it through such a movement (towards the feminine) that postmodernism is figurable *as* woman? In this chapter, I suggest that we should not assume that there is something *within* postmodernism that renders its alliance with the feminine automatic. In other words, the relation between 'woman' and postmodernism is not essential, but is determined in specific sites of inscription.

In *Patterns of Dissonance: A Study of Women in Contemporary Philosophy*, Rosi Braidotti discusses the crisis of the discourse of modernity and the Cartesian subject as opening up new possibilities for re-figuring sexual difference or, at least, for making visible the problematic of the relation between women and philosophy (Braidotti 1991: 10). The subject of modernity, she argues, occupies a specifically phallocentric order: the rational subject is masculine and achieves its identity through an expulsion or repression of its physicality. The identity of the thinking subject is achieved through a repression of the ambiguity and contingency of the body (Braidotti 1991: 8). The 'return of the repressed' in the crisis of modernity is an opening up of the identity of the Cartesian subject to the feminine – as that which refuses incorporation into the realm of truth and rationality, and that which remains other to its law. Braidotti writes, 'it is as if the modern subject, the split subject, discovers the feminine layer of his own thought just as he loses the mastery he used to assume as his own' (Braidotti 1991: 10). A philosophy which plays amidst the heterogeneity of the bodily, and of the materiality of the signifiers (of desire) is a philosophy which is *becoming woman*, refusing the Law and Truth of modernity in a celebration of the otherness (of the feminine).

However, while this relation between a critique of identity thinking and sexual difference is constructed through the philosophical, I think the relation can be seen as a difficult one. What is required is not so much a general theory of the relation between postmodernism and sexual difference – which accepts the narrative at work that conflates femininity with difference – but a closer and engaged reading of how postmodernism has aligned itself with the feminine through the re-figuration of woman. The two crucial texts that have been debated by feminists such as Elizabeth Grosz, Elspeth Probyn, Alice Jardine and Rosi Braidotti as posing 'woman' as the crisis of modernity are Derrida's *Spurs: Nietzsche's Styles* in which 'woman' is inscribed as catachresis (as a name without an adequate referent), and Deleuze and Guattari's *A Thousand Plateaus* in which 'becoming woman' is privileged as the becoming through which all other becomings must pass. Through engagement with these authorising texts, I will pose the question of how feminism itself can theorise the instability of 'woman' as a signifier without losing sight of the over-determined relation between 'woman' and women as historically constituted and embodied subjects.

Becoming woman

It is not an over-estimation to say that the reception of *A Thousand Plateaus* within feminism has been controversial, and has produced polarised responses in which it has either been taken on board or dismissed. My own reading is not organised by the desire to dismiss this text (for example, as 'male theory', or as a symptom of the 'masculine' crisis of identity perhaps nameable as postmodernism), though neither am I simply interested in what it might mean for feminism to 'take it on board'. Hence I broadly support the engaged readings of Deleuze and Guattari offered by writers such as Rosi Braidotti, Elspeth Probyn and Elizabeth Grosz.

Because of the nature of this polarisation within feminism, I think we need to return to some of the issues I raised in the introduction regarding the problem of belonging. My own reading is not motivated by issues of 'belonging' – does feminism 'belong' inside or outside the texts of Deleuze and Guattari (should feminism become Deleuzian?)? Such a question assumes that feminism can be fixed in a singular place and that feminism has, so to speak, a proper object and trajectory (often a curiously modern narrative of progress is in play here, whereby feminism is liberated – perhaps by Deleuze and Guattari, or by post-modernism in general – from its embarrassing roots in modernity). In so far as I am not interested in questions of belonging, I am also not interested in authorising what some might call 'a Deleuzian feminism'. Such a conjoining of terms suggests that feminism can be successfully incorporated into another critical discourse without destabilising or displacing its terms. Hence for me, reading Deleuze as a feminist involves a form of dialogue in which something other than simply the reproduction of critical terms takes place. This desire for 'something other', must involve a refusal to position *A Thousand Plateaus* as a master-discourse which can be used to 'help' feminism discover its own identity. Indeed, Braidotti uses the term 'great help' when she talks of the relation between Deleuze and Guattari and feminism (Braidotti 1994a: 163). Elizabeth Grosz also uses the word 'help' – suggesting that they may 'help clear the ground of metaphysical concepts' (Grosz 1994a: 192). This model of Deleuze and Guattari 'helping' feminism is not a politically enabling one; it positions them as the subjects who can *authorise* a 'better' space for feminist critical thinking. Such authorisation can be disrupted through close and critical engagement.

First of all, we need to begin with the very question of 'becoming' rather than the particular narrative on becoming woman. What constitutes a philosophy of becoming? In *A Thousand Plateaus* becomings have a very particular structure. Becomings involve a movement between entities, a passing from one to an-other that is beyond the meeting of two points. Becomings are not imitations, identifications or evolutions; they are not anything that implies a correspondence amongst relations. Becomings involve a movement in which the real is the 'becoming' and 'not the supposedly fixed terms through which that becoming passes' (Deleuze and Guattari 1992: 238). Given this, becomings are irreducible to identity; they traverse the (supposedly inviolable) distinctions upon which identity thinking relies: 'Starting from the forms one already has, the subject one is, the organs one has, or the function one fulfils, becoming is to extract particles between which one establishes the relations of movement and rest, speed and slowness that are *closest* to what one is becoming, and through which one becomes. This is the sense in which becoming is the process of desire' (Deleuze and Guattari 1992: 272). Becomings activate *zones of proximity*; they are the movement of a desire in which surfaces meet, and particles slide into each other. Since becomings involve two entities, then becomings involve otherness, a division in-between which forms the 'middle' that becomings always inhabit.

Deleuze and Guattari state very explicitly that becomings are not phantasies. They write: 'Becomings . . . are neither dreams nor phantasies. They are perfectly real' (Deleuze and Guattari 1992: 238). Earlier in the text, they are critical of psychoanalysis for translating everything into phantasies (Deleuze and Guattari 1992: 151). When they consider Freud's reading of Little Hans, they argue that psychoanalysis 'has no feeling for becoming' precisely because of its interpretation of phantasy, whereby the phantasy itself is interpreted symptomatically as being organised around the Oedipal crisis (psychoanalysis sees the father and not the horse in Hans's story). So what is at issue is not simply psychoanalysis's perceived over-reliance on phantasy, but on the particular ways of interpreting phantasy in which all 'objects', 'events' and 'images' have significance only in so far as they 'stand in for' a prior (master) narrative. This means that psychoanalysis 'botches' the real (Deleuze and Guattari 1992: 151) and overlooks or 'fails to see' the movements of becoming, the forces of matter, which matter.

What I want to do here is to problematise the model of phantasy that Deleuze and Guattari are using which, in part, will provide some qualification of their critique of psychoanalysis. In the first place, the opposition they rely upon is between phantasy and the real: becomings are not phantasies precisely because they are real. In psychoanalytic terms, phantasy is not easily explained in terms of the opposition between imagination and reality. According to Jean Laplanche and Jean-Bertrand Pontolis, the third term which destabilises any simple opposition between imaginary and real in Freud is 'psychical reality' (Laplanche and Pontolis 1986: 7–8). In Freud's *Interpretations of Dreams*, this concept is introduced to describe how the dream is not a 'fantasmagoria', but a text to be deciphered. As Laplanche and Pontolis explain, the term does not represent the whole of the subjective (as in 'psychological field'), but functions as a heterogeneous and resistant element within the subjective (Laplanche and Pontolis 1986: 8). Inevitably, as they point out, the term psychical reality cannot 'resolve' the problematic tension between imaginary and real; rather it traces the problem of how the relation between the 'inner' psychic field and the 'outer' external field comes to be determined as the site of instability and crisis. Hence, a psychoanalytical understanding of phantasy does not, as Deleuze and Guattari assume, suggest that meaning is simply locatable elsewhere, in a prior master narrative (or in the unconscious) which is represented symptomatically. Rather, the relation between the literal scene and the elsewhere posits the over-determination of the text by elements which are not simply absent or present.

Such an approach clears the way for a critique of the assumption that matter and the image are separable. Becoming, as I have pointed out, involves a movement between two material entities. Those entities also involve over-investment as images – 'wolf' for example, as a material entity is inseparable from the fascination with 'wolf' as image. Images do not fully saturate material entities, but convey their investment with a significance which moves beyond them. Phantasy names this opening out as an instability – it hesitates between the domains of the material, the imaginary and the social. How then does becoming, as a movement between entities which is transformative, rely for its effects on the motivated nature of the images of 'the other entity' (which one does not become, but enters a relationship with through becoming)? By posing such a question, we are moving away from a model of becoming as separable from the motivated nature of the image (of the other) – becoming is not freed from 'the image', though neither is it reducible to it.

Deleuze and Guattari use the language of 'fascination' to discuss becomings. They write: 'We do not become animal without a fascination for the pack, the multiplicity. A fascination for the outside? Or is the multiplicity that fascinates us already related to a multiplicity dwelling within us?' (Deleuze and Guattari 1992: 339–40). What fascinates is the multiplicity that cannot be simply grasped or placed as 'inside' or 'outside'. Phantasy names this fascination; it names this fascination with an otherness which cannot simply be relegated to the outside. The very language of 'fascination' links the question of the other, with an excess of affect and desire, that causes ripples and movement. But what fascinates – what, in this limited sense, causes the movement of becoming – is always already an image of the otherness of the other. To understand fascination in terms of phantasy would be to refuse to see the movement of becoming as 'freed' from particular self–other relations. Reading 'fascination' in terms of phantasy can lead us from simply being fascinated by the text: instead we may ask, how does fascination (with the other) constitute the implication, rather than the separation, of phantasy and becoming?

To speak then of phantasies of becoming is to raise the following questions. First, to what extent do the narratives of becoming discussed by *A Thousand Plateaus* involve a fascination with otherness in a way which re-inscribes an identity-through-becoming? Second, to what extent do the accounts of these narratives of becoming themselves install particular phantasies of otherness (the motivated nature of the 'other entity')? Third, to what extent is the philosophy of becoming itself a phantasy; not in the sense of being imaginary, but in the sense of re-producing dominant social identities through its fascination with otherness, and its very desire to become other (or to get closer to the other)? It is here that we can begin to address the difficult question of becoming woman *as phantasmatic*.

Becoming woman has certainly been a main point of contention in the debate amongst feminists about the status of *A Thousand Plateaus* (see Braidotti 1994b: 116–22; Grosz 1994b: 161). Although becoming woman does not take up much of the section on becoming, it is given priority and privilege in the text. Crucial to an understanding of this privileging is the division between molar and molecular. A molar entity is, for example, 'the woman as defined by her form, endowed with organs and functions and assigned as a subject' (Deleuze and Guattari 1992: 275). A molecular entity is fluid and beyond the form and structure of this identification. Hence becoming woman is not imitating woman, or transforming oneself into a woman – defined as a molar identity (Deleuze and Guattari 1992: 275). Indeed, woman as a molar identity must first become woman, in order that the man can become woman (Deleuze and Guattari 1992: 276). Although Deleuze and Guattari accept that it is important for women to conduct a molar politics, and hence to become 'subjects of enunciation', they also suggest, 'it is dangerous to confine oneself to such a subject, which does not function without drying a spring or stopping a flow' (Deleuze and Guattari 1992: 276).

The narrative of becoming woman offered by Deleuze and Guattari works through another coupling – not just molar/molecular, but also majoritarian and minoritarian. One cannot 'become man' – man is the absolute majoritarian; the face against which all other identities are defined (Deleuze and Guattari 1992: 178, 292). Hence the other entity which one moves towards in becoming is always minoritarian: it is always less powerful. It must be noted here that the narrative at this level is very simplistic. There is a struggle between two things – the more powerful and the less powerful, the totalising and the dispersing. As a model of relationality this is extremely inadequate. In some sense, power becomes defined as a struggle between identity and its partial collapse (becoming). This sets up a hierarchy between identity/totality and difference: a hierarchy which returns us to the methodological limitations of Lyotard's *The Postmodern Condition* discussed in my introduction. Indeed, becoming is set against the BIG institutions (or molar powers): the family, the church, the state. This model obscures how identity and the 'failures' of identity (difference, fluidity, dissipation) form a necessary relation to each other. We could consider, for example, how the perpetuation of 'identity thinking' relies on the threat of the 'collapse' of identity – for example, the language of 'crisis' over identity (national, familial, sexual) enables it to become more rigidly policed. The model also obscures the antagonistic and complex nature of differentiated power relations which cannot be simply subsumed into each other.

This 'first-ness' of 'becoming woman' on the surface, then, does not relate to a particular philosophy of femininity. Rather, becoming woman is simply an instance of the privileging of the molecular: 'becoming woman is the first quantum, or molecular segment' (Deleuze and Guattari 1992: 279). One could have assumed, for example, that 'becoming woman' is privileged due to the perceived *nature* of woman; her position as hysteric, as excessive, and as beyond the masculine structures of rationality (woman *as* desire, difference and fluidity). However, 'becoming woman' relates supposedly not to femininity as a molar identity – this in itself must be lost by the woman. Here, woman must 'become woman' in order that becoming in general can move through and between. But what is the relation between the molar and molecular? Becoming woman is not about ending up as 'a molecular woman'. This much is clear. Becomings do not relate to end points: they are the movements through which the distinctions between such points become difficult to discern. Becoming moves through proximity, by getting close enough to 'the other entity' to release the positivity of desire. So what is the material entity here? What zone of proximity is being activated?

The need for woman as a molar entity to 'become woman' (molecular) suggests that the zone of proximity must constitute the activation of the space of the feminine which is only partly excluded from the construction of feminine identity (that is, 'molar woman' and 'molecular woman' must be close enough to enable activation). For the argument to make sense, becoming woman must activate 'woman' herself (although it does not end with her), even if 'woman' remains 'beyond' the molar identity of femininity. This is clearly evident in the following passage:

writing should produce a becoming-woman as atoms of womanhood capable of crossing and impregnating an entire social field, and of contaminating men, of sweeping them up in that becoming. Very soft particles – but also very hard and obstinate, irreducible, indomitable. The rise of women in the English novel has spared no man: even those who pass for the most virile, the most phallocratic, such as Lawrence and Miller, in their turn continually tap into and emit particles that enter the proximity or zone of indiscernibility of women. In writing, they become-women. The question is not, or not only, that of the organism, history and subject of enunciation that oppose masculine to feminine in the great dualism machines. The question is fundamentally that of the body – the body they *steal* from us in order to fabricate opposable organisms. The body is stolen first from the girl: Stop behaving like that, you're not a little girl anymore, you're not a tomboy etc. The girl's becoming is stolen first, in order to impose a history, a prehistory, upon her. The boy's turn comes next, but it is by using the girl as an example, by pointing to the girl as an object of his desire, that an opposed organism, a dominated history is fabricated for him too. (Deleuze and Guattari 1992: 276)

Here, becoming woman is irreducible to woman; it does not belong to the woman (it is not a question of the specificity of her writing). Becoming woman is, instead, activated in such a way that it is transformative of the social field (the absoluteness of this transformation is indicated by the use of two 'phallocratic writers' as examples of becoming-woman). That 'impregnating' of the entire social field takes place at a molecular level – it is the emission of atoms or particles that perform and stage the crossings. But those particles are, in some sense, 'within' woman: they are 'atoms of womanhood'. That is, the molecular particles that can be 'very soft' or 'very hard' (atoms) are fragments of the molar (womanhood). So becoming woman gets close to the molar entity of woman; it is something about the nature of the woman (= womanhood) that enables these particles (atoms) to be emitted and to activate the social field.

The second part of the passage tells a story which is breathtaking in its simplicity. In this story, gender – as the organising of subjectivity into two organic sexes – is the enemy of becoming. The girl is *made to be* a woman, which means that the multiplicity and beyondness of her embodiment is appropriated and stolen from her. In this sense, becoming (the movement, lines of flight and so on) precedes gender, but is negated (even repressed?) by it. One wonders why the girl's body is stolen first. The implication is that gender itself renders the girl 'the first victim'. If this is the case, then becoming woman as 'the first becoming' *repeats* the formation of gender relations, by rendering woman the passage through which the man becomes woman, rather than being man. This repetition is curious and has implications for the difficult relation being forged here between gender and becoming.[1] For it is the girl who is then positioned as becoming woman – as the molecular woman – it is her movement and rest, her speed and slowness (Deleuze and Guattari 1992: 276). It is her body (= Body without Organs). The separating out of gendering from becoming leads to the following contradictions. On the one hand, becoming woman releases atoms from womanhood and hence activates the nature and body of the woman. At the same time, becoming is suggested to pre-exist gender (as a structure of identification – the girl is hence implied to be ungendered). Becoming is reducible to the body of the girl that is repressed or 'stolen' by womanhood. As a result, the phantastic figures of girl and woman hesitate in relation to each other, as the pre-gendered and post-gendered woman.

The hesitation between girl and woman – later 'becoming woman' produces the universal girl – is a symptomatic one (Deleuze and Guattari 1992: 277). The narrative fascinates itself with the feminine body as being *simultaneously* inside and outside, or before and after, gender (femininity). The collapse of becoming woman and the girl helps demonstrate that the 'proximity' of 'becoming woman' rests precisely on a phantasy of the feminine body as both prior to, and in excess of, the nature of womanhood. The phantastic feminine body released by becoming woman is hence irreducible to, and yet close enough to, 'womanhood'. So although at one level the text severs any connection between becoming woman and women by separating becoming from either end points or molar identities, at another level becoming woman *brings into play* phantasies of womanhood (where she is already endowed with organs). The phantasy of becoming woman (bodies without organs) is *close enough* to the phantasy of being woman (bodies with organs): indeed, it is this doubling or movement from one to the other which is the structure of the phantasy itself.

So while on the surface, becoming woman does not seem to rely on a philosophy of femininity, through the emphasis on becoming as a proximity between material identities, it returns to some notion of 'woman' as in-excess. The privileging of becoming woman implies a fascination with 'molecular woman' (the girl/woman beyond women) as the space in which the logic of molar identities must, *in the first place*, meet its limits. Here, 'becoming woman', in some sense, 'clears the way' for becoming itself, for the very philosophy of becoming as a critique of philosophies of either presence (metaphysics) or psychoanalysis (negative metaphysics). Woman becomes then a 'key to all the other becomings' which unlocks something other to the very opposition presence/absence upon which identity thinking rests (Deleuze and Guattari 1992: 227). This position of the woman as a 'key', as the necessary condition for the movement from the opposition presence/absence through the zone of imperceptibility activated by becoming, reifies the link between woman and difference (the molecular), as it renders woman the radically other (the key to becoming). This fascination with woman as radically other to masculinity/femininity and all the dualisms that this carries with it, can be seen as implicated in a long history of fascination with woman as a figure for alterity within Western philosophy. 'Woman' herself, as that which is activated by becoming, is over-invested as an image. She becomes then a phantasy of the very necessity and impossibility of philosophy itself through the figuring of its other.

Becoming woman, moves from figuring woman as a 'danger' or 'risk', to woman as the key to the positivity of desire. But in this very event of privileging woman as the becoming through which others *must* pass, it keeps that phantasy (against which the masculinity of the philosopher remains defined) in place. To this extent, she is the means through which masculinity announces its impossibility and is re-inscribed other-wise (through her, he undoes his gender). That re-inscription still constitutes the passivity of the woman, her positioning as a means through which the masculine subject is in dialogue with (him)self. Indeed, if the movement through and beyond masculinity is, in the first instance, equatable with becoming woman (the becoming woman of woman through which man becomes woman) then 'woman' stands for the very phantasy of masculinity over-coming itself: not only can he make but he can unmake the border between self and other.

It is this relation between becoming and over-coming that I now want to address. If becoming woman has ontological privilege as the 'first' becoming, the becoming through which all other becomings pass, then 'woman' herself does not remain distinguishable as a figure for be-coming. The narrative of becoming offered by Deleuze and Guattari does not just offer a re-inscription of the feminine other-wise. It does not end with becoming woman. It ends with 'becoming imperceptible'. One must first re-think the relation between imperceptibility and woman. An aspect of imperceptibility is the collapse of identities-as-distinctions. Becoming woman is linked precisely to indiscernibility, to being unable to differentiate at the level of the organic body (hence the phrase, 'the proximity or zone of indiscernibility of women' (Deleuze and Guattari 1992: 276)). Becoming woman in this sense obliterates its own trajectory; woman ceases to be the figure through which becoming can appropriately be named: 'If becoming-woman is the first quantum, or molecular segment, with the becomings-animal that link up with it coming next, what are they all rushing toward? Without a doubt, toward becoming-imperceptible' (Deleuze and Guattari 1992: 279). There is a link made between imperceptibility, indiscernibility and impersonality: 'By process of elimination one is no longer anything more than an abstract line' (Deleuze and Guattari 1992: 280). This (progressive?) narrative shift from woman to imperceptibility, suggests that 'woman' is positioned as a means through which a radical transformation of the conditions of possibility for both philosophy and living-as-movement takes place. In other words, 'woman' is first privileged as a figure of radical alterity and then subsumed in a generalised process of becoming other-than-identity.

Furthermore, what is interesting here is the use of the personal pronoun 'one': 'one is no longer anything more than an abstract line' (Deleuze and Guattari 1992: 280). This 'one' begs the question of the link between the position of whom or that which is becoming in relation to the process of becoming-imperceptible. How does the imperceptibility of becoming – the movement which cannot be seen and yet which constitutes the force of perception – relate to differentiated subjects? Of course, you may say, becoming is not, and cannot, be a question of subjects – it is a question of surfaces meeting, of particles being activated through touch, of subjects themselves being lost or erased from the surface. The very distinction of subjects is what becoming-imperceptible moves beyond. Yet I would argue that this 'moving beyond' the discernibility of subjects is in itself implicated in the writing of a certain kind of subjectivity; a subjectivity that can move, that is unfettered, and that has the privilege of fluidity and transformability. This is clear in Marcus Doel's paper, 'Bodies without Organs' where he affirms that, 'the subject swarms with these modalities of disappearance which Open onto the motionless voyaging of Becoming-other' (Doel 1995: 240). Here, becoming other, as the disappearance of the subject, is also its voyage: that is, a journey of the subject through the other and towards the imperceptible. As such, subjectivity is re-written through the other: the other becomes a means through which the subject announces its disappearance. Becoming other, in this sense, is the movement through which the dominant subject commands the otherness of the other.

I do think it is important to contextualise the narrative of becoming/over-coming offered by Deleuze and Guattari precisely because of how it has been positioned as a way out of the stasis of philosophies of either being or not being, and even as a way of 'freeing' the image from Law, lack and signification (Probyn 1996: 59). Hence I have raised various issues by re-reading becoming woman as phantastic and as implicated in the cultural fascination with an otherness which cannot be relegated to the outside. Firstly, I have argued that becoming woman involves phantasies that saturate the 'woman' with a significance beyond the material ('atoms of womanhood'). Secondly, I have argued that becoming woman re-constitutes the (masculine) philosophical subject other-wise through engagement with this other identity. Thirdly, I have argued that becomings in general can involve phantasies of over-coming in which the privilege of the masculine subject to move across and in-between is re-asserted. To the extent that I have contextualised becoming woman as a phantasy of otherness, I have argued that philosophies of becoming (woman) do not necessarily resolve the problems implicit to philosophies of being (woman). That is, a philosophy of desire, difference and fluidity can easily support the structures of privilege which authorise certain 'beings' over others.

Woman as catachresis

Significantly, it is when philosophical texts that have become part of the canonical 'heritage' of postmodernism have announced their relation to the question of 'woman' – indeed, have announced themselves through this question – that they have been treated with the most suspicion, by both feminists and non-feminists (see Norris 1993: 184–5). At the same time, feminists have been criticised for making decisions about the politics of such texts without reading them closely. This crisis over reading is certainly evident in relation to Jacques Derrida's *Spurs: Nietzsche's Styles*: a text that has been read as symptomatic of a post-modern inscription of woman as catachresis (Jardine 1985: 40). Derrida himself has accused feminists of not reading the text in their judgement of it (Derrida and McDonald 1982: 69). While I agree that Derrida's text deserves a closer reading, I am concerned about the status of his accusation against feminists and feminism. While there is inevitably violence in judging any text without reading it, I must also point out here that Derrida's response to feminists, or to feminism in general, very rarely proceeds through direct citation, or evidence of actual reading and engagement with feminist work. So while I want to respond more justly to *Spurs*, I also want to respond more ungratefully to this injustice that surrounds the (non)reading of feminism. As a result, my reading will first concentrate on how the difficulties of reading *Spurs* relate to the question of 'woman'.

What are the kinds of judgements that have been made about *Spurs* and will they be justified by a closer reading? Linda Kintz argues that the status of woman as textual enigma in this text covers over our absence as women and, in particular, our status as female readers (Kintz 1989: 121). Michael Ryan argues that, in the process of making philosophy female, Derrida is positioned as quintessentially male himself (Ryan 1989: 63–4). Sally Robinson argues her case more strongly. She claims that the proliferation of woman-effects functions as an attempt to recuperate the 'feminine' in the service of masculine self-representation (Robinson 1990: 206). According to Robinson's reading, the affirmative woman becomes a figure of male desire who is appropriated in order to mask the masculine with heterogeneity (recuperating the threatening feminine into a safer discursive space). However, it could be argued that the textual project of *Spurs* complicates readings such as these which may assume the transparency of the authorial signature as masculine. But such an argument does not necessarily disqualify their judgements.

Importantly, the subject of *Spurs* is, from the beginning, under question. The text begins with what was to have been its title, '*the question of style*' (Derrida 1979: 35). But the next sentence acts as a qualification, 'However – it is woman who will be my subject' (Derrida 1979: 37). And then a further qualification of the qualification, 'Still, one might wonder whether that doesn't really amount to the same thing – or is it to the other' (Derrida 1979: 37). The series of qualifications of what is to be situated as the subject of the text entails a blurring of the questions of woman and of style. The uncertainty of what is the subject of the text opens up the text to its other, to the spurring operation of its style that hesitates upon the uncertainty of sexual difference. The subject of the text is a non-subject: its condition of possibility remains a question, a question which qualifies its own operation, constituting, then, an enigma.

The blurring of the questions of woman and style takes place around and through the proper name of Nietzsche, 'by way of a first glimpse of some exchange between Nietzsche's style and Nietzsche's woman' (Derrida 1979: 41). Through the citing of Nietzsche the question of woman (as a question which raises issues of truth interior to the structure of metaphysical philosophy) becomes one of style, which opens up the spurring operation which is the title of the text: 'the style-spur, the spurring style, is a long object, an oblong object, a word, which perforates even as it parries' (Derrida 1979: 41). This spurring operation is engaged by the graphic and visual effect of the quotation marks that Derrida uses in the event of citing Nietzsche's texts. These marks (<< >>) become spurs, dividing as well as spacing, cutting through the text to interrupt its flow with their double points.

As such, the very citing of Nietzsche opens up the spaces and intervals which constitute the field of writing. The difficulty of demarcating Nietzsche's text becomes a part of the problem of defining what is to be the subject of the text (of *Spurs*). This difficulty has structural implications for any model of reading the text, becoming inscribed and enacted within the very reading process. Derrida takes the phrase, 'I have forgotten my umbrella', from the unpublished writings of Nietzsche and asks whether or not this phrase inhabits the authorised work of Nietzsche, whether it is signed by Nietzsche, and to what extent that signature (or its non-event) guarantees the meaning of the text (Derrida 1979: 123–39). Here, the impossibility of ever knowing the context of its writing becomes inscribed in the very structure of its mark. That impossibility cannot be eliminated by a proper 'recovery' of its context, for its repetition remains irreducible to that context. The uncertainty as to the meaning and intentionality of the phrase becomes a mark of the refusal of texts to be fully bound by any notion of context or signature. The textual body of Nietzsche refuses to be confined to the proper name, refuses to have the form of a secret or veil to which we, as readers, may have access. The non-event of the signature rebounds to open the text of *Spurs* to the play of signifiers between contexts of utterance and interpretation whose demarcation remains temporary and partial.

The structural non-availability of any intentional or proper meaning to the sign (the possibility of its non-meaning, that is, being essential to its circulation as a sign) is always already implicated, here, in the field of sexual difference. The signifier 'umbrella' itself is carried over into the text of *Spurs* as a 'spur', a structure which confuses sexual opposition, with the double/doubling possibility of aggression and defence. The umbrella may function as a sign that is contained by a particular Freudian analysis as 'having' a symbolic meaning of sexual (or, specifically phallic) desire. However, in *Spurs* 'the umbrella' refuses to be contained by the notion of a symbol. The umbrella may be a phallus, or like a phallus, and yet, when opened, it may have the function of a sail, adrift and floating in a sea of signifiers, open, receiving and feminine. The double possibility of the masculine and feminine is inscribed in the structure of its meaning, which leaves 'this elytron to float between the masculine and the feminine' (Derrida 1979: 39). The umbrella deconstructs the opposition masculine and feminine upon which the regime of sexual decidability relies. What implications, then, does this textual and sexual in-determination have for a model of the politics of interpretation or, more specifically, for our politics in interpreting the text?

Derrida shows that any strategy of reading or politics of interpretation (of Nietzsche's text) which exercises the concept of 'belonging' is contained within the structure of metaphysics. For example, Heidegger's argument that Nietzsche has failed to overcome metaphysical philosophy effectively attempts to put Nietzsche's text in its 'proper place'. Heidegger's general project of deciding where the texts of Nietzsche properly belong – inside or outside of metaphysics – effects a totalisation of the body of Nietzsche's texts, presuming not only their exhaustibility but also their accessibility in the form of a secret to be unveiled. Derrida comments: 'In presuming to penetrate to the most intimate reaches of Nietzsche's thinking will . . . Heidegger concludes that this will, because it aimed to culminate it, still properly *belonged* to the history of metaphysics' (Derrida 1979: 115). This notion of belonging effaces, then, the uncertainty of where the textual body of Nietzsche begins and ends.

The metaphysics of Heidegger's own textual project and reading strategy is linked by Derrida to the effacement of the question of woman. Heidegger's reading 'missed the woman in truth's fabulous plot-ting' (Derrida 1979: 109); he 'skirts the woman, abandons her there' (Derrida 1979: 85). The fantasy of possessing Nietzsche's texts is the very desire to master the woman – the impossibility of that fantasy's fulfilment becomes then the necessity that the woman must take flight, must escape the regime of philosophical decidability which pins her down to a conceptual essence.

The textual project of *Spurs* is hence clearly differentiated from the Heideggerian analysis. Derrida's project is, 'to decipher this *inscription of the woman*' (Derrida 1979: 87), rather than position her as some 'mythological flower' which we 'pluck' in order to 'dissect' (Derrida 1979: 85). In this sense, the woman that inhabits the text of *Spurs* does not properly belong to either the proper names of Nietzsche or Derrida, but occupies the (inter-textual, potentially endless) space between them, as the interval of their very textual relation. She cannot be attributed to either, in so far as either name functions as an indicator for an exhaustible conceptual and semiological space.

Are arguments such as Sally Robinson's complicated and disrupted by the explicit textual project as it is articulated in *Spurs*? The position that this text involves the recuperation of the feminine in the interests of masculine self-representation invokes notions of proper meaning and belonging, as well as presupposing a model of biographical desire as being recoverable through the transparency of the sign. It attributes not only an absolute and intentional significance to the inscription of woman in the text, but also sustains an automatic link between that inscription and the proper name 'Derrida'. But to say that the textual project of *Spurs* disqualifies reading strategies such as Robinson's is, of course, to accept the text on its own terms. Those terms can, in themselves, be open to a further complication.

This complication, as one would expect, is anticipated by Derrida. The opposition that my analysis has exercised, between models of reading (woman) which merely decipher her play, and those which impose a structure of belonging, is in itself problematised. Derrida writes: 'In its turn the opposition between metaphysic and non-metaphysic encounters its limit here, the very limit *of* that opposition and of opposition's form . . . if the form of opposition and the oppositional structure are themselves metaphysical, then the relation of metaphysics to its other can no longer be one of opposition' (Derrida

1979: 117; 119). Given this non-opposition between metaphysics and its other, then the reading strategies based on belonging and decipherment can no longer be opposed. Derrida's own decipherment of the inscription of woman in Nietzsche's text entails an interpretation of her play and a mastering of her enigma, however much that mastery is deferred and that enigma structurally returned to inscribe her mark. For example, Derrida reduces the multiple women of Nietzsche's text through a formalisation. He writes, 'rather than examine here the large number of propositions which treat of the woman, it is instead their principle, which might be resumed in a finite number of typical and matrical propositions which I shall attempt to formalise – in order to mark then the essential limit of such a codification and the problem that it entails for reading' (Derrida 1979: 95). Here, the relation between Nietzsche's cited text, and Derrida's *Spurs*, is one which imposes a structure of interpretation, an active and positive gesture of re-reading that necessarily de-limits the play of significance (of the woman).

The politics of a reading which interprets the politics of Derrida's reading becomes necessary as well as impossible (in the form of the impossibility of staging any absolute resolution of the text's play). This implies that although the woman cannot be attributed to either the proper names of Derrida or Nietzsche she remains inscribed and *de-limited* by their textual relation, opening up a potential for us, as readers, to interpret the politics of her decipherment within specific inter-textual and ideological formations. Although woman does not *properly belong* to the text of *Spurs*, or to the cited text of Nietzsche, her inscription in this text remains *specific and productive in its effects*, and, given this, her meaning and politics remains partially stabilised, contained and de-limited in the interval of her articulation, and in the event of our reading.

The interval of her articulation involves a narrativisation of woman's relation to philosophy itself. Derrida summarises the narrative of 'Women and Their Effect at a Distance' offered by Nietzsche in the text *Joyful Wisdom* (Derrida 1979: 41). Here, the philosopher knight stands 'in the midst of the surging of the breakers', where there is only undifferentiated sound, 'howling, threatening, crying and screaming at me' (Derrida 1979: 43). But, then, 'suddenly, as if born out of nothingness, there appears before the portal of this hellish labyrinth, only a few fathoms distant – a great sailing ship (*Segelschiff*) gliding silently along like a ghost' (Derrida 1979: 45). The appearance of a visual and physical presence, creates the philosopher's desire for meaning, which then becomes figured as his desire for women:

When a man is in amidst of his hubub (*Lärm*), in the midst of the breakers (again *Brandung*) of his plots and plans, (*Würfen und Entwürfen*) he there sees perhaps calm, enchanting beings glide past him, for whose happiness and retirement (*Zurückgezogenheit*: withdrawing in oneself) he longs – they are women. (Derrida 1979: 45)

The entrance of women into the literal scene of Nietzsche's narrative functions here to gender this allegory of philosophy's quest for truth (as presence). Into the empty scene arrive objects which tantalise the male philosopher with their fullness. They carry with them a lure and promise of an identity which transcends the undifferentiated signifiers that serve only to baffle and confuse, to overwhelm his senses and deprive his rationality of stable objects for contemplation. But his longing *for* them is figured here as a desire to *be* them, to have and possess their retirement, their self-possession. This displacement, this lack of being (them) which energises his desire, represents its impossibility; that fullness remains at a distance, a promise, a lure, which divides the philosopher (or the rational subject) from himself. The lure of woman is the lure of that which cannot be realised: it becomes the impossibility of philosophy itself.

The conflation of woman and (impossible) truth that is at work in this passage is carried over into another narrative that is offered to represent the history of the relation between woman and truth. Here, the male philosopher moves from a conceptual world where he *is* truth (Plato says <<I Plato, *am* the truth>>) to one where 'the philosopher is no longer the truth', where, 'severed from himself, he has been severed from truth' (Derrida 1979: 87). This is represented as the beginning of history and narrative, and also as the beginning of woman, 'Distance-woman-averts truth-the philosopher' (Derrida 1979: 87).

But why is the beginning of history and narrative already defined as woman? Why is history already gendered in this way? The asking of such questions introduces the contexts surrounding philosophy itself, the power relations that involve the definition and demarcation of 'who' (or 'what') is the subject and object of a discursive and philosophical exchange. To ask why is history gendered in this way is to open out the non-essential nature of that gendered relation, the way in which it occupies a specific regime of force relations that are contestable and partial in their fixation. In relation to Nietzsche's narrative, we can recognise that contestability in the over-determination of the philosophical gaze (where he sees women and longs for them *as* the longing for truth) by the social legitimation of male voyeurism. That is, the power of the look is not the expression of what constitutes the philosophical contemplation of presence *per se*, but is that which brings the borders between philosophy and the social into contention (as the unstable border between text and con-text). We may ask, how is this look organised in terms of modes of subject formation that are both within and beyond the philosophical? It is through situating the philosophical within the force relations of the social, that we can recognise how the relation between truth and the figuration of woman becomes determined, but also how that relation *is not fully determined*. Hence, when Derrida writes, 'it is impossible to resist looking for her' (Derrida 1979: 71), I would suggest that such an impossibility over-looks the possibility of looking otherwise precisely by assuming the necessity of this mode of the philosophical.

What I want to argue in my interpretation of *Spurs* is that the absence of a contextualisation of woman's determination as truth has structural consequences for a reading of the text. For contextualising woman's determination is not about fixing woman into a pre-designated place (into an already mapped out history of the subject). Rather, contextualising the determination of woman is about complicating the very *event* of her figuring, whereby she becomes *over-determined* as a name within masculine and Western philosophy. I emphasise Western to introduce the way in which the contexts which surround the repetition of woman as both signifier, name and subject involve cultural and racial difference. To re-think the way in which 'woman' is determined within a racialised context may halt the event whereby woman is inscribed in the form of a singular signifier in the first place. The collision of race and gender may interrupt the very designation of woman as a figure, halting the singularity of woman as both signifier and subject. We can return, for example, to chapter 2, to our discussion of how the subaltern woman is not subsumable under a postmodern figuring of radical otherness. The collision with racial difference halts the event of figuring and the singularity it shapes through the re-tracing of a signifier. Indeed, it is interesting and perhaps symptomatic that Derrida's inscription of 'woman' is separated from 'women'. Women may introduce not simply the question of reference, but may also serve to *pluralise* and *divide* the status of the signifier 'woman'. The problem of Derrida's exclusion of broader contexts in which woman becomes determined as 'women' is precisely that this enables a resistance to complicating the *singularity* of woman as signifier, subject, or even as the enigma of philosophy itself.

In my interpretation, the repetition of 'woman' in the form of a singular signifier may participate in itself, in a protection of the masculine as a mode of enunciation. That is, in the very event of taking a position in relation to the question of woman as enigma, whereby she is circulated in the form of a 'signifier' within the text, *Spurs* may protect the discursive space in which the male subject enunciates the terms of an exchange by naming woman with the impossibility of a name. The production of masculinity as a subject of (and within) the text may be enabled precisely by conflating the determination of woman with that exchange in which she is the enigmatic object of an (impossible) quest for truth. This framing of the philosophical exchange entails 'self'-reflection – philosophy becomes reproduced in its very introspective reflection upon its impossibility in relation to the question of woman. The circulation of 'woman' as a singular signifier is here enabled by the rendering invisible of the context of her enunciation (the power of naming her difference). While the repetition of the signifier 'woman' is in itself subject to iterability, by being re-inscribed in relation to the determination of philosophy's impossibility, her potentiality may serve to enable the reproduction of the masculine as the subject of the text.

What does it mean to introduce the question of the relation between 'woman' and the plural 'women'? At one point in the text Derrida discusses the question of the woman's figure. He writes:

by way of an emphasis on what impresses the mark of the stylate spur in the question of woman (note that this is not (according to a well-turned phrase) *the woman's figure*. It is not the figure of the woman precisely because we shall bear witness here to her *abduction*, because the question of the figure is at once opened and closed by what is called woman). (Derrida 1979: 41)

The abduction of the figure of woman represents her liberation from a certain discursive economy which reduces her to the biological, to the shape and form of a body which is pre-discursive. The absence of a figure to woman suggests that she no longer refers to a specific body, or is tied to a specific linguistic unit (as in 'a figure of speech'). The loss of a literal referent is hence staged by this abduction: the woman has no figure because the very possibility of a figure, with the implication it carries of a discrete unit, either biological or linguistic, is negated by her meaning. In so far as the question of woman is not a question of her figure, then woman comes to stand for the impossibility of figuration as such (her abduction). Woman signifies the very impossibility of women as referent, the very absence of figures to ground her meaning and de-limit the play of her difference. Although it is not a question of the woman's figure, the figure of 'woman' nevertheless stalks the text as a figure for that which cannot be contained within philosophy; it is *through* her figure that masculine philosophy is speaking about the impossibility of speech.

Derrida explicitly differentiates his re-inscription of 'woman' from models of essentialism and fetishism, which return her to biologist notions of the body as an integral unit and as providing the basis for the ontological truth of the subject. He writes:

That which will not be pinned down by truth is, in truth – *feminine*. This should not, however, be hastily mistaken for a woman's femininity, for female sexuality, or for any other of those essentializing fetishes which might still tantalize the dogmatic philosopher, the impotent artist or the inexperienced seducer who has not yet escaped his foolish hopes of capture. (Derrida 1979: 55)

Here, Derrida's inscription of 'woman' is freed from notions of reference as they are exercised by the discourses of essentialism (the founding of woman's conceptual essence in the bodies of women) and fetishism (over-investment in the object or body as referent). This non-referential character of 'woman' is constructed through the association made between woman and 'that which will not be pinned down'. There are some major problems with this passage, however, particularly in the kinds of elisions and slippages it enables the rest of the text to make. For the question of reference or, more generally, the problem of the relation between woman and women, is immediately and automatically reduced to assumptions of naïve or literal reference – as represented by the discourses of essentialism and fetishism. In the terms of the text, to assume a relation between woman as signifier and women as subjects would be, 'to pin her down'. Through this assumption, the text avoids dealing with the issue of the nature of the relation between woman as signifier and women as subject-effect, and the degree to which the meaning of woman is stabilised by this very relation. There is an opposition implicitly set up here between naïve models of literal reference and non-reference (such that her very meaning becomes the very impossibility of reference), where woman is severed from *any* connection with women, or any notion of a historically specific group of sexed subjects.[2]

Later Derrida cites Nietzsche on women: 'If we consider the whole history of women [that history which oscillates between histrionics and hysterics will come to be read a little later as a chapter in the history of truth], are they not *obliged* first of all, and above all to be actresses?' (Derrida 1979: 69). So although woman signifies the impossibility of reference, she remains in this text saturated with or over-determined by these cultural representations in which woman is obliged to inhabit a certain space (the actress). This over-determination of 'women' by cultural constructions of 'woman' suggest a way of conceiving their relation beyond literal reference and beyond the staging of the impossibility of reference. Here, such a relation could be understood as involving the function of the trace, whereby both signs invoke a history of their determination within a mutually grafted structure of discourse. Women does not pin 'woman' down as a literal referent (women is also a signifier), but may evoke how the figuring of 'woman' has an effect on the constituting of subjects (women as subject-effect). We should not, therefore, as Derrida does, turn the absence of a simple, referential link between woman and women into a refusal to engage with their relation as being an aspect of woman's meaning (and therefore involving its *de-limitation* through modes of subject formation).[3] Such a de-limitation is also, paradoxically, a widening or opening out of the contexts in which 'woman' is enunciated.

The effacing of woman's wider more complicated history of enunciation has further implications for the representation of the female body in *Spurs*. The insistence on woman as a non-figure, as being no-where with no-place, turns into a negation of the historical specificity of female bodies. The female body is either conceived in terms of an essence, or it disappears, through the presupposition of the impossibility of reference.

And yet, importantly, the female body reappears on the side of the male philosopher, as a way of radically symbolising his over-coming of his own history of metaphysics and phallogocentrism to which he does not belong, but from which he cannot escape. So, for example, when discussing Nietzsche's relation to his own thought, Derrida writes, 'he is the thinker of pregnancy which, for him, is no less praiseworthy in a man that it is in a woman. Indeed one might imagine Nietzsche, who was so easily moved to tears, who referred to his thought as a pregnant woman might speak of her unborn child, one might well imagine him shedding tears over his own swollen belly' (Derrida 1979: 65).[4] Here the female body is figured *as a way of representing masculine philosophy's over-coming of itself through a love of its otherness.* In the process of its metaphoricisa-tion, however, the historical specificity of the female body's determina-tion disappears: it is emptied out of the limits imposed in the process of that determination, becoming an empty space through which philosophy can speak of its otherness. He comes to write himself as inhabiting her empty space. In representing the phantasy of its own over-coming as becoming woman, masculine philosophy denies the specificity of woman's determination in a wider, more complicated history of enunciation, which de-limits and regulates spaces which are productive of the subject-effect women, of female bodies and corporeality.

Feminism and woman

In the previous two sections I have provided careful and close readings of *A Thousand Plateaus* and *Spurs* in order to demonstrate the difficulties sustained by narratives which assume the figure of 'woman'. I have suggested that in these texts, 'woman' becomes a phantasy of the over-coming of philosophical and masculine identity, but an over-coming which is more a coming-over, in that identity comes to be figured in different terms over the body of the woman. That phantasy fills woman with the very meaning of difference (from him) as it assumes that woman is precisely the impossibility of meaning *per se*. The relation of 'woman' to women as embodied (molar) subjects is denied, a denial that enables the philosopher to claim her figure and inhabit her (swollen) body. Such judgements of texts which have authorised the relation between postmodernism and woman have been produced through close readings, a closeness that has enabled distanciation rather than absorption or immersion in the texts.

But what implications do such judgements have for feminism? Partly, such judgements call for a different form of theorising in which 'woman' is not detached from women as embodied subjects. Indeed, Jane Flax has suggested that the problem with the postmodern de-essentialisation of woman is that it leaves it without reference 'to any historical, specific beings constituted by and through different sets of social experience' (Flax 1990: 213). Is this critique a call for a return to essentialism, for a new theory of referentiality, in which there is no dangerous detour between woman and women, and where 'women' becomes a signifier whose meaning is assured or a name whose referent is given in the material world? However, a critical reading of such postmodern narratives of woman does not necessitate a 'return' to this form of essentialism.

Such a critical reading demands a different return: that is, a return to why feminists themselves have engaged in a substantive critique of both essentialism and referentiality in theorising 'woman'. The strongest critique has come from Black feminism and the recognition that what is meant by woman as such usually refers to 'white woman'. Elizabeth Spelman suggests that the notion of a generic 'woman' functions in feminist theory in a similar way to how the notion of a generic 'man' has functioned in Western philosophy – it works to exclude an analysis of the heterogeneity that inflects the category, and so cuts off an 'examination of the significance of such heterogeneity for feminist theory and political activity' (Spelman 1990: ix). Indeed, woman as a generic term is predicated on violent exclusions. Audre Lorde argues this point powerfully: 'as white women ignore built-in privilege of whiteness and define *woman* in terms of their own experience alone, then woman of Color become "other", the outsider whose experience and tradition is too "alien" to comprehend' (Lorde 1980: 117). The violence of such othering demonstrates *what is at stake* in the assumption that woman has an essential and stable meaning. Such an assumption conceals the very borders that mark out the meaning of woman (whereby woman comes to stand for white woman). To assume the stability of woman is to conceal the borders that police what is inside and outside the meaning of 'woman'. As such the stability of woman is an effect of power relations: that is, an effect of those who have the power to define or authorise the criteria for what constitutes woman. Such criteria are not only racialised; other women such as lesbian women, disabled women and working-class women have also become the other through which norms of 'woman' are policed. Such normalisation clearly takes place within the social field as a way of regulating identity. It is hence of strategic importance that feminism makes visible, rather than keeps concealed, the borders which constitute the category of 'woman' (just as, returning to my argument in chapter 1, feminism needs to make visible the borders which constitute the signifier 'women's rights'). By recognising that definitions of 'woman' are exclusive rather than inclusive, Black feminism challenges forms of essentialism embedded in the assumption that feminism simply speaks for all women.

Such a recognition of the violence implicated in the designation of an essential meaning to woman, also opens out possibilities for social change. This brings us to the other main feminist critique of essentialism: to assume that 'woman' has an essential meaning is to negate the possibility of transformations in that meaning (Butler 1990). Here, the critique of essentialism involves a critique, not simply of normative ideas of 'woman', but also of 'women': the latter no longer can be used to simply refer to already constituted historical subjects. To assume essentialism, then, may be to fix women in an already designated space. The instability of the categories of 'woman' and 'women' is the condition of possibility for feminism as a transformative politics.

However, what follows from this position should not be a simplistic opposition between anti-essentialism and essentialist forms of feminism. As Teresa de Lauretis has noted, such an opposition swiftly converts into a hierarchy, a way of delineating better (sophisticated) and worse (naïve) forms of feminism (de Lauretis 1990: 255–7). Indeed, one of the most powerful 'accusations' within feminist theorising has become the accusation of essentialism. Diana Fuss has argued against such a use of 'essentialism' as a signifier of that which contaminates feminism. She suggests, in *Essentially Speaking: Feminism, Nature and Difference*, that the assumption that there is an essence to essentialism, that it is always already reactionary in its appeal to a reality which is pre-discursive and hence unchangeable, enables the theories of social constructionism to assume that their own narratives of cultural determinism escape or suspend the normative (Fuss 1990: 2–16). All theories may inscribe some form of essentialism in that they are all

constituted by certain assumptions which remain essential (both defining and determining) to them. To some extent, then, we need to
qualify our arguments by a recognition that essentialism is not a
conceptual horizon that can be simply transcended. However, I would
also add here that essentialism is itself impossible as such. Any positing
of pure essence always requires contingent and non-essential details and
so is always already contaminated by its other. The non-opposition
between essence and contingence may demonstrate for feminism the
importance of a *continual* reflexivity over how the borders which sustain
conceptual entities such as 'woman' and 'women' are constituted
through acts of exclusion or othering (essentialism is always a risk that
one has and has not taken).

Does my argument suggest that feminism may have something to gain
by the postmodern narratives of becoming woman or woman as catachresis? I want to argue that the feminist debate around the problematic
of essentialism may lead to a very different narrativisation of 'woman'
where the impossibility of designating her meaning (as sign) or referent
(as name) leads, not to the absence of relation between signifier
'woman' and subject-effect 'women', but the over-determination of that
relation. In my feminist narrative, the relation between 'woman' and
'women' is not one of a direct, unmediated reference, nor one which
assumes an essential link between signifier and a signified. Rather, as my
critical reading of Derrida suggested, both are mutually determined
through a generalised field of discursivity.

Theorising the over-determined relation between signifier and
subject-effect enables us to consider how the meanings of 'woman'
become stabilised or fixed in time and space in a way which constitutes
the boundaries of women as embodied subjects. So while the instability
of the category may be a condition of possibility for feminism, so too is
the stabilisation of the category. What brings different forms of feminism
into being is surely the recognition of how gender relations are stabilised
in the form of violence and hierarchy. Indeed, the difficulty of achieving
more equal social relations makes the political necessity of understanding how stabilisation operates very clear. We can understand the
relation between signifier and subject-effect in terms of processes of
stabilisation and fixation whereby 'woman' comes to acquire certain
meanings over others. It is through being fixed in intelligible forms that
'woman' comes to have certain effects that constitute the boundaries of
embodied subjects ('women'). But rather than seeing stability and
instability as in opposition, we need to understand how they are
mutually constitutive: to talk of stabilisation is to imply the possibility of
destabilisation.

What is required here is an understanding of the social as constituted through antagonism. Take Laclau and Mouffe's model of the social. They argue that:

> The impossibility of an ultimate fixity of meaning implies that there have to be partial fixations – otherwise, the very flow of differences would be impossible . . . If the social does not manage to fix itself in the intelligible and instituted forms of a society, the social only exists, however, as an effort to construct that impossible object. Any discourse is constituted as an attempt to dominate the field of discursivity, to arrest the flow of differences, to construct a centre . . . The practice of articulation, therefore, consists in the construction of nodal points which partially fix meaning; and the partial character of this fixation proceeds from the openness of the social, a result, in its turn, of the constant over flowing of discourse by the infinitude of the field of general discursivity. (Laclau and Mouffe 1985: 112–13)

Here, the social is understood as an impossible object that cannot command the play of difference. However, such a play would not take place without the partial fixation of meanings (in the form of intelligibility and institutionality). The process of fixation itself constitutes the instability of the signifier. We can hence recognise that the category of 'woman', as an over-determined category, is partially fixed into intelligible forms. However, that fixation cannot be halted, command over her meaning cannot secure her as a object. The possibility of her otherness is the very impossibility that command over her meaning can be had or maintained. The general field of discursivity within which woman is articulated cannot be arrested, but remains partially fixed or stabilised by relations of force.

Furthermore, to argue that 'woman' is over-determined – which brings into play the borders which constitute 'woman' in certain forms over others – is to suggest an intimate relation between the signifier 'woman' and the materialisation of women's bodies. The war of signification takes place at the level of embodiment. This understanding of the relation between the fixing of the signifier 'woman' and embodiment is clear in the work of Luce Irigaray. In Irigaray's work, embodiment is *simultaneously* differential and textual, as well as material and fleshy. Irigaray forges a metonymic connection between language and the body, which attempts to link the signifier 'woman' to the bodily and material experience of women in a way which is complex and over-determined. The body (for example, the 'two lips' of women's multiple and diffuse sexuality) does not have here the status of a referent to which we have a privileged access, but is contingent on, and merges with, the spacing and intervals which constitute language as differance (Irigaray 1985: 26). The body is not reduced to either an anatomical/biological entity or a text, but is a morphology which is constituted by both and hence which exceeds both.

Understanding the traces of signification of the fleshing of bodies requires a shift from both essentialism and from the postmodern narrativisation of woman as an impossible figure or as a molecular segment through which all becomings must pass. Thinking of the relation between 'woman' and embodiment in terms of over-determination (the function of the trace) is a direct critique of any attempt to empty the signifier woman from the open and complicated history of its enunciation which over-determines the lived, corporeal experiences of women. Woman, as signifier, becomes a trace of the weight of female bodies: a weight which returns to these postmodern narratives, as a reminder of the impossibility of assuming her figure by inhabiting an empty space.

4   Subjects

If postmodernism is, as Lyotard argues, a crisis of legitimation, then that crisis has been most consistently expressed as a crisis of the founding subject of modernity. Indeed, perhaps crisis is too weak a term here: an association has been set up between postmodernism and Death (the Death of the subject) such that the paradoxical question, 'who comes after the subject', is askable.[1] This crisis or Death of the subject is a way of signalling the effect of a substantive theoretical interrogation of Enlightenment assumptions of an instrumental relation of subject to object world, the dichotomy of mind and body, the predication of identity on rationality, and a consciousness that is fully autonomous and present to itself. The crisis of the subject is precisely a crisis of the *Cogito*: 'I think therefore I am.' If postmodernism signals a shift from a model of the subject as disembodied, unified and rational, and towards a model of the subject as textual, contradictory and in-process, then surely postmodernism and feminism have more than some-Thing in common? Doesn't feminism's critique of the modern rational subject as predicated on masculinity mean that feminism is part of this general postmodern onslaught?

Of course, such questions are difficult, if not impossible, to answer without considering the role and effect of psychoanalysis on this challenge to the unified, self-present subject of modernity. Psychoanalysis provides the critical horizon in which the question of the subject returns to the subject as a division within it-self. Lacan's 'return' to Freud is especially significant for this theorisation of a cleft that is always-already within consciousness. My entry into the debate on postmodernism and feminism in relation to the question of the subject must first commit itself to posing a more primary question of the relation between feminism and Lacanian psychoanalysis. Having more than two players on the stage (just to remind you of the theatrical metaphor with which I opened the book) is, in some sense, a symptom of the difficulty of staging the question of the subject through any such coupling.

In this chapter, I will consider the significance for feminism of the

intersection between psychoanalytical, postmodern and feminist challenges to the subject. I will focus on the way in which feminism
simultaneously presupposes *and* dis-places the critique of Cartesianism
central to the projects of both psychoanalysis and postmodernism. I will
hence not ask the general question, 'what is the subject?' (for the
discreteness of the subject may be precisely what is put under question),
but rather ask the particular question, 'how is the subject produced
within this theoretical frame?' This chapter will assume that it is
inadequate to talk of one general onslaught on the onto-theological
subject of modernity. In other words, there are different ways the
modern subject can be dis-placed and these differences can also be
traced at the level of effect. As a result, postmodernism cannot be
equated with the destruction of the onto-theological subject *per se*.

Of course, it is a commitment of this book precisely *not* to assume that
there is a subject which 'belongs' to postmodernism: postmodernism
lacks such a subject, even if it is produced through narrativisations of its
subject. Indeed, we could ask: how is postmodernism produced through
the announcement of a crisis in the subject? For example, Paul Rodaway
links 'the crisis of the subject' to 'significant change(s) in the contexts of
the mass media, consumer-oriented, technologically dominated societies of the late twentieth century' (Rodaway 1995: 241). Mark Poster
suggests that the historical outcome of a 'postmodern society' is a
transformation in identity itself: 'if modern society may be said to foster
an individual who is rational, autonomous, centred and stable . . . then
perhaps postmodern society is emerging which nurtures forms of identity different from, even opposite to, those of modernity' (Poster 1995:
80). To avoid assuming this subject of crisis (the subject which arises
from crisis) *as* a postmodern subject, I will examine how such narratives
of postmodernism, which assume that there has been a historical shift in
modes of subject formation, produce their subjects. That is, I will
examine the kinds of constructions of the subject that are produced in
theories that presuppose there is something out-There called postmodernism which has shifting ways of being-in-the-world. This meta-
discursive approach to how theories have constructed 'their' subjects
will lead us to an analysis of how identification becomes central to a
feminist politics of the subject, within the context of the challenges
posed by both psychoanalysis and postmodernism.

Detour through Lacanian psychoanalysis

Why psychoanalysis? Why Lacan? Firstly, this detour is an attempt to
recognise the influence of psychoanalysis upon postmodern construc-

tions of the subject. For example, Arthur Kroker and David Cook's *The Postmodern Scene: Excremental Culture and Hyper-Aesthetics*, includes Lacan's 'psychoanalytics of the bourgeois ego' within the nomenclature of postmodern theorisations of the body as a site of subjugated knowledge (Kroker and Cook 1988: 25). Secondly, the detour recognises the importance of psychoanalysis in providing the critical horizon in which the question of the subject can be addressed *as a question* by both feminism and postmodernism. As my opening comments suggested, it is in Lacan's work that the crisis of the subject returns most powerfully to the subject as a division within it-self.

In Lacanian psychoanalysis, subjectivity is understood in terms of a primary act of identification. In 'The Mirror Stage as Formative of the Function of the I', the child sees itself in the mirror, and misrecognises the image as itself. This act, 'rebounds in the case of the child in a series of gestures in which he experiences in play the relation between the movements assumed in the image and the reflected environment – the child's own body, and the persons and things, around him' (Lacan 1977: 1). The play with an image structures the relation of the child to its body and to others, in the form of an identification, that is, in 'the transformation that takes place in the subject when he assumes an image' (Lacan 1977: 2). Such an identification is imaginary and phantasmatic, projecting from the fragmentation of the bodily state a specular and Ideal-I, understood as the agency of the ego (Lacan 1977: 2). The importance and value of the Lacanian notion of the mirror stage is precisely that it 'leads us to oppose any philosophy directly issuing from the *Cogito*' (Lacan 1977: 1). The unity and Ideality of the I is a misrecognition which, while structuring the relation of the I to others (in the forms of the projection of the ego onto others), conceals the lack that inflects its own coming into being, returning to disrupt the self-presence of the imago in the discordance and alienation of the fractured body. The notion of misrecognition helps us to investigate the passage of the subject into an identity as entailing phantasy, projection and the concealment of otherness, in the irreducibility of the body to its specular imago. As Lacan summarises:

The *mirror stage* is a drama whose internal thrust is precipitated from insufficiency to anticipation – and which manufactures for the subject, caught up in the lure of spatial identification, the succession of phantasies that extends from a fragmented body-image to a form of its totality that I shall call orthopaedic – and, lastly, to the assumption of the armour of an alienating identity, which will mark with its rigid structure the subject's entire mental development. (Lacan 1977: 4)

The disruption of the *Cogito* is, however, centrally performed through the formulation of a theory of the unconscious. Shoshana Felman provides us with an excellent reading of the unconscious as determined by Lacan's rereading of Freud:

The unconscious is thenceforth no longer as it has traditionally been conceived – the simple outside of the conscious, but rather a division, *Spaltung*, cleft within consciousness itself; the unconscious is no longer the difference between consciousness and the unconscious, but rather the inherent, irreducible difference between consciousness and itself. The unconscious, therefore, is the radical castration of the mastery of consciousness which turns out to be forever incomplete, illusory, and self-deceptive. (Felman 1987: 57)

The notion of 'having an unconscious' implies that the unconscious is a place, and in this sense, an identity (however supplementary to the conscious self). In contrast, in 'The Agency of the Letter in the Unconscious', Lacan argues that the unconscious is structured like a language, understood in post-Saussurian terms. Lacan explicitly defines the limits of Saussure's model as the limits of the sign, understood as 'the illusion that the signifier answers to the function of representing the signified' (Lacan 1977: 150) – leading to a linear and closed model of significance. He elaborates: 'There is in effect no signifying chain that does not have, as if attached to the punctuation of each of its units, a whole articulation of relevant contexts suspended "vertically", as it were, from that point' (Lacan 1977: 154). Here, the polyphonic nature of the agency of the signifier, which is inseparable from, if irreducible to, the contexts which surround it (both linguistic and otherwise), can be read in terms of the function of metaphor or condensation (word-for-word) and metonymy or displacement (word-to-word) (Lacan 1977: 157–8). It is this agency of the letter which Freud 'called his discovery of the unconscious' (Lacan 1977: 159).

To say that the unconscious is structured like a language in the Lacanian schema, is to outline the function of the linguistic process of condensation and displacement as the dynamics of desire, whereby the contextualised play of the signifier prevents the fixing of meaning (or the signified) as presence, and the subject as self-presence. The sliding of the signifier divides the moment of interiority that invests the Cartesian subject with self-mastery and mastery over others (both the other in transference, as well as the Other). Meaning is not in any literal place, but remains elsewhere, not in a singular place or repository, but in the divisions and relations of language, and the instability of the desire for presence it necessarily deflects as lack of being.

It may be on the issue of the relation between Lacan's theory of language and his theory of subjectivity or desire that my reading may expose certain difficulties. Jean-Luc Nancy and Philippe Lacoue-Labarthe in *The Title of the Letter: A Reading of Lacan* examine the way in which the logic of the signifier settles into a theory of the subject. They argue that, if the subject is simply the 'locus of the signifier', then it follows literally that it is in '*a theory of the subject* that the logic of the signifier settles' (Nancy and Lacoue-Labarthe 1992: 65). Indeed, Lacan's very definition of the signifier as 'that which represents a subject for another signifier' seems to presuppose the there-ness of the 'subject', as that which the signifier represents, and as unable to represent anything but for another signifier. Nancy and Lacoue-Labarthe conclude: 'the subject staged in Lacan's text – on one level – as subject of enunciation, must be referred in fact to this other subject: the one which, caught in the separation between the subject of the statement and of enunciation, posits or imposes itself as a pure signifier' (Nancy and Lacoue-Labarthe 1992: 70). The subject is instituted in and by a signifier. This returns the theory of the letter to a theory of the subject, in which the maintenance of the name 'subject' stops the letter on its travels. Nancy and Lacoue-Labarthe argue that the return of the letter to the subject reinstates a metaphysics of the subject – albeit a negative one. The subject is de-centred, disrupted and subverted, but only through the presupposition that the letter returns to it in the first place.

If, as we have discovered, the Lacanian narrative settles into the singularity of the signifier of the subject, then we can establish the limits of identification as defined in 'The Mirror Phase'. For here, the act of the child seeing itself in the mirror and misrecognising the image as itself is a singular process, however much that act is taken figuratively to signify that which structures the impossibility of 'becoming' a subject, in the sense of being an image. What is the significance of a theory which takes its *figure* of subjectivity in such a singular act? I use 'figure' here deliberately. I am not claiming that this figuring exhausts the terms of psychoanalysis (which complicates the discreteness of the subject again and again) but rather that the reliance on the 'mirror phase' and the figure of the child's encounter and projection of an image is over-determined by the status of the subject as signifier. In this sense, the narrative reliance on the figure enables the return of the letter to the subject whose singularity as signifier is already assured (the complication of identification is hence contained by the outlines established by this metaphoric reliance).

That figure is certainly associated with the whole question of the nature of the subject: the child's misrecognition of its image comes to *stand for*, 'the assumption of an alienating identity, which will mark with its rigid structure the child's entire mental development' (Lacan 1977: 4). The limitations of the Lacanian model which sutures the divisions it

recognises in the relations of language and the unconscious by centring
on the subject (and its lack) may establish the limitations of a theory of
identification itself, which can no longer be figured in terms of a singular
(visual or otherwise) encounter with an image.

What we may need to investigate is not simply the status of the
signifier 'the subject', but also the irreducibility of the gap between the
theory of the signifier and the theory of the subject (and its desire). This
irreducibility may be decisive upon considering the role or dynamics of
desire. Returning to the axis of metonymy, it can be noted that the shift
from signifier to signifier with its contiguity and fluidity, means that the
signified is constantly deferred, is always already lacking. Lacan locates
the axis of metonymy as one of desire. Indeed, 'The Agency of the
Letter in the Unconscious' ends by declaring, 'desire *is* a metonymy,
however funny people may find the idea' (Lacan 1977: 175). The
linguistic trope of metonymy becomes reducible to the dynamic of the
subject's desire, *vis-à-vis* an analogy: both shift from signifier to signifier
without halting that signifier into a signified or object. But I think their
relation is stronger than mere likeness. In the Lacanian narrative, desire
and metonymy form an identity: it is a copula that joins and hence
divides them (desire *is* a metonymy). What divides metonymy and desire
is, then, a metaphor. The division between metonymy and desire,
between the theory of subjectivity as the axis of desire and the theory of
language as the axis of metonymy, meets its limit precisely through
metaphor, through the substitutions of language which are symptomatic
of the bar which frustrates the realisation of the identification forged
between the subject and signifier. The non-identification of subject and
signifier moves the narrative into a different place in which the subject
loses its place (even if it already means this loss, here it is no longer the
means through which that loss is signified as the always-already).

This loss beyond the loss of the subject may precisely introduce the
question of the border between the subject and the social as a site of
instability and crisis. Rather than such loss belonging to 'the subject', it
may open out the relation between the subject and the sociality in which
it is already immersed. As a result, our critique of the model of
identification offered by Lacan may suggest a different way of thinking
through the relation between psychoanalysis and sociology. Psychoanalysis and sociology have traditionally defined themselves against each
other: both of them, defined here in reductive terms, can be understood
to involve acts of translation whereby either the psyche is read through
the social or the social is read through the psyche. But if we begin to see
the border between the psychic and the social as undecidable and yet
determined, then we can begin to see that neither psychoanalysis nor

sociology can successfully translate their own subjects; there is always something left out of the psyche or the social which constitutes the trace of the other or *each other*. It is this opening out of psychoanalysis to an understanding of the social which has the function of a trace (which resists the mapping of the psyche as such) which may enable psycho-analysis to avoid fetishising the signifier 'the subject' through a discourse on its lack.

By focusing on the division that prevents Lacan's narrative being instituted into Law as the foundation of a 'true' theory of subjectivity, my reading may dislodge its apparent role as Master (of the other), which has frustrated the possibility that psychoanalysis could deal with the demands and concerns of feminism. The Lacanian narrative is structured by its own suturing operation, in which the gap between its theory of the signifier and its model of the subject and of desire, is covered over through a metaphoric elision. This does not lead us to reject the text, nor psychoanalysis in general, although perhaps we may question its status as Law or as a universal theory. Rather, an analysis of the gaps and divisions which structure Lacanian psychoanalysis may help us to re-negotiate its movements as a textual and performative operation which is *constructing its own subject*. And indeed, through dividing the theory of desire and metonymy we may re-stage the debate over the role of the phallus that has been the central focus for the articulation of a relation between feminism and psychoanalysis.

In 'The Meaning of the Phallus' Lacan moves from a theory of the signifier as having 'an active function in determining the effects in which the signifiable appears as submitting to its mark, becoming through that the passion of the signified' (Lacan 1990: 78), to a theory of the phallus as privileged signifier. He writes:

The phallus is not a fantasy, if what is understood by that is an imaginary effect. Nor is it as such an object (part, internal, good, bad, etc. . . .) in so far as this term tends to accentuate the reality involved in a relationship. It is even less the organ, penis or clitoris, which it symbolises . . . For the phallus is a signifier. (Lacan 1990: 79)

The phallus is not merely a signifier, but one that is responsible for the whole effect of there being a signified, through its necessary appearance as veil (Lacan 1990: 80). As such, 'the phallus is the privileged signifier of that mark where the share of the logos is wedded to the advent of desire' (Lacan 1990: 82). This separates the phallus as a signifier of potency and power (though, as veil, the presence of the phallus is constituted by the trauma of nothing-being-there) from the biological difference of men and women. For the phallus as a signifier of power and presence can never be possessed or had. Rather, it is what creates the effect of power in the form of presence, or the realisation of desire (the elimination of the divisions of the signifier). It organises the relation between the sexes, in the form of having or being the phallus (which crucially rests on the realisation of the mother's lack of, and desire for, the phallus). But is not the theory of the sliding of the signifier – where the only point of intelligibility is understood as a *mythic* fixing of a signified, as the function of the *point de capiton* (Lacan 1993: 267–8) – halted precisely here, *in the singularity of the phallus as a signifier?*

This is precisely Derrida's point in his reading of Lacan's 'The Purloined Letter', which is dedicated to interpreting Poe's short story of the same name. Here, Lacan focuses quite literally on the passage, circularity and agency of the letter, which is purloined, or missing from its proper place. The letter becomes the object of desire, although it 'doesn't have the same meaning everywhere, is a truth which is not to be divulged' (Lacan 1988: 198). But as Derrida argues, the letter, or place of the signifier, is found where Dupin and the psychoanalyst expect to find it, 'on the immense body of a woman – between the "legs"' (Derrida 1987: 440).[2] According to Lacan, the trajectory of the letter must return to its proper place, it must arrive at its destination. With the link between its property and woman's lack (of a phallus) the letter's agency becomes reducible to the law of castration. Derrida writes: 'Something is missing from its place, but the lack is never missing from it . . . The phallus, thanks to castration, always remains in its place, in the transcendental topology of which we were speaking above. In castration, the phallus is indivisible, and therefore indestructible, like the letter which *takes its place*' (Derrida 1987: 441).

What Derrida is outlining here as the truth-discourse of Lacan (the truth of the phallus as the law of castration), can be read more strongly as symptomatic of the shift from a theory of the signifier to a theory of the signified, in which the content or signified of the phallic signifier is already assured, *whether or not the signified is in itself the lack of a signified.* The singularity of the phallus as a signifier halts the Lacanian narrative into a theory of the sexual relation, at the point in which the theory anchors itself in a notion of indivisibility. The status of phallus as a privileged signifier can be seen as symptomatic of the more general collapse of a theory of signification into a theory of the subject as locus of the signifier, and into a theory of desire as metonymy.

Perhaps there is a need to move beyond Derrida's reading to investigate exactly why the Lacanian narrative privileges the phallus as the signifier which effects the illusion of presence. Can a closer reading accept the disassociation of phallus and penis? The reason tentatively given by Lacan for the role of the phallus is that it, 'stands out as most easily seized upon in the real of sexual copulation' and also that, 'by virtue of its turgidity, it is the image of the vital flow as it is transmitted in generation' (Lacan 1990: 82). The emphasis on the visual and on physicality returns the privileged phallus to the penis, as organ, suggesting that the privileging of the phallus may connect *in some way* with the penis, and the clitoris, when construed as a little penis. Judith Butler defines the connection in terms of symbolisation. Lacan does declare that the phallus is not the organ, *which it symbolises*. Butler points out that, if the relation of phallus to penis is of symbol to symbolised, then the phallus is not the penis, given that symbolisation presumes the ontological difference of that which symbolises and that which is symbolised (Butler 1993: 84). Indeed, the phallus must negate the penis in order to symbolise – their relation relies therefore on a *determinate negation*. The disconnection of the phallus and penis, despite their necessary dependence, implies that the phallus is necessarily transferable, and can transfer itself from the Lacanian economy which masters its movement by sustaining the dichotomy of being/having the phallus according to the scene of castration.

While Butler's emphasis on symbolisation links the determinate relation of the phallus and penis to its negativity, and hence to the potential for transference and displacement, there are limits to this reading. These limits are determined by the separation of the linguistic relation of phallus and penis from the issue of the power embedded in symbolisation. It is only given this, that she maintains the strategy of *inscribing transferability to the singular signifier of the phallus*, rather than putting the status of that signifier or letter, as a privileged and determinate mark of sexual difference, more radically under question. Jane Gallop provides us with an alternative reading, which emphasises the strategic element of the disassociation:

The question of whether one can separate 'phallus' from 'penis' rejoins the question of whether one can separate psychoanalysis from politics. The penis is what men have and women do not, the phallus is the attribute of power which neither men nor women have. But as long as the attribute of power is a phallus which refers to and can be confused (in the imaginary register?) with a penis, this confusion will support a structure in which it seems reasonable that men have power and women do not. And as long as psychoanalysts maintain the separability of 'phallus' from 'penis', they can hold on to their 'phallus' in the belief that their discourse has no relation to sexual inequality, no relation to politics. (Gallop 1982: 97)

Here, the disassociation of the phallus from the penis is defined as a strategy for concealing the relation of power that the marking of penis as privilege inevitably carries with it. This still begs the question of how we are to define their relation. To suggest an identity (the phallus *is* the penis) would also seem problematic. It would imply that the penis, as organ, could only signify power and potency, hence eliminating the possibilities of the biological being inscribed in a different order of meaning. I want to return here to my conclusion in chapter 3 where I introduced Irigaray's reading of the body in terms of a morphology, in which the relation between language and the body is conceived as metonymic. To inscribe the phallus (as signifier) and penis (as signifier) as having a metonymic relation would locate the dynamic whereby sex is invested with meaning and value, that is, whereby bodies become sexed, and *become identified as having organs.* Such an approach would historicise the role of the phallus as the privileged mark of sexual difference as being specific to a formation of power, and would emphasise the irreducibility of the penis (as signifier of the body) to the phallus (as signifier of a metaphysics of presence), as well as their contingent relatedness. The association of phallus and penis as metonymic, as a relation of word-to-word that opens out the temporal and historical dynamic in which bodies are identified as sexed, may enable us to theorise the stabilisation of gender relations, as well as the possibilities of a displacement, whereby the signifier 'phallus' loses its privilege, becoming one mark amongst many. The Lacanian schema which keeps the 'phallus' in its proper place (however much that place is the impossibility of the proper as such) would in itself be displaced, not by the transferring of that signifier to another organ (or to another relation beyond being or having), but through a giving up of its proper name in the division between it and the signifier 'penis'.

The shift in thinking through how sexual difference is organised in the Lacanian narrative of the subject cannot simply stay with the question of sexual difference. For psychoanalysis is also problematic in the very assumption that sexual difference is *the difference* that marks the subject. Indeed, Judith Butler suggests that it is the assertion of the priority of sexual difference over racial difference that marks psychoanalytic feminism as white (Butler 1993: 181). The use of psychoanalysis has invariably meant that other differences are explained through an act of translation back into the model which elaborates the division of subjects into sexes (the resolution of the Oedipal crisis, castration anxiety and the phallic logic of fetishism). Such a translation is even evident in the work of a theorist who occupies the difficult terrain of the post-colonial. Homi Bhabha argues that: 'fetishism is always a "play" or vacillation between the archaic affirmation of wholeness/similarity − in Freud's terms: "All men have penises"; in ours "All men have the same skin/ race/culture" − and the anxiety associated with lack and difference − and again for Freud "Some do not have penises"; for us "Some do not have the same skin/race/culture"' (Bhabha 1994: 74). Here, the recognition of racial difference as constitutive of the subject is enabled only through a re-working of the Freudian logic of fetishism. Racial difference is hence positioned as secondary to a logic of sexual differentiation which comes to function as a self-evident way of explaining *in itself* the structuring of desire and difference *in general*. As Anne McClintock argues, 'reducing racial fetishism to the phallic drama runs the risk of flattening out the hierarchies of social difference, thereby relegating race and class to secondary status along a primarily sexual signifying chain' (McClintock 1995: 183).

The translation of racial difference into the logic of the Freudian topology can only mean that the 'unmarked' language of that topology is held in place (whereby 'the subject' becomes implicitly conflated with 'the white subject'). To avoid the violence of translation, psychoanalysis must refuse to ontologise sexual difference as the difference that marks the subject. Such a refusal means complicating the model of (primary) identification as such – it means recognising the instability of the relation between 'the psychic ' and 'the social' in the conflict *between* identificatory practices. The subject is *already* marked by differences which exceed the domain of the psychic. In other words, if identification involves 'the transformation that takes place in the subject when he assumes an image' (Lacan 1977: 2), then we need to consider how the transformation depends on the already differentiated nature of the 'images' assumed by subjects.

In this section, I have drawn attention to the importance and value of Lacanian psychoanalysis. Its key concepts of misrecognition and the unconscious (as the sliding of the signifier) enable a politics of the subject which stresses the phantasmatic nature of the specular and Ideal-I, and the impossibility that (sexual) identity is ever successfully or completely achieved. But I have also located some divisions in Lacan's narrative of sexual identification, which may demonstrate how the narrative functions as an ideological frame. The text sutures a variety of gaps, between the signifier and the subject, metonymy and desire, as well as the psychic and the social, in order to halt the contingency of the linguistic process it identifies in the law of castration. The privileging of the phallus is not simply incidental to this theory, but is in itself symptomatic of the elisions it performs in halting the contingency of signifiers by abstracting them from the temporality of their contestation. This contingency which is irreducible to the law of castration may hence open out the vertical contexts which surround and enable the polyphony of signifiers as the open and pragmatic field of the social itself.

Postmodern subjects

As previously mentioned, Arthur Kroker and David Cook include Lacanian psychoanalysis within postmodern narratives of the body as a site of subjugated knowledge (Kroker and Cook 1988: 25). In this section, I want to examine such postmodern narratives more closely, asking: how do such narratives, in which the crisis of the subject is related to 'contemporary experience' (Rodaway 1995: 241), produce their own subjects? What differences exist between these narratives and Lacanian psychoanalysis as ways of reading and identifying the subject? What is the significance of these differences for a specifically feminist theory of the subject? I will consider the work of Jean Baudrillard, one of the most influential of the writers who argues for the existence of a contemporary 'postmodern' situation, alongside Arthur Kroker and David Cook's *The Postmodern Scene*.

Jean Baudrillard's *Seduction* deals with the issue of subjectivity and sexual difference within the context of a thesis on postmodernism as the loss of the real. It opens with the sentence: 'Nothing is less certain today than sex, behind the liberation of its discourse' (Baudrillard 1990: 5). Uncertainty is here relegated to a condition of the present ('today') and as constitutive of sexuality ('nothing is less'). Baudrillard suggests that the proliferation of sexual images involves the extension of the principle of uncertainty from political and economic reason to sexual reason (Baudrillard 1990: 5). He argues that we are in a state of 'sexual indetermination' where there is, 'no more want, no more prohibitions, and no more limits: it is the loss of every referential principle' (Baudrillard 1990: 5). The passage from determination to 'general indetermination', and to the neutralisation of structure, involves a '*flotation of the law that regulates the difference between the sexes*' (Baudrillard 1990: 5–6).

The passage towards indetermination, neutralisation and flotation is represented also as a movement towards seduction. But seduction is, more specifically, a metaphor for that which resists nature and essentialism, for artifice, appearance and the dispersal of truth and ideology. Seduction 'continues to appear to all orthodoxies as malefice and artifice, a black magic for the deviation of all truths, an exaltation of the malicious use of signs, a conspiracy of signs' (Baudrillard 1990: 2). Seduction is figured as the feminine which, rather than being considered as the negation or opposite of masculinity, becomes associated with the deconstruction of the masculine/feminine opposition. Seduction becomes a sign for the indeterminable and undifferentiated subject, *the subject in and of free play*. The shift from production to seduction involves a shift from a theory of the subject as active agent to a theory of the subject, 'as fascinated, entranced and entangled within the technologies and images of the contemporary objective world' (Rodaway 1995: 251–2).

Baudrillard hence rejects ideologies which argue that the subject is determined in the last instance. According to his reading, 'anatomy is destiny' signifies such a postulation of the subject as determined by a particular structure within Freudian psychoanalysis while, in Marxism, class becomes such a structure, and in feminism, gender. But it is here that the postmodern gesture can itself be problematised. For rather than refusing the concept of destiny, the concept of determination in the last instance, Baudrillard offers an alternative. He argues, 'seduction is destiny' (Baudrillard 1990: 179–81). That is, the very structure of free play becomes the normative account of subjectivity. The subject is determined by indeterminacy (rather than by anatomy, class or gender). As such, Baudrillard's postmodernism can be read as a normative and positive reading of the subject, rather than as a rejection of its limits, a reading which refuses to recognise the determining influence of structures of power, but sees the subject as governed only by the radical free play of its own (in)difference. The subject is determined (it has a destiny), but by nothing positive which exceeds it or is beyond it. The subject is determined then by its own undetermined possibilities, by its own limitless potential for dispersal and betrayal. In this sense, determination by indetermination separates the play of the subject from the relations in which it is embedded. Despite dethroning the subject as a rational agent, Baudrillard's theory of seduction implicitly assumes the subject's primacy over these relations (the subject becomes a fetish rather than a trace).

Baudrillard's interpretation of transvestism, for example, as the exposure by the male of the artifice of femininity (not the female subject but that non-referential other of sexuality/production), refuses to recognise power relations as operative within the determination of subjectivity (Baudrillard 1990: 12–15). The transvestite is radical and powerful in so far as it retrieves the symbolic power of the feminine (for Baudrillard patriarchy is a mere trivial and pathetic defence against the austere power of the feminine to disperse and betray truth itself). The transvestite is a sign for the radical refusal of truth and production and hence the free floating of the sign. Baudrillard writes:

What transvestites love is this game of signs, what excites them is *to seduce the signs themselves*. With them everything is makeup, theatre, and seduction. They appear obsessed with games of sex, but they are obsessed, first of all, with play itself; and if their lives appear more sexually endowed than our own, it is because they make sex into a total, gestural, sensual, and ritual game, an exalted but ironic invocation. (Baudrillard 1990: 12–13)

In Baudrillard's argument about the play of transvestism, the subject is 'seduced' in a 'game of signs' and hence rendered indeterminate rather than referential (Baudrillard 1990: 13). The arguments here about transvestism and seduction relate more generally to Baudrillard's arguments about hyper-reality and the simulacra, where 'the reference to an original is lost in a continuous play of signs and the subject is fragmented' (Rodaway 1995: 248). I do not disagree with Baudrillard's analysis of transvestism (or sexuality more broadly) as a signifying system rather than as referential. But the opposition implied here, between indeterminacy and referentiality, is in itself a false one. Indeed, one could question Baudrillard's narrative of the hyper-real or simulacra as the loss of the referent/original on two counts. First, such a narrative implies that the sign had a referent in the first place (a nostalgic narrative which assumes reference through designating it as a loss). Second, such a narrative assumes that the lack of a referential relation means that signs are not determined. Determination does not necessarily take place at the level of referentiality, where the referent itself is outside the text. Rather, determination takes place pragmatically, in stratified discursive (rhetorical/syntactical), political and ethical situations (Derrida 1988a: 148).

As such, one could argue in contradistinction to Baudrillard, that the signs intrinsic to the production of the transvestite subject are material and determined. They form part of a generalised discursive economy which stabilises meanings in the form of the de-limitation of subject positions. The signs used by the transvestite subject (as the signs of a fully negotiated, although unstable femininity), hence entail the de-limitation of the play of its meaning via their occupation in an already over-determined cultural space. The subject here, while not unified or self-present, is also not simply fragmented through free play. The sexual subject is here constituted through the pragmatic limits to the play (of the signifier).

In a feminist analysis, transvestism may be shown as functioning at the level of the material dynamic of the sign, over-determining the subject effects produced by a signifying system, rather than at another order suspended from material effects and determinate meanings. The system of gender may be seen to be relatively stable, to involve the determination of patterns of intelligibility (what it might mean to identify as 'male' or 'female'), *from which* a play in the terms is made possible. That play can hence be viewed as an aspect of (in the sense of being framed by) a pre-existing, determined and material system. In Judith Butler's work, there is a shift from a model of transvestism as a voluntaristic performance which disrupts a system of differences in *Gender Trouble: Feminism and the Subversion of Identity*, to an emphasis on the regulatory and normative mechanisms through which subjects are identified and which de-limit the potential for transgression through the re-incorporation of difference into systematicity in *Bodies That Matter: On the Discursive Limits of 'Sex'*.[3] The absence of a referent to secure the regime of the subject does not lead to a mere 'flotation' of the law regulating differences. That law may not be a referent, but its stabilisation is pragmatically and normatively regulated through the very structures of identification whereby subjects are constituted as such. Such a model does not exclude the possibilities of degrees of flotation, precisely because the social is an open and non-totalisable field, where subjectivities are under contestation.

The thesis of a generalised indetermination structuring contemporary subjectivities is also central to Arthur Kroker and David Cook's *The Postmodern Scene: Excremental Culture and Hyper-Aesthetics*, but here that process is not simply celebrated. It is instead identified as an aspect of the commodification process which neutralises and appropriates all differences into the in-difference of consumerism:

The fascination of capitalism today is that it works the terrain of Lacan's 'sliding of the signifier', it thrives in the language of sexual difference, of every difference, and it does so in order to provoke some real element of psychological fascination, of *attention*, with a system which as the emblematic sign of the Anti-real, must function in the language of recuperation, of the *recyclage*, of every dynamic tendency, whether potentially authentic or always only nostalgic. (Kroker and Cook 1988: 20)

This logic of recuperation and *recyclage* is suggested here to organise the regime of sexual difference leading to an androgynous sexual subject which cannot be contained by the dichotomy man/woman. Indeed, Kroker and Cook argue that, '*The absorption and then playing back to its audience of the reversible and mutable language of sexual difference is the language of postmodern capitalism*' (Kroker and Cook 1988: 20, original emphasis). This entails both the death of natural sex (the idea that sex could be had without the mediation of discourse) as well as the death of sociological sex, in the creation of a type of sexuality which is *experienced as an endless semiury of signs*. Thus postmodern sex is a *panic sex*, a sex without secretions. This virtual sex fears secretions (such as excrement) as signs of bodily desire which may threaten the integrity of the consuming subject, and enact the loss of the unifying principle of the social itself. The hysteria surrounding AIDS is here the panic site of postmodernism, which 'feeds on the fear of sex itself as emblematic of excremental culture driven onwards by the projection onto the discourse

of sexuality of all the key tendencies involved in the death of the social'
(Kroker and Cook 1988: 24).

Here, there is a shift from the Lacanian model of the impossibility of
identification as such to an argument about history, that is, about the
state-of-affairs in the modern world. But the thesis that sexuality is
virtual and mutable, and that it lacks either a basis in real or material
social relations, or the intelligibility of a system (such as gender) departs
from a 'psychoanalytics of reception' with which it is identified (Kroker
and Cook 1988: 25). For in the Lacanian model the phantasmatic (and
necessarily unsuccessful) nature of identification does not exclude its
role in marking subjects in real terms, that is, in producing systematic
and material effects. So although the notion of sexual identity, of the
intelligibility of sex, remains imaginary, it nevertheless organises the
relations between subjects. Indeed, Lacan develops the notion of *point
de capiton* (quilting) where there is a temporary (although mythic) fixing
of the relation between signifiers and signified, leading to the securing of
patterns of intelligibility, without which difference would become sheer
indifference (Lacan 1993: 267-8). Kroker and Cook's claims cannot,
therefore, be grounded in a theory such as psychoanalysis. Their argument is an empirical one which can only be contested empirically. Is sex
in contemporary Western, late capitalist society simply virtual? Is there
no pattern to subjectivity? Has all systematicity been 'lost' (presupposing it was there in the first place) in an explosion of signs?

I will address these questions by looking at one of the examples
Kroker and Cook use to ground their claim. They argue:

What makes the *Eurythmics*, Madonna, and Carol Pope with *Rough Trade* so
fascinating is that they play at the edge of power and seduction, the zero-point
where sex as electric image is amplified, teased out in a bit of ironic
exhibitionism, and then reversed against itself. They are artists in the big
business of committing sign crimes against the big signifier of Sex. (Kroker and
Cook 1988: 21)

I want to focus here on the representation of Madonna as postmodern,
because there has been considerable debate over the politics of the
representation of Madonna's sexuality, with her use (some would say
appropriation) of marginalised sexualities (such as sado-masochism and
lesbianism) and her reversal of the male gaze, allegedly 'deconstructing'
the convention of femininity by pushing it to its sexual, bodily limits.
Susan McClary, for example, argues that 'Madonna's art itself repeatedly deconstructs the traditional notion of the unified subject with finite
ego boundaries. Her pieces explore . . . various ways of constituting
identities that refuse stability, that remain fluid, that resist definition'
(cited in Bordo 1993: 272). As Susan Bordo suggests, this reading

isolates the politics of Madonna as a representation from the contexts of both its production and reception (Bordo 1993: 273). That production not only situates Madonna's text as a commodity (circulated by industries largely dominated by men), but also as part of a tradition of rock videos which reduce the female body to a spectacle. Bordo elaborates: 'many men and women may experience the primary reality of the video as the elicitation of desire *for* that perfect body; women, however, may also be gripped by the desire (very likely impossible to achieve) to *become* that perfect body' (Bordo 1993: 273).

Indeed, Bordo's text *Unbearable Weight: Feminism, Western Culture and the Body,* dedicates itself to an analysis of the ways in which gendered bodies are produced through disciplinary regimes, such as diet and exercise, by the act of an identification with an idealised figure of man/woman. Pointing out that the production of Madonna as body (rather than simply as image) inhabits this disciplinary and normative regime (which converted her body into acceptably slim and firm contours), Bordo argues that her meanings and effects are stabilised and (at least partially) regulated by a pre-existing system which constitutes bodies as gendered, and hence, as already inscribed in a system of value and power differentiation. Bordo's critique of this idealisation of Madonna as a postmodern sign, which calls for an analysis of the social contexts and consequences of images from popular culture, does not assume that identification is ever fully assured and totally stable, nor does it exclude the possibility that transformations and departures from dominant identifications could take place within popular culture. Returning to Lacan, it could be argued that the vertical contexts surrounding the signifier of Madonna render her a nodal point or *point de capiton*, a mythic point where the intelligibility of sexual identification may itself be contested. This contestation is open, contingent and pragmatic, but it is nevertheless structurally mediated by general formations of power embedded in consumerism, industry, and the gendering and disciplining of bodies and spectator roles.

Kroker and Cook address feminism itself as postmodern – they call feminism *'the quantum physics of postmodernism'* (Kroker and Cook 1988: 22). Although they define feminism as postmodern in its notion of power as localised and its emphasis on difference, Kroker and Cook also define their position against feminism, suggesting that feminism assumes sexual difference is a privileged zone of difference (Kroker and Cook 1988: 26). Sexual difference is hence re-figured as one difference amongst many, in a power grid, 'where all ontologies are merely the sites of "local catastrophes"' (Kroker and Cook 1988: 26). Power is quite literally a form of body tattooing where all signs of cultural excess are inscribed on the body (Kroker and Cook 1988: 26). This does not simply repeat Foucault's notion of technologies of the body, for Kroker and Cook's body is in pieces, becoming *undifferentiated* through the excess of signs.

Here, the refusal of any understanding of privilege – where some differences are understood as more important than others – leads to an in-difference. The problem here is the assumption that a theory of privilege (and with it, both hierarchy and inequality) requires the existence of privilege at an ontological or foundational level. In contrast, I would argue that privilege is determined pragmatically through the formation of social relations and identifications. Which differences matter more than others is determined by the formation of relations of power through which embodied subjects are constituted. That is, the de-limitation of difference through privilege, through the maintenance of relations of domination and subordination, can be understood as the grid through which bodies become intelligible. So here, feminism may privilege gender by recognising that gender itself is a privileged site of power differentiation. A feminist privileging of gender does not necessarily assume that privilege at the level of ontology and, as I have already discussed in this book, much recent feminist work has focused on the mutually constitutive relation between gender and other differences which matter, such as race and class (which is not to deny that some feminists continue to privilege sexual difference over other forms of difference).

Kroker and Cook's analysis of technological embodiment is important in so far as it challenges the opposition between the organic and technological. Indeed, the cyborg as a figure, which first became visible within contemporary theory through the work of Donna Haraway (1991), has become a figure for the postmodern subject. Postmodernism comes to express the very crisis of 'the human' as a boundary crisis – the impossibility of separating the subject from its prosthetic limbs. Although the destabilisation of the relation between organism and machine is important, I think the status of the 'body' in some of these 'postmodern' narratives is questionable. While the body is inscribed as a form of cultural excess in Kroker and Kroker's work, it also becomes undifferentiated as 'a passive screen for the hystericizations and panic mythologies of the (disappearing) public realm' (Kroker and Kroker 1988: 28). While feminism may also challenge the assumption of the body as ground, root or given, it strikes me there are differences that matter between such feminist and postmodernism concerns. Within such postmodern narratives of the subject, the body is valued only then to disappear: the disappearing postmodern body is a body without material limits or constraints. The body which knows no limits – which appears unmarked as such – conceals the mark of the masculine. To this extent, postmodern technological embodiment is structured around an (elided) masculinity.

Indeed, a disappearing body is no-body at all (or the process of no-bodying): and as such, postmodern embodiment constitutes a flight from the body as the site of social and cultural inscription. Anne Balsamo expresses this point well:

Postmodern embodiment is not a singularly discursive condition . . . In offering the matrix of forms of technological embodiment, I argue that the material body cannot be bracketed or 'factored out' of postmodern body theory. This is not an argument for the assertion of a material body that is defined in an essentialist way – as having unchanging, trans-historical gender or race characteristics. (Balsamo 1995: 233)

To speak then of the body as implicated in the overloading of the technical is *not* to over-come the body whose materiality may always belong to the future (that is, whose matter may not be already-there, but which, as a process of material-ising, is coming-there). If (technological) embodiment is always in the process of becoming materialised, then it is neither reducible to, nor freed from, matter as such.

Such a critique of the disappearing postmodern body could be extended more generally to theories which assume contemporary tech-nologies 'liberate' subjects from the constraints of embodiment, such as theories which assume that cyberspace allows subjects to re-make their (sexual) identity. For example, Sherry Turkle, who defines the relation of the subject to the cyberscreen as expressive of the 'postmodern fragmentation of the subject' (Turkle 1995: 49), suggests that in cyber-space, 'the self is not only decentred but *multiplied without limit*' (Turkle 1995: 185, emphasis mine). Turkle argues that role playing on the Internet leads to a fluid and multiple identity, especially in relation to sexual identity – where subjects can assume the identity of 'the opposite sex' (Turkle 1995: 49). She later describes such a postmodern shifting of identities as a form of 'gender-bending' which leads to a recognition of the constructedness of gender itself (Turkle 1995: 223). However, in assuming a different sexual identity in cyberspace one is not suddenly freed from constraints. Subjects are already constituted as embodied before they enter such a space, however much that already-ness does not lead to a fixed or fully determined identification. This negative model of freedom (freedom from constraint) in such theories of liberation-from-identity-through-technology provides ideological support for neo-liber-alism, where self-making becomes the obligatory expression of the new 'ethics' of consumerism. It is here the disappearing postmodern body may re-appear (embedded in the phrase, 'let's make or have a new body').

In this section, I have shown how some postmodern narratives have worked from the assumption of the textual and constructed nature of subjectivity and sexual identity. Despite this, significant problems exist in these postmodern narratives. Baudrillard, as well as Kroker and Cook, collapse a theory of textuality into a theory of indetermination, in which the absence of a referent or ontology to subjectivity is taken to mean that subjectivity is indeterminate and unintelligible. In both cases, this also functions as a historical argument that embodied and sexed subjectivity in late consumer capitalism ('postmodernism') is indeterminate and free floating. In contrast, my reading has suggested that the contextualisation of the process in which bodies become intelligible, understood as the mythic (but material) fixing of a signified to signifiers along a vertical plain, opens out the pragmatic constraints to subjects as constitutive of the social itself.

Identifying the subject of feminism?

In this section, I want to examine how a feminist theory of the subject as constituted through identificatory practices may be developed through this critical engagement with both psychoanalysis and postmodernism. Feminists such as Judith Butler have already provided us with a model of phantasmatic sexual identification. Butler argues, 'if the immutable character of sex is contested, perhaps this construct called "sex" is as constructed as gender; indeed, perhaps it was always already gender with the consequence that the distinction between sex and gender turns out to be no distinction at all' (Butler 1990: 7). She further suggests that gender is the discursive/cultural means by which 'sexed' nature or 'a natural sex' is produced and established as pre-discursive (Butler 1990: 7). In terms of an analysis of sexual identification, this would suggest that gender is the process whereby identifications become solidified into identities, into possessions. Gender is hence simultaneously phantasmatic *and* material, an illusion of presence that marks the subject, unattainable in any ideal or integral form, but which is normative and regulative in its constitution of subjects as already sexed.

However, returning to my critique of psychoanalysis, we must be careful not to assume the primacy of sexual identification and to focus only on divisions within rather than between identificatory practices. To illustrate the divisions between identificatory practices more concretely I want to re-read Althusser's re-working of Lacan's concept of misrecognition, alongside an autobiographical example. Althusser writes:

ideology 'acts' or 'functions' in such a way that it 'recruits' subjects among the individuals (it recruits them all), or 'transforms' the individuals into subjects (it transforms them all) by that very precise operation which I have called *interpellation* or hailing, and which can be imagined along the lines of the most commonplace everyday police (or other) hailing: 'Hey, you there!' (Althusser 1971: 162–3)

Althusser argues that the individual's 'recognition' that he or she is being addressed, represents the point of entrance into subjectivity, and perhaps, into the authority of Law, where the potential for the subject to be *suspected* is inscribed by the possibility that the police are hailing. This links accession into subjectivity with the maintenance of a system of prohibitions and regulations. I want to stress two issues raised by Althusser's thesis that are often neglected. Firstly, the act of interpellation is a relation between subjects (or, to be more precise, the event of becoming a subject involves a relationship with another – equally imaginary – subject whose speech authorises this instant of becoming). Interpellation entails an addresser and addressee: the constitution of the subject is predicated upon an (elided) inter-subjectivity. Secondly, Althusser argues that hailing hardly ever misses its mark, 'the one hailed always recognises that it is really him who is being hailed' (Althusser 1971: 163). We may need to rethink the implications of *the structural possibility that hailing may miss its mark*, and that the subject, sexed or otherwise, may think she or he is being hailed or addressed (when they are not) or not think they are being hailed or addressed (when they are). This may suggest that the process of becoming a subject is more fractured and potentially unsuccessful than Althusser's schema may seem on the surface to suggest, and that this fracturing and failure is a way of theorising differences *between* structures of identification. I will hence focus on the way in which that identification does not fully or adequately name the subject, or divides subjects by naming them in contradictory and conflicting ways. Given this, the subject as such is never the subject as such, because its point of excess to the very name or signifier of 'the subject' locates it precisely as marked or named by colliding regimes of address which attach (asymmetrical) value and meaning to specific subject positions.

The example I want to use to illustrate the overlapping of identifications relates to an incident when I was 14 years old, walking around the streets of Adelaide without any shoes on (I was in a 'scruffy' phase). I was stopped and addressed by two policemen in a car. They called me over, asked me what I was doing (I said I was walking) and then asked me why I wasn't wearing shoes (I can't remember my reply, but I was indignant about my rights). The policeman closest to me asked me if I

was Aboriginal. Again I was indignant, replying 'no'. The other policeman interrupted, gave me a wink, and said 'It's a sun tan, isn't it?' I
smiled, but did not identify my racial 'background'. I was at the stage
when I longed to fit in, and be white. They asked me where I lived and I
told them, and mentioned which school I went to (a private girls'
school). They said that was fine, but to wear shoes. I asked them why
they had stopped me. They said there had been some break-ins in the
area recently, and that they were checking it out. When I arrived home
and told my mother and sister, my sister suggested that if I lost weight I
wouldn't be 'suspected' of being an Aboriginal. Needless to say, this
incident ended in tears, and left me angry and resistant.

It seems to me now that the policemen addressed me, in the first
instance, as working class (from dress), and as Aboriginal (from colour).
This identification *read* me as a subject, *by rendering me a suspect*, as a
danger to the Law (of property), a potential robber. Here, the absence
of shoes becomes fetishised as an object which signifies not simply a lack
of proper dress, but an improper status as somebody who does not
belong to this middle-class and respectable suburb, somebody whose
presence can only have the function and effect of a threat. Indeed, the
address shifts immediately from the absence of shoes to a query about
race. The address of the policemen in the first instance, their positioning
of me as a suspect, somebody to be queried and interrogated, was on the
mistaken assumption I was Aboriginal. Their question demanded to
know the extent of my threat by demanding to know whether my racial
origin was Aboriginal. In this sense, Aboriginality becomes figured as
the most threatening or disruptive presence. But the error of their
address gave me a space to address them, through denial and disavowal.

Through returning their address a shift occurred which forced a dis-
identification from my identity as suspect. Not an Aboriginal (but
perhaps only sun-tanned), not working class (but at home in the middle-
class suburb). My denial of being Aboriginal and my failure to name or
declare my race (which of course was unnoticed or invisible to them)
implicated me in their structure of address, by rendering Aboriginality
something to be disavowed. The gesture of smiling can here be figured
as a collusion, a desire in some sense to be figured as white, as
respectable, as somebody who has a legitimate right to walk in these
leafy suburbs. My disavowal thus suggests an implicit desire for 'whiteness'. That desire creates an imaginary (and impossible) conception of a
purified and ideal self, as well as a coherent social order (to which I
could 'fit in'), by assigning certain values to 'whiteness'. Such an assignment entails a disavowal and repudiation of the other, of 'blackness', or
Aboriginality. As such, desire itself projects an imaginary presence

through a process of exclusion. The temporality of the act of disavowal stages the impossibility of desire's fulfilment generally, but also the racialist logic that demands the purification of colour, as a reminder of an-other that refuses to inhabit these terms and returns (to walk the streets) only as a threat.

This disavowal was also structured by a class dynamic whereby legitimacy was restored to my presence through naming my school (a private girls' school). This information was not asked for – but projected by me onto them as a sign that I was 'with them', that they were policing for me, rather than against me, as an owner rather than a taker of property. The disavowal and repudiation of Aboriginality hence structured a desire to be taken as inhabiting the policing demand, as somebody worthy of protection, as white and middle class; a taxpayer not a dole bludger or a waster.

The structure of identification which involved the exchange of a wink and the quip about being sun-tanned caused me the most discomfort. Although inspired by my dis-identification as Aboriginal (which was implicated in the assigning of certain values to Aboriginality, as something to be disavowed), and my refusal to identify my race, this quip both made light of their mistake (their hailing of the wrong person, their error of reading) while positioning me as a woman, as a recipient of a wink (and of a gaze), and as someone who sun-bathes, who tans her body. The entrance of the body into the explicit terms of the exchange shifted me from being suspect to object, from a threat to property, to property itself. While defining the body in terms of leisure, where colour is a sign of a 'higher' class, the quip shifted my attention from the social relation of policeman to suspect, to the sexual relation of man to woman. The colour of my body was evoked as an adornment rather than a stain, as 'a paying attention to the body'. Here, colour is literally a detachable signifier, inessential to the subject, and hence acceptable. By rendering colour inessential rather than essential, the exchange inscribed my body as something to be valued, adorned, protected. Colour becomes inscribed as a detachable signifier, positioning me as essentially white, as truly and properly white underneath the luxury of a brown veil. Inscribed as a white woman, I was the legitimate object of the policeman's protective gaze.

I dealt with this anxiety over my body and colour by addressing the policeman in the structure of a demand. That demand gave me a point of entry into identifying them as racist. For it linked their project (fighting street crime) to their identification of me as Aboriginal, which made me a suspect. Through identifying the racism that constituted their primary identification, I withdrew from the situation very angry and ashamed that I had disavowed being Aboriginal, and had so been implicated in a racist structure of identification. By returning their address, I hence read the policemen and assigned them to a place in my own self-identification as non-white and non-racist. It was this role in identification (which I still think made its mark) that, when walking away from the police car, shifted me from the anxiety over my sex and body, to a sense of being a subject. That sense, again, was only to be shattered by my sister's evocation of 'fatness' as a sign of Aboriginality and hence of error. Read the text implicit here: laziness, indulgence, excess. Fatness not only inscribes certain negative values to Aboriginality, but also positions me as a woman who has failed, who has failed to police and discipline her body into acceptable 'feminine' contours. Within this structure of address, the fat woman is (like) an Aboriginal, in excess of the norms and values inscribed by a proper social and sexual order. Again, identified in this way, I was returned to a feeling of anger, to not being a (legitimate) subject.

What this example may evoke is the complexity of the identification process. The very temporality of identification ensures not only that it can miss its mark, but that it always already does miss its mark, by enacting the divisions that frustrate the identity of the subject in the first place. The overlapping of the issues of race, class and gender in this recalled event, suggests that the relation of power to identification is constitutive but divisive, where the position of the subject is perpetually assigned and threatened by their designation in related, but distinct, regimes of difference. The constant negotiation of identifications temporarily assign the subject to a fixed identity (both gendered, racialised and classed) through a reading of the body. Such readings are open to contestation in the everyday encounters with the Law, family and others.

This model I am tentatively offering here, in which the phantasmatic nature of identifications are perpetually re-negotiated in an inter-subjective context, entailing the temporary fixing of values to sliding signifiers (such as Aboriginality, woman, class) both presupposes and displaces the narratives offered by psychoanalysis and postmodernism. This model of identifying subjects assumes, following Lacan, that identity is phantasmatic and perpetually under threat by the sliding of signifiers along vertical plains, enacting the division and the repression which institute the unconscious elements of subjectivity. But it displaces the Lacanian theory of the subject as locus of the signifier, as well as the phallus as privileged signifier, by arguing that the contingency of the signifier is only halted by the temporary fixing of the signifieds in the intelligibility of the social itself. Hence, my model does not suture the gap between language and the subject, or between privilege and the phallus: the status of the subject and the phallus as signifiers may, in itself, become suspect. This approach also presupposes that subjectivity is textual and constructed, as argued in the postmodern narratives offered by Baudrillard and Kroker and Cook. However, it displaces the notion of the subject as indeterminate and radically unstable, by stressing that de-limitation and fixation occur, however temporarily. The processes of fixation mark and divide the embodiment of the subject. This feminist model of the subject hence moves through and beyond psychoanalysis and post-modernism: a movement which, at once, opens up the possibility for a different kind of dialogue between these subjects (these subjects who are no longer subjects in any proper sense).

5   Authorship

If postmodernism announces itself as a crisis of the subject, a crisis that returns to postmodernism as a crisis in its subject, then postmodernism signals a shift in thinking concerning the nature of authorship. Indeed, the 'death of the subject' is haunted by another death announced so famously by Roland Barthes in his polemical essay, 'The Death of the Author'. There exists a crucial connection between the critique of the foundational subject, the subject that stands above or outside the contingent world of matter, and the critique of a model of the author as the originator of creative works. Hal Foster, for example, discusses how postmodernism 'assumes "the death of man" not only as original creator of unique artefacts but as the centred subject of representation and history' (Foster 1984: 67). Here, the critique of Cartesianism is directly associated with a problematisation of the notion of the author as an original creator. As Patricia Waugh suggests, postmodernism engages in a repudiation of the discourses of modernity by 'proclaiming "the death of the author" and the end of humanism' (Waugh 1992: 129). Barthes's pronouncement of the 'death of the author' has been read in this way as *signalling* a postmodern suspicion of the human subject as a founding principle of modernity. So while we may question any assumption that there is an author of postmodernism, we can nevertheless recognise that postmodernism may become (ironically) authorised through the narrativisation of the author's death.

Authorship has functioned differently within various traditions of literary criticism, becoming especially significant in conceptions of literature and poetry specific to Romanticism. For example, in M. H. Abram's *The Mirror and the Lamp*, the poet/author is located at the centre of the text, as its imaginative interiority. Criticism comes to function as a desire for proximity to the latent interiority which is the genius of the poetic mind. That mind is figured as a 'lamp', as 'a radiant projector which makes a contribution to the objects it perceives' (Abrams 1953: vi). Here, the author is to his text as God is to man: 'the unitary cause, source and master to whom the chain of textual effects must be traced, and in whom they find their genesis, meaning, goal and justification' (Burke 1992: 23).

Both postmodernism and feminism have become associated with substantive critiques of this romantic construction of the author. But how exactly do postmodern and feminist critical readings of author-centred criticism intersect? Are they necessarily consistent? Are there differences that matter between them? Since narratives of post-modernism have employed the metaphor of 'the death of the author' as constitutive (where postmodernism comes to be read as signalling the death of the author, or even where the death of the author comes to be read as signalling postmodernism), I will discuss Barthes's and Foucault's essays on authorship, which introduce this metaphor, as instances of postmodernism. I will examine their texts on authorship in order to trace the genesis of this postmodern concern with writing, death and authorship. I will suggest that, despite a shared critical ambivalence to the tradition of authorship as a recoverable intention-ality, a feminist intervention departs from these postmodern narratives precisely through its enquiry into the gendering of the authorship function and effect. A feminist reading may in itself complicate and displace the narrative of the death of the author offered by post-modernism by focusing on the critical (but not essential) difference of women's writing. However, the final section of the chapter will qualify my claims about the difference of women's writing by discussing the relation between authorised writing and auto/ethno/graphies of empire.

The death of the author

In Roland Barthes's 'The Death of the Author', the figure of the Author is located within the modern discourse of individualism, which centres on the autonomy and interiority of the 'human person'. Barthes writes, 'the Author is a modern figure, a product of our society insofar as, emerging from the Middle Ages with English empiricism, French rationalism and the personal faith of the Reformation, it discovered the prestige of the individual, of, as it is more nobly put, the "human person"' (Barthes 1990: 142–3). Barthes locates authorship as func-tioning ideologically within literary criticism by working to close off interpretation in the supposed unity of the poetic self. He suggests: 'The *explanation* of a work is always sought in the man or woman who produced it, as if it were always in the end, through the more or less transparent allegory of fiction, the voice of a single person, the *author* "confiding" in us' (Barthes 1990: 143). For Barthes, a critical refusal of the ideology of authorship is necessary in order to open up the text to a plurality of interpretations. Such a plurality is predicated on the opaqueness and complexity of the text itself. Released from notions of a theological meaning, the text becomes re-figured as 'a multi-dimensional space in which a variety of writings, none of them original, blend and clash' (Barthes 1990: 146). Reading becomes a process of disentanglement, where meaning is no longer limited or closed off by 'the Author' as a transcendental signified (Barthes 1990: 147).

Barthes's essay introduces issues of sexual difference only then to suggest that such differences themselves no longer matter as the author is always already dead or lost to the text. He begins his polemic by citing an excerpt from Balzac's story *Sarrasine*, which hovers around the issue of sexual identity: 'This was woman herself, with her sudden fears, her irrational whims, her instinctive worries, her impetuous boldness, her fussings, and her delicious sensibility' (Barthes 1990: 142). Taken on its own, this sentence asserts the unproblematic nature of sexual identity, it identifies woman as 'herself' – a figure who is easily assigned a place within (or as) the truth of sexual difference. Placed within Barthes's essay, however, this 'truth' is quickly called into question. The essay opens with the sentence: 'In his story *Sarrasine* Balzac, describing a castrato disguised as a woman, writes the following sentence' (Barthes 1990: 142). Through foregrounding the citationality of the literary sentence, Barthes draws our attention to how the apparent assertion of the truth of sexual identity is open to complication, that such identity is always vulnerable to the possibility and threat of disguise and artifice. By contextualising the sentence cited from Balzac, the possibility of 'arriving' at a knowledge of sexual identity in the process of reading is questioned.

However, Barthes's citation of Balzac seems to lead to an argument, not so much concerning the complications of context, but rather the loss of origins:

Who is speaking thus? Is it the hero of the story bent on remaining ignorant of the castrato hidden beneath the woman? Is it Balzac the individual, furnished by his personal experience with a philosophy of Woman? Is it Balzac the author professing 'literary' ideas on femininity? Is it universal wisdom? Romantic psychology? We shall never know, for the good reason that writing is the destruction of every voice, of every point of origin. Writing is that neutral, composite, oblique space where our subject slips away, the negative where all identity is lost, starting with the very identity of the body writing. (Barthes 1990: 142)

Here, the absence of a singular voice is shown to be constitutive of writing, which functions by *cutting* itself off from any supposed origin. Writing's opaqueness is precisely the destruction of a point of origin, any true authorial voice. The citation from *Sarrasine* is used here to *demonstrate* the negativity of writing, and the loss of the identity of the (authorial) subject. But by turning this sentence into an illustration of the death of the author, Barthes effectively elides the question of woman it raises. In this sense, Barthes's use of the excerpt from *Sarrasine* to demonstrate 'the death of the author' means that he overlooks the question of 'woman herself' (Barthes 1990: 142).

An emphasis on the literary production of 'woman' as a site of meaning (woman-as-text) may lead us to an alternative to either the author as originary or the author as dead. That is, the question of 'woman' may help to convey that it does matter who is writing: the text may not belong to the 'who' as a marker of authorial and sexual identity, but the 'who' opens out a broader social context which is neither inside or outside the text itself. Indeed, the essay seems to conflate the loss of identity *per se* with the loss of context. Such contexts of utterance may constitute the field of writing. To address these contexts of utterance, would not be to assume that the 'who' is a marker of a 'real individual' who has his own 'philosophy of Woman' (Barthes 1990: 142). Rather, it would be to argue that the written text is implicated in broader relationships of power predicated on distinctions between the subject and object of a discursive formation. The question of 'woman' raised by the cited excerpt from Balzac's *Sarrasine* may function to remind the reader that a dominant history of literature and criticism has involved the privileging of male authors and the relegation of femininity to a constitutive enigma (the man as speaking, the woman as spoken for). In other words, Barthes's citation of *Sarrasine* may demonstrate, not simply the impossibility of (sexual and authorial) identity, but the way in which identity can only be sustained as an illusion *when the literary sentence is isolated from its contexts of utterance*. The shift from the author-god to the death of the author is itself a narrative which represses certain contexts of writing. It is those contexts of writing which help to undermine the assumption of an ontological authorial and sexual identity.

The issue of the relationship between the body and writing may serve to problematise the terms of Barthes's argument. The body appears early on in his text in an ambiguous fashion, as that which is lost in writing, 'starting with the very identity of the body writing' (Barthes 1990: 142). The ambiguity of the phrase 'body writing' is instructive. Is the body here the author (the body of the author or, as synecdoche, the body as author)? Or is it the body of writing? Is the identity of the body of writing lost in the event of being found without an author? The uncertainty of *which* body is lost in writing could be read as symptomatic. The loss of a specific body, a specific figure which is writing and written into the body of writing, suggests that, within the context of Barthes's piece, writing is written by no-body, no-body who is identifiable either as subject or body.

This very detachment of writing from bodies is problematic. As I've suggested previously, the universalism of the masculine perspective relies precisely on being disembodied, on lacking the contingency of a body. A feminist perspective would surely emphasise the implication of writing in embodiment, in order to re-historicise this supposed universalism, to locate it, and to expose the violence of its contingency and particularity (by declaring some-body wrote this text, by asking which-body wrote this text). A feminist approach cannot afford to collapse the issues of embodiment and subjectivity with the ontology of identity. In other words, we need to ask: is it possible to theorise the relationship between writing and embodiment without assuming an ontological authorial identity?

What is at stake, in 'The Death of the Author', is a shift from a model of authorship as biographical intentionality to a refusal that authorship matters at all, where 'the author is never more than the instance of writing' (Barthes 1990: 145). So while I agree with the critique of the author as a 'theological' principle within the text (Barthes 1990: 146), I would also suggest that what is required is a historicisation and con-textualisation of the author as an embodied subject. By opening out the process of writing to the contexts of authorship, such a feminist approach would not de-limit or resolve the text, but complicate it. Here, the relation between writing and auto/biography becomes constitutive: the border between work and life is unstable, an instability which points to the contextualisation of the text (the life that is not inside or outside the work) and the textualisation of the context (the work that is not inside or outside the life). If an authorial subject is understood as not properly outside the text (not cut off from it), then that text becomes more difficult to govern and de-limit. The relation between the literary, the embodied subject and the social becomes an issue that troubles the demarcation of one text from another. In this sense, the question of text and context is posed, not as a resolution of the text (its founding explanation), but as a principle of uncertainty and difficulty.

Michel Foucault also announces the death of the author in 'What is an Author?' He posits a general relationship between writing and death manifest in the effacement of the writing subject's individual character-istics (Foucault 1980: 143). Foucault argues, 'the mark of the writer is reduced to nothing more than the singularity of his absence; *he must assume the role of the dead man in the game of writing*' (Foucault 1980: 143, emphasis added). However, with Foucault there is a more rigorous emphasis on the status of authorship as a discursive function and effect which cannot simply be dismantled through a critical refusal of an ontology of the subject. Foucault focuses on the specificity of the author's name as a proper name that performs a certain classificatory function, allowing the differentiation of texts and 'marking off the edges of texts' in a way that partakes of a mode of being: 'The author-function is therefore characteristic of the mode of existence, circulation, and functioning of certain discourses within society' (Foucault 1980: 148). The author serves as a unifying principle, neutralising contradictions that may structure any clearly demarcated set of texts (Foucault 1980: 151) .

Foucault's emphasis on authorship as a function and effect separates the issue of authorship from the individual writer or producer of a text, literary or otherwise. Indeed, he explicitly argues that the author-function, 'does not refer purely and simply to a real individual' (Foucault 1980: 153). What I want to raise here is the question of the relation between the author function and this 'real individual' or, at least, the specific or particular subject who writes. Foucault's focus on authorship as a social and discursive function does not explicitly deal with this question, beyond the acknowledgement that the relation between the individual and the author-function is not one of pure and simple reference. If the relation between the author-function and 'a real individual' does not take the form of pure and simple reference, then what form does it take? How does the individual or empirical writing subject participate in the institution of authorship?

My suggestion that the relation between the subject who writes and the social function of authorship entails its own problematic can be explored when considering the last few pages of Foucault's text. Here, Foucault discusses the way in which his approach calls into question 'the absolute character and founding role of the subject' (Foucault 1980: 158) in the process of examining the subject itself as a mode of functioning, a discursive effect. Within this horizon of de-centred subjectivity:

All discourses, whatever their status, form, value, and whatever the treatment to which they will be subjected, would then develop the *anonymity* of a murmur. We would no longer hear the questions that have been rehashed for so long: 'Who really spoke? Is it really he and not someone else? With what authenticity or originality? And what part of his deepest self did he express in his discourse?' Instead, there would be other questions, like these: 'What are the modes of existence of this discourse? Where has it been used, how can it circulate, and who can appropriate it for himself? What are the places in it where there is room for possible subjects?' And behind all these questions, *we would hear hardly anything but the stirring of an indifference: 'What difference does it make who is speaking?'* (Foucault 1980: 160, emphasis added)

In this statement, Foucault confirms that the shift from the individua-
listic model of the author enables the issue of authorship to be politicised. Rather than address the author as an individual being, Foucault
asks crucial questions about the modes of existence of discourses and
how the circulation of discourses may produce subject positions. But the
model of the author/subject as a discursive function also leads to, 'the
stirring of an indifference', a questioning of what difference it makes
'who' is speaking. I would argue that the 'who' does make a difference,
not in the form of an ontology of the individual, but as a marker of a
specific location from which the subject writes. The individual and
empirical subject may not write without the orderings and disorderings
of the entire structure of authorship, but the inclusion of the 'who'
within that structural relation means precisely that it does matter. An
alternative critical project would not be indifferent to empirical authors,
as the 'who' that writes, but would document how the event of writing
participates (by both supporting and complicating) in the structural and
institutional relation of authorship itself. Indeed, a feminist reader may
want to suggest that it is Foucault's own questions about modes of
discourses and the terms under which they circulate which lead to the
importance of recognising the *difference* of the 'who' that writes. What
difference that difference makes is another matter (it is certainly not a
difference that secures the transparency of the text).

The necessity of contextualising and addressing the empirical subject,
the 'who' that writes and is written, at once a subject effect and an effect
of a subject, may indeed return to complicate Foucault's own text.
Naomi Schor, for example, suggests that Foucault effaces the sexual
specificity of his own narrative and perspective as a male philosopher
(Schor 1989: 55). The refusal to enter the discourse as an empirical
subject, a subject which is both sexed and European (Spivak 1988:
294), may finally translate into a universalising mode of discourse,
which negates the specificity of its own inscription (as a text). The
effacement of the authorial subject within Foucault's narrative may
produce this potential of indifference. An investigation into the status of
the 'who' that writes may involve a politics of reading for difference.

Does the signature have a sex?

How can sexual difference be theorised as a critical difference, as a
difference that matters, within the structure of authorship, without
relying on a foundational, ontological or biological authorial identity?
Within feminist literary criticism the question of authorship has been
significant, in part because the theological or romantic conception of the

author reinforced a gender hierarchy. Susan Gubar, for example, in ' "The Blank Page" and Issues in Female Creativity' discusses how the relation of author and text has been figured, both within literature and criticism, as a relation of man and woman. The woman becomes the text upon which the agency of the male author is literally inscribed. Gubar concludes: 'This model of the pen-penis writing on the virgin page participates in a long tradition identifying the author as a male who is primary and the female as his passive creation – a secondary object lacking autonomy, endowed with often contradictory meaning but denied intentionality' (Gubar 1989: 295).

Authorship has also been important to feminism due to the desire to inscribe women as writers. The importance of constructing the category of 'women's writing' (which is indeed central to many university English curricula) has led to a suspicion of the postmodern refusal of the author as a critical tool within feminist literary criticism. Nancy Miller, for example, writes 'the postmodernist decision that the Author is Dead and the subject along with him does not . . . necessarily hold for women, and prematurely forecloses the question of agency for them' (Miller 1989: 6).

Hence, the stress on women's writing has led to a qualification of the postmodern narrative of the death of the author, despite the feminist critique of Romantic conceptions of the author-figure. In 'Feminist Criticism in the Wilderness', Elaine Showalter defines what she per-ceives as a shift from androcentrism to gynocentrism within feminist literary theory. This entails a shift from a critical approach which puts forward revisionary readings of male-authored texts to 'the study of women as *writers*, and its subjects are the history, styles, themes, genres and structures of writing by women; the psychodynamics of female creativity; the trajectory of the individual or collective female career; and the evolution and laws of a feminist literary tradition' (Showalter 1989: 248). Such an approach posits sexual difference as an 'essential ques-tion' asking, 'what is the difference of women's writing?' (Showalter 1989: 248). What is fundamental to Showalter's differentiation and privileging of gynocentrism is the assumption that the relation between sexual difference and the signature is unproblematic. Even if difference is to be looked for (put forward as a question leading to an analysis of style, genre and theme), it is nevertheless already to be found *within* certain texts. The signature of the woman writer, in this sense, *guaran-tees* the value of the critical approach of gynocentrism.

The reliance on the signature as already sexed does indeed structure a critical approach and strategy of reading. 'Women's writing' does not function simply as a category within and for itself. Rather, something is always done to this category; it is enlisted within an argument or interpretation. This is evident, for example, in Judith Kegan Gardiner's 'On Female Identity and Writing by Women'. Here, Gardiner enlists a psychological theory of the specificity of female identity (derived largely from Nancy Chodorow's *The Reproduction of Mothering*) to examine women's writing. She argues, 'women writers and readers tend to approach texts differently from men . . . . That is, the woman writer uses her text, particularly one centering on a female hero, as part of a continuing process involving her own self-definition and her empathetic identification with her characters' (Gardiner 1982: 187). Gardiner's reading approach assumes the transparency of women's texts: continuities between women's texts are read as signs of a pre-existing identity. The sex of the signature functions to stabilise Gardiner's reading strategy precisely because it is attached to assumptions about what female identity (or indeed, 'woman' herself) already is.

The problems with relying on 'women's writing' as an unmediated and transparent category are, indeed, similar to the problems with relying on 'woman' as an unmediated and transparent category. As I discussed in chapter 3, 'woman' always operates within broader contexts of difference, including race and class. To use 'woman' as a foundational or essential category would serve to make invisible these broader contexts of difference. Crucially, the question of sexual difference remains in Gardiner's analysis a hypothesis, a formulation arrived at within the process of critical appraisal. Although the sex of the signature is assumed as already available in a pre-existing sexual and authorial identity, it remains inscribed by the feminist reader, projected as prior (already there) from the position of posterity. And, indeed, it is the question of the status of the feminist reader that may begin to complicate the notion that the sex of the signature is both prior and transparent, determining or guaranteeing the meaning of the text.

The shift from authors to readers is the concern of more 'deconstructive' feminist literary approaches.[1] For example, Mary Jacobus in *Reading Woman* asks the question: 'What would "reading woman" mean if the object of our reading (woman as text) and the reading subject (reader as already read) were gendered only as a result of the reading process?' (Jacobus 1986: 3). Jacobus suggests that the category of 'women's writing' is problematic, and calls for a shift of emphasis from writers to readers. Interestingly, Jacobus provides a rigorous critique of Elaine Showalter's article, 'Critical Cross-Dressing: Male Feminists and the Woman of the Year'. Here, Showalter argues that, 'Without closing the door on male feminists, I think that Franco-American theory has gone much too far in discounting signature and gender in authorship'

(Showalter 1987: 132). According to Showalter, a feminist critical practice cannot (or should not) forget that the male author occupies a different literary place (Showalter 1987: 132). Jacobus criticises Showalter for being essentialist, for 'it is surely essentialism – whether theoretical or professional – that we glimpse here, for without essentialism identity comes into question, and with it the importance of "signature and gender in authorship"' (Jacobus 1986: 12).

Reading Woman relies on the construction of an opposition. Either there is a feminist critical practice which focuses on the author and assumes that sexual difference exists prior to the act of reading (as a form of 'essentialism'), or there is a feminist critical practice which focuses on the reader and assumes that sexual difference is constructed through the process of reading (as a 'deconstructive' mode of reading). I contend that it is the very status of this opposition, as it is constructed in *Reading Woman*, that needs to be questioned. In other words, I do not think that all arguments that assume gender and signature matter in authorship are simply essentialist. What matters, is how those differences are perceived to matter in the first place. I would argue that the question of sexual difference does not reside entirely within the figure of the woman writer or the woman reader, but perhaps may exist in the very determination of their textual relation. If sexual difference is critical or constitutive of the interpretative process, then perhaps it lodges itself between the before and after, between the signature and the reading. Such a notion of in-between-ness, of a space neither held in the past (guaranteed by the woman who writes) or in the present (made real by the woman who reads as woman reading) would suggest that sexual difference is both structural, delimiting or binding what is possible within a textual relation, and open to being displaced and transformed, in the process of being read differently.

In some attempts to problematise the relation between gender and the signature there has been a considerable emphasis on the deferral of meaning – both literary and sexual. Take Jonathan Culler's use of Peggy Kamuf's approach to the woman writer to re-figure the place of the woman reader. Kamuf's famous phrase 'writing as a woman as a woman as a woman' implies the endless deferral of the sexual identity of the writer (Kamuf 1980: 298). The meaning of what it is to write as a woman is hence itself deferred in the very unavailability of any essence or substance to the signifier 'woman'. Indeed, for Kamuf, to affix a sexual signified to the text is to assign an intentionality to the text and thus to contain or foreclose it (Kamuf 1980: 285–6; Kamuf 1988). Culler turns this phrasing of a sexual and authorial non-identity into a statement about the non-identity of the reading subject. He writes:

For a woman to read as a woman is not to repeat an identity or an experience that is given but to play a role she constructs with reference to her identity as a woman, which is also a construct, so that the series can continue: a woman reading as a woman reading as a woman. (Culler 1982: 64)

The deferral of 'woman' as reading subject is here a deferral of a series of constructs and roles which are played out in an endless negotiation of meanings. 'Reading as a woman' itself becomes a phrase without substance, an empty or vacant space. Where I think both Culler's and Kamuf's approach can be complicated is on the question of 'what happens' to the (writing and reading) subject when one does not rely on notions of an originary identity. I would argue that the chain 'reading as – writing as' does not endlessly defer itself. That chain of endless deferral, that seemingly open fluidity, is halted at certain points, partially fixed in the process of becoming intelligible. The signifier 'woman', as writing and reading subject, remains partially fixed by its location within a relatively stable structure of discursivity. I agree with Showalter's critique of Culler for his refusal to locate the difference between 'a woman reading as a woman reading as a woman' and 'a man reading as a woman reading as a woman' (Showalter 1987: 125–6). The difference between these two phrases is critical (but not essential). Such a critical difference suggests that the act of reading is not a pure and self-legislating moment, but brings into play already constituted definitions of writing and reading that are clearly gendered.

The question of what is the nature of this critical difference has yet to be addressed and to some extent this question remains an impossible one (if the difference is organised through the pragmatic field of force relations, then we cannot talk about its 'nature'). How is this difference manifest, if it is not guaranteed by the signature of the one who writes? Shoshana Felman takes up the question of sexual difference in relation to the engendering of speech acts. In *What Does a Woman Want? Reading and Sexual Difference*, Felman addresses the significance for a feminist politics of Freud's question, 'what does a woman want?' She asks if it is the power of the question, 'to engender, through the literary or psychoanalytic work, a woman's voice as its speaking subject' (Felman 1993: 3). Felman does not simply address this question as an enigma that returns to haunt Freud's text, disrupting its internal movement towards self-presence, and so breaking it apart. Rather, Felman asks whether this enigma is placed differentially according to the scene of a sexual relation. That sexual relation is, of course, a structure of address: the male speaker asks the question *of* woman rather than *to* her. To ask the question of sexual difference as a structure of address (which is also already a relation of writing) does not foreclose interpretation in Felman's own text. Rather it serves to displace the literary sentence (the integrity of the question 'what does a woman want?') by locating the resistance to interpretation of what woman is (for whom): a resistance which marks both male and female authored texts.

It is here that Felman pays attention to the question of 'getting personal' and the status of female auto-biography as a speech act rather than re-presentation – where women speak to, rather than of, other women (Felman 1993: 14). This auto-biographical mode *for women* forms a tension with the Freudian question and male desire for an interpretation of woman-as-text. She writes: 'To the extent that women *"are* the question," they cannot *enunciate* the question; they cannot be the speaking *subjects* of the knowledge or the science that the question seeks' (Felman 1993: 43). To clarify the question of sexual difference that structures the mode of address which enables this question, Felman asks, 'What does the question "What is femininity – *for men* ?" mean *for women* ?' (Felman 1993: 43).

Here, the enigma of woman (that in a psychoanalytic framework makes impossible the sexual relation), as an enigma which structures the opaqueness of the text and its resistance to a final interpretation, becomes inflected with the dynamics of sexual difference. It is not an enigma in itself, but an enigma that is opened out through the very relation of address that renders woman the object of male enquiry. The effect of this differentiation of the scene of woman-as-textual-enigma according to a scene of gender, is that it shows how the complication of the transparency of woman-as-text is precisely how sexual difference becomes critical. The author is not, then, simply there as a sexed being we have access to. The author is sexed in the process of being positioned according to the enigma of woman-as-text, according, that is, to the *demand* both for interpretation and sexual identity.[2] To make critical the relation of woman-as-text to the sexing of the authorial subject is to enable a feminist politics of reading for sexual difference as a complication of the scene of interpretation and analysis. To posit a woman or man 'speaking' the text is to raise the *structural location* of the question 'what does a woman want?' in which an enigma becomes constitutive of a critical difference.

To exemplify how reading for sexual difference may work to complicate notions of both authorial and sexual identity, I will examine Willa Cather's *My Antonia*, which was one of the texts I studied on my first 'women's writing' course as an undergraduate. *My Antonia* is a fascinating text, whose narrative follows or traces the movements of Antonia as a heroine. The reader's access to Antonia is mediated through a male

narrator, a narrator who claims possession of her in the event of the title
(*My* Antonia). Book 1 of *My Antonia* begins with the 'I' of this narrator,
who hears the name of Antonia on his travels (Cather 1991: 3). It is her
name that flashes across the scene of the text in the form of an enigma.
Indeed, in the italicised introduction to the text, Antonia is introduced
as a nameless character by an anonymous narrator: 'During that
burning day when we were crossing Iowa, our talk kept returning to a
central figure, a Bohemian girl whom we had both known long ago.
More than any other person we remembered, this girl seemed to mean
to us the country, the conditions, the whole adventure of our childhood'
(Cather 1991: ii). Here, the nameless girl is inscribed as the essence of
an experience, as a way of identifying and locating a given moment in
time. Her meaning becomes inscribed as essential to the text itself.

The Introduction to *My Antonia* also provides us with a narrative of
the origins of the manuscript 'My Antonia':

'Here is the thing about Antonia. Do you still want to read it? I finished it last
night. I didn't take time to arrange it; I simply wrote down pretty much all that
her name recalls to me. I suppose it hasn't any form. It hasn't any title, either.'
He went into the next room, sat down at my desk and wrote across the face of
the portfolio the word 'Antonia.' He frowned at this a moment, then pre-fixed
another word, making it 'My Antonia.' That seemed to satisfy him. (Cather
1991: iii)

Here, the re-naming of the text draws attention to the gendered
discourse of property: 'she' is constituted through being marked as his
property (and through the signing of his proper name). Our access to
her name is hence mediated through the signifier of the male writer
(the 'my' which institutes 'his' text). The implication that the writing is
without form implies a phantasy of direct, unmediated relation
between the narrative and the object which inspired it, the figure of
woman.

The exchange that takes place in the Introduction is between a male
writer and a male reader, to whom the manuscript is given, and whose
eyes we, as readers, are led to imagine are crossing the words of the text,
as we cross them in our own reading. The male reader is also the
narrator of the Introduction, the anonymous 'I'. The male narrator of
the Introduction exchanges his 'I' to 'Jim', who is introduced simultaneously as a male character and as the male author of the manuscript/
text 'My Antonia'. The exchange of narrators, the shift from one 'I' to
another, between the Introduction and Book 1, may suggest the 'I' is
constituted around the terms of a male exchange of woman as textual
enigma.[3] To define that exchange as male is not to foreclose its potential
for destabilising the text, for the exchange can only take place given the

impossibility of securing any 'I' in a proper ontology of authorial or sexual identity (the 'I' is transportable, it does not stay in one place). But the repetition or transfer of the 'I' suggests at the same time the determination of an enigma through a gendered modality of address in which woman remains the object of the naming quest.

My Antonia therefore has an important gendered dimension manifest in the very relation between the narrative 'I' and the central female character. But, in one scene, in which a coiling snake makes the letter 'W', that forming of a gendered dimensionality involves a de-forming. In this scene, a snake arrives, whose loose coils form the letter 'W'. Judith Butler provides us with a strong reading of this scene: 'The truncated 'W' introduces an abbreviated Willa into the text, and connects her with the loose waves of the letter, linking the question of the grammatical morphology with the morphological figure of the snake that bears the movements of desire' (Butler 1993: 150). The snake that arrives in the form of a 'W' is one that produces a relation between the narrator and Antonia as one of protection, when Jim strikes the snake down to save Antonia, whose screams announce the existence of its threat: 'I saw his coils tighten – now he would spring, spring his length, I remembered. I ran up and drove at his head with my spade, stuck him fairly across the neck, and in a minute he was all about my feet in wavy loops' (Cather 1991: 46). The snake introduces in its physicality the connotations of a phallic sexual threat and, in terms of plot, serves to instigate a sexual relation which produces the male narrator as a heroic figure 'saving' the woman. So why read the snake in terms of the figuring of the woman writer's authorial presence?

To read the 'W' formed by the coiling of the snake as a sign of authorial presence is an active gesture of interpretation that reads from the letter a broader context of writing. It makes a metonymic connection between the grammar of the letter and the morphological question of who is writing. This is an important way of opening out the instabilities of the narrative in *My Antonia*. As I have discussed, the text traces the name of Antonia through the narrative which produces her as both enigma and object of a male quest. The snake centres the masculinity of that enunciative frame in a singular trope (or perhaps in the determination of a relation between the image and the narrator) at the same time as it abbreviates the woman writer through the materiality of a letter. It is the linkage that is important. Through breaking the masculinity that determines the writing of woman through the fissure and materiality of an authorial letter, the text opens up a gap in the male identification of woman as an object or enigma. To read the letter 'W' as a sign of an authorial presence is precisely to disrupt the narrative whereby woman is secured as an object in writing. It is to interrupt the enunciative frame in which 'Antonia' is claimed by the male narrator, breaking that open, by enabling woman to become present in the form of a body writing rather than as an object. Here, the woman writer is made present in the graphic form of a letter that stops the narrative of male desire on its travels, however much it cannot in itself halt that narrative and 'liberate' the woman from the text.

The figure of the snake cannot be contained by its phallic connotations (although neither can it be freed from them). By having a metonymic relation to the woman writer, the snake crosses over the text to prevent the securing of woman in an expression of either authorial or sexual identity. Reading for 'women writing' is, here, to interrupt the very enunciation of woman by the trajectory of male desire which may demand of her a presence. In this sense, the 'I' of the male narrator is transported and transferred to the woman writer, whose claiming of the text may operate only in terms of its transportability, of the 'shifting' and crossing constitutivity of the 'I'. The contiguous letters cross over the text, opening out the materiality of the body of woman as that which resists entrapment in an authorial or sexual identity. It is in this travel and crossing of letters and names that the figure of the woman writer becomes discernible as a woman who resists the heterosexual exchange which fixes woman as an enigma *for men*. That resistance may work to open out a space in which woman exceeds her narrativisation *as* enigma, becoming a speaking subject who names as well as is named, so dividing the enigma from itself (Spivak 1989: 220).

A story from Angela Carter's *Fireworks* collection, 'The Flesh and the Mirror', contains an image which may clarify how 'women's writing' involves the engendering of speech acts for women through the displacement and non-resolution of an enigma. This image associates this inscription of woman as speaking subject with the opening out of an otherness within woman, posing a difference as well as identity between herself and herself: 'Women and mirrors are in complicity with one another to evade the action I/she performs that she/I cannot watch, the action with which I break out of the mirror, with which I assume my appearance' (Carter 1987: 65). Here, the relation between woman and her image (as returned by the opaqueness of the mirror) is made undecidable by the gap between an action or a performance and its appearance. The gap enacted by the difference between woman and her image is expressed in a complex morpheme, 'I/she'. The oblique that associates the first person and third person pronoun, existing between the 'I' of a speaking subject and the 'she' of woman, creates a division and a connection. It is a telling signifier of that which stands between and enables the transformation of woman as enigma into a speaking subject, a subject which performs itself through commanding itself to interrogate and question the 'she', as well as to love it. Indeed, earlier in the story the heroine 'moved through these expressionist perspectives in my black dress as though I was the creator of all and myself, too, in a black dress, in love, crying, walking through the city in the third person singular, my own heroine, as though the world stretched out from my eye like spokes from a sensitized hub that galvanized all to life when I looked at it' (Carter 1987: 62). Here, the relation of woman to herself is the site of a necessary division, which creates a 'she' from the spacings and travels of an 'I'. The unnamed heroine who is both an 'I' and a 'she', both connected to, and disassociated from, the location and image of her body is, perhaps, a figure for the woman writer, whose embodiment cuts across the text rather than is contained within it. The woman writer, hesitating between an 'I' and a 'she', between inscribing the text and being inscribed within it, does not have an essential identity, but is a figure which can locate itself only in a textual difference. Reading such texts as inscribing a space for women to speak (to) their otherness, in order to dislodge the relation of address in which woman's enigma is a question for man, poses this textual difference as another difference that matters.

Auto/ethno/graphies

In the previous section, I complicated the postmodern narrativisation of the author's death by discussing how an understanding of the difference of women's writing keeps the author in place as a formation, at the same time as it challenges notions of authorial and sexual identity. To this extent, this feminist approach to women's writing takes us beyond the opposition between the author as living (modern) and the author as dead (postmodern). The author is in-between life and death, made alive after the event of that life's possibility: made alive through a kind of death which is itself a gift to the living (the reader who finds the materiality of the letter, 'W', as a trace of the author that will have been).

However, in this section, my concern will be to undermine any such privileging of sexual difference – as the difference that matters – by considering the relation between authorship, writing and empire. I have already mentioned the relation between writing and auto-biography: whereby the latter comes to signify the difficulty of separating work from life. In Jacques Derrida's work, the instability of such a border between work and life (auto/biography) does not simply displace the signature as a pure event – as an event which can be, at any given moment, in the present as such – but also comes to embody the relationship to the reader as other (Derrida 1988b: 5). The auto-biography can only take place through an-other's hearing of the text: through an-other which receives the gift of writing. Such an approach is closer to my feminist concern with the ethics of reading through the impossible figuration of the woman writer, than the metaphor which has been more expressive of postmodernism within literary criticism, 'the death of the author'.

Within traditional forms of criticism, however, auto-biography is only used to describe a certain kind of writing about life. It is only privileged texts that are read as auto-biographies: as writings of a self that transcends the contingency of historical or social relations. This critical differentiation of auto-biographical writing from other personal writings – as a differentiation that belonged to the Romantic ideology of individualism – was a way of maintaining the property embedded in conceptions both of the self (the self which is proper) and writing (the writing which is proper). Auto-biography as individuation – as a story of the gradual separation and perfection of the individual self – has been identified by feminists as a specifically masculine genre, as a way of writing that marks, and is marked by, privilege and social agency. As Susan Friedman puts it, 'The emphasis on individualism as the necessary pre-condition for auto-biography is thus a reflection of privilege, one that excludes from the canons of auto-biography those writers that have been denied by history the illusion of individualism' (Friedman 1988: 39).

In Jenny Sharpe's *Allegories of Empire*, the analysis of the exclusive nature of the auto-biographical self is taken further. In her reading of *Jane Eyre*, Sharpe argues that the story of the individuation of the female narrator relies on a racialising of the authorial signature. She writes: 'One way to consider the power relations in *Jane Eyre* is to read the writing of a female self and the voicing of women's oppression as a privileged mode of address for the feminist individualist. It is a mode of address that is unavailable to the subaltern women who are represented in the novel' (Sharpe 1993: 32). The white woman gains partial access to the privilege of the authorial 'I', through the negation or exclusion of Black women. They become signs of that which she is not – an abject and irrational embodiment which she can speak of through the discourse of enlightened authority (for example, the white woman as missionary). Her gesture of 'speaking for' the Black women presupposes their violent effacement as subjects. In this sense, auto-biography as individuation functions as a racialised as well as gendered practice. I would take this point further and argue that auto-biography as individuation never quite takes place. It is precisely those marginalised and abject figures which return to haunt the authorial self and to remind her of her immersion in a violent sociality. Here, Black women are present as a trace of the impossibility of the female signature, or of any ontologically secured category of 'women's writing'.

Indeed, my concern with the relation between self and writing is an attempt to recognise how race and gender are mutually implicated as differences that matter within the discursive formations of authorship. Whose (life) stories matter? Whose stories are authorised as such? My attempt to defend the importance of the question, 'who is writing here?' which, as argued in section one, necessitates that we shift from an analysis of the origins of writing to the contexts in which writing and reading takes place, is an attempt to bring our attention to how writing is always implicated in a discursive relation of address which is irreducible to sexual difference. So, returning to Spivak's work, we can consider how the subaltern woman does not speak or write, but is always spoken for, or written about. The discursive relation of address in which authorship is implicated involves both colonial and gendered dimensions. In light of such a relation, we must ask: would it be possible to read her (the subaltern woman's) auto-biography as a gift that cannot be reduced to colonial and gendered exchange? Can we hear a voice that is not speaking? Is there a potential for a gift, in which the other no longer confirms the auto-biography as the violence of individuation?

Then again, does not reading the auto-biography of an-other install the phantasy that we can get inside the skin of the other: that we can simply hear her story and so witness a truth that was lacking? But auto-biography is irreducible to the intimating of the self-in-writing. On the contrary, it is auto-biography's movement *outward and across* from any individuated phantasy of being-in-the-world that is so important. Auto-biography traces how a writing of the self cannot simply exist as such, how the self is always implicated in relations with others who cannot be relegated to an outside. Kamala Visweswaran begins her text *Fictions of Feminist Ethnography* with a note on how the conflation of auto-biography and ethnography takes place at particular conjunctures (Visweswaran 1994: 6–7). Here, a writing of the self intrudes into a writing of the other. The confusion resides over what is the 'proper object' of writing. As one 'proper object' is set up as constitutive of a discipline (auto-biography as the self, ethnography as the other), then what it excludes and designates as other-to-itself necessarily remains internal and constitutive of its limits. In auto-biography, 'others' inflect the self, rendering it impossible to designate this story as 'my story'. Interestingly, Visweswaran argues that: 'the confluence of race and gender is one juncture at which the boundaries of a newly emergent ethnographic genre are burst by personal narrative; that the rhetorical devices of "objective" ethnography are somehow inadequate to deal with the difficulties and contradictions of writing about race' (Visweswaran 1994: 7). This image of 'bursting' is easily reversible: one could discuss how any personal testimony on the intersection of gender and race necessarily brings into play the outward movement implicit in the writing of 'otherness'. What these arguments about the complicated relation between auto/biography and ethno/graphy suggest is the importance of the 'who' that writes: not the author as individual hero, but the author as located in a context (which is at once a text) which involves the demarcation of boundaries between self and other that are implicated in both gendered and colonial histories.

Such a confusion of what is the proper object of writing in the 'bringing together' of auto/biography and ethno/graphy is clearly evident in Sally Morgan's *My Place*. As Ken Gelder points out, 'Sally Morgan who collects that information, is not only intimate with her informants, she is related to them: no ethnologist could be more at home with her subjects, and it is doubtless this collapsing of the difference between ethnographic discourse and the other that has made *My Place* so popular' (Gelder 1991: 359). I read *My Place* when I was still at school in Adelaide. It is a text that affected me. It caused me to think again about some of my ideas concerning Australian history, and my own relation to the 'racialised form' of Australian nationhood. An autobiographical text by a young Aboriginal woman, *My Place* is a personal testimony that calls into question many of the assumptions that are central to the phantasy of how 'Australia' came-into-being. The violence which is unspeakable is traced as a story of intimacy, of becoming intimate with one's (lost) family in order to write something other.

At one level, *My Place* could be read as a story of Sally Morgan's individual discovery of her Aboriginal identity. The reader is told how Sally did not know that she was Aboriginal: 'For the first time in my fifteen years, I was conscious of Nan's colouring. She was right, she wasn't white. Well, I thought logically, if she wasn't white, then neither were we. What did that make us? What did that make me? I had never thought of myself as Black before' (Morgan 1995: 97). Sally has to 'find out' what it means to be Aboriginal. However, the quest does not involve her individuation. This narrative of discovery of a past which is absent from the surface involves a community. It involves speaking to her family who tell her their stories. Sally becomes the subject of the text as an Aboriginal woman only through hearing others speak and re-tracing their partial and fractured stories. The story of assuming a lost Aboriginality demands a collective memory which forms the materiality of the text itself. The act of remembering through engagement with others creates the present identification as one that lives for the future of a displaced community. Given this, Sally's claiming of an 'I' does fully account for the production of this auto-ethno-graphy. On the contrary, authorship within *My Place* can only take place through partially giving up any such authorial 'I'.*

The act of 'discovering Aboriginality' becomes then a story not of truth *but of love*. The process of remembering involves a form of closeness and proximity to each other in order to deal with the tragedy of 'the stolen generation' – the generation of half-caste Aboriginal children who were taken away from their mothers and introduced into white communities as part of a policy of assimilation. This policy (which constituted the sanctioning of miscegenation) involved the assumption that eventually all traces of Aboriginality (as Blackness) would be erased from the faces of Australia. In speaking to each other about the history of enforced separation, the generation of women in *My Place* resist their silencing. But it is a painful process:

It took several months to work through Mum's story and, during that time, many tears were shed. We became very close.

Although she'd finally shared her story with me, she still couldn't bring herself to tell my brothers and sisters. Consequently, I found myself communicating it to them in bits and pieces as it seemed appropriate. It was, and still is, upsetting for us all. We'd lived in a cocoon of sorts for so long that we found it difficult to come to terms with the experiences Mum had been through. (Morgan 1995: 307)

Here, the sharing of stories is like breaking out of a cocoon of assumed whiteness. That 'breaking out' constitutes a form of closeness arrived at through the pain of loss. The act of sharing allows the re-forming and trans-forming story of a 'we' which had been made impossible, which had become erased from the surface of any living community. The 'we' doesn't constitute the smoothness of the narrative: it doesn't abolish the distances and divisions. The narrative becomes increasingly disjointed as it attempts to forge the links of a new community. Sally, as a narrator, wants other members of her family to tell their side of the story. We have

---

* One must note here how the reading of *My Place* within White Australia has authorised a discourse of appropriate(d) otherness. The fact that *My Place*, has been accommodated within White Australian literary self-representation, and 'Sally Morgan' has been individuated as the acceptable face of Aboriginality, needs to be addressed. Rather than dismissing *My Place* itself, we need to recognise the potential and irreducible danger of such reading practices in which the figuring of the author as an individual and autonomous hero enables the radical contingency of the textual relation to be effaced. Here, the other can be domesticated and appropriated, precisely in so far as it is assumed to be known or read *in the text*.

then incorporated into her narrative *My Place*, the stories of these other 'I's', told in the first person singular. The 'I's' within her 'I' do not emerge through appropriation or absorption. The reader passing through, gains a sense of the discontinuities between subjectivities that informs the force of the community. Through narrating the act of speaking to each other, the reader is reminded that the 'we' is unnarratable beyond the disjointed patching of 'I's' whose status in the narrative cannot be rendered equivalent. The community lives through this impossibility: *it becomes a force through a recognition of that which cannot merge into one.*

In the unspeakable gaps between the stories, Aboriginality gets reconstructed as a politics of resistance, a politics based, not on a concealment, but a revelation that there is 'more than one' (story) that opens up the future. This re-creation of the possibility of community and collectivity occurs through the pain and hope of speaking to each other, of desiring to hear each other's stories. But that gesture of 'getting closer' does not abolish the distance, rather, it becomes liveable through it. Claiming the authorial 'I' for the Aboriginal woman can only involve giving it up as the origin of the text: her story can only be told through the recognition of the immersion of the 'I' in a 'we'. The author, then, is not the 'I' or the 'we' but the very division between 'I' and 'we', the very division between self and community. Is it through such a division that the reader can hear the Aboriginal woman speaking?

Of course, though, there is something that still does not get across. However much *My Place* provides an alternative to the ethnographic construction of Aboriginality as other, it also admits to its own limits, to the 'secret' which it cannot speak of. For Nan, Sally's grandmother, must take her secrets to the grave: 'Well, Sal, that's all I'm gunna tell ya. My brain's no good, it's gone rotten. I don't want to talk no more. I got my secrets, I'll take them to the grave. Some things, I can't talk 'bout. Not even to you, my granddaughter' (Morgan 1995: 349). Here, even the intimacy of 'being related' is not enough for a complete story. There are secrets which simply cannot be named. Sally admits knowing, 'she would never plumb them' (Morgan 1995: 350). As a reader, Nan's admission of this impossibility of telling is also a reminder of the incompleteness of *My Place* itself. It is a reminder that we, as readers, cannot get close enough to 'know' the truth about the story. The movement towards (we get closer, we hear more) and away (we get close enough to find out there are secrets) animates our relation to the text. The movement between proximity and distance (through proximity, distance) renders the process of reading *My Place* one which confounds and unsettles the reader. What cannot be said, throws away any sense of security, unsettles that phantasy that we can know and represent the story for ourselves. Touched by the text, the other presents itself *without being presented as such.*

The ethics of reading *My Place* as beyond the opposition between the auto/biographical and the ethno/graphic take us to a different model of authorship. The author is not here an intentional subject which 'owns' the story and legislates on our behalf. Authorship is only possible through giving up the realm of property: by opening out the writing of the self to an-other whose secret one cannot possess. In other words, the speech acts that are always addressed to an-other are engendered through the necessity and impossibility of claiming an 'I' (I speak to you only in so far as I do not know). This reminds me here of Shoshana Felman and Dori Laub's work on testimony. They write: 'As readers, we are witnesses precisely to these questions we do not own and do not yet understand, but which summon and beseech us from within the literary texts' (Felman and Laub 1992: xiii). Felman further suggests that one does not have to own or possess the truth in order to bear witness to it (Felman 1992: 15). *My Place*, as a testimony, bears witness to a truth which it cannot possess. The reader, in reading this as auto/ethno/graphy, is also in the position of a witness: the reader is beseeched into an impossible act of witnessing. But again, what we witness is the unrepresentable: an unrepresentability which does not necessarily lead to over-representation (the enigma which demands that we keep looking), but to a recognition of the limits of what can be got across (we cannot claim ownership of our reading). This limit, then, does not belong to the text, or to ourselves as readers, but is constitutive of our relation to it.

To become an author of a story is to withdraw from the authorisation of the story through possession of the other. The relationship between work and life is an instability which involves the relaying of a gift: it is a gift that is received by the author (from Nan) and then received by the reader (from Sally). But the gift, which constitutes the possibility of *My Place* as speech act or testimony, is also at the same time a secret: a gift that cannot be reduced to an exchange between author and reader, yet takes place through the determination of their critical relation. The secret lodges itself as a reading of the gift of writing.

In this chapter, I have argued that postmodern narratives become authorised through a discourse on the author's death. Despite feminism's shared critical ambivalence to the romantic construction of the author, I have argued that the feminist concern with the difference of women's writing displaces any notion of the author as either living or dead. In between life and death, the gendered author is a difference that matters: a difference that is not found within the text, but is constitutive of our relation to it (as a relation to an impossible enigma). At the same time, the concern with the critical difference of women's writing does not produce a resolution to the problem of the author's life or death. I have also argued that the author function has a colonial dimension, and that the question, 'what difference does it make who is writing here', opens out that dimension in terms of the instability of the relation between work and life and the instability *within* both 'work' and 'life'. Here, auto-biography and ethno-graphy do not have the structure of an opposition: the border between self and other is destabilised. In *My Place* the writing of the authorial subject takes place through the relaying of gifts between others. Reading for an authorial difference is not reading here for a difference that is within the text, but a difference that commands an ethics of reading in which there are limits to what can be got across. This ethics of reading might return us to the ethics of reading postmodernism. How to bear witness to the postmodern without assuming that one can possess or own the truth? Perhaps this question demands another opening: perhaps it is here that the author's death proclaimed by postmodernism as signalling its own arrival becomes a question that is living.

6   (Meta)fictions

Can we speak of postmodern literature? What does it mean to read literature as postmodern? These questions are more complicated than they might appear on the surface. In much use of postmodernism within literary theory, postmodernism is taken for granted as a generic term for a certain kind of writing. Postmodernism is assumed to have a referent – it is assumed to refer to writings that complicate and destabilise the narratives of classical realism. However, as I have discussed so far in this book, postmodernism is constructed through the very readings which take it for granted as having an object or referent that is already in place. This approach to postmodernism may have important consequences for theories of postmodernism in relationship to literature. It may suggest that what is important is not so much postmodernism as a kind of writing, but postmodernism as a way of reading. Postmodern literary theory does not so much describe a set of fictions, but constructs itself through a critical dialogue with the fictions it names or designates as postmodern.

Why is such a shift from postmodernism as a generic term for writing to postmodernism as a way of reading and constructing 'the generic' important? Why might this shift be important to feminism? To account for my desire to enter these debates, I will provide you with an anecdote. My first encounter with postmodernism was through taking a course on American literature at the University of Adelaide in 1989. I remember a tutorial that took place in my women's writing course the following year. The tutorial had a powerful effect on me. In the tutorial we were speaking about postmodernism. I was taking the position that I often assumed: I was re-presenting postmodernism through making claims about its radicality. I remember speaking about how postmodernism destabilised our very notion of 'the real' and with it notions of gender identity. My tutor questioned me at this point and herself told an anecdote about another student who had, like me, taken the course on American literature the previous year. That student had been upset and angry about how postmodern fictions were taught on that course. Her anger related in particular to how Robert Coover's 'The Babysitter' had been discussed. This story involves the plot of the multiple rape of a female character, but no one within the tutorial had mentioned this at all. I cast my mind back to that course. She was right, the rape, within the tutorial, was not spoken of. All that was spoken of was how the story undermined the very notion of 'representation', how it drew attention to its constructedness as a text, and how it refused the very possibility of plotting as a sequencing of events in time. In this instance, reading a text as postmodern meant that the question of violence was elided. We must ask: what violence is at stake in this non-reading of violence?

Of course, opening a chapter with an anecdote provides a very particular way of organising one's narrative: self-presented as discrete moments in time, anecdotes mark out a line in the text like the route of a journey (through this, I discovered). Indeed, my anecdote is an anecdote of an anecdote: it is a second-hand account in which a student's distress is doubly removed. What I am remembering is a story that was already told at least twice: there is no event at which I was present, but only a relaying of stories. One must be cautious of how the anecdote can become an absent centre, not only by being given the status of an event that simply happened, but also by being used as a justification for a given argument (as a justification which belongs 'outside' the text).

At the same time, this pedagogical encounter became very important to me as a way of unlearning any simple equation of postmodernism with a radical politics (a politics of 'transgression' and 'subversion'). To provide this anecdote is to account for what affected me, that is, what moved me to write this, here and now. Through the telling of the anecdote, I have implicated myself in the subject of my research and any such implication always invokes an-other who cannot be named.

And yet events that have not simply taken place, can still repeat themselves. I have since, as a teacher, encountered students who have also been upset as they have not been allowed to speak of the role of sexual violence in postmodern fictions. Indeed, students have been accused of being unsophisticated readers in being upset by such texts. Their concern with issues of violence against women has been read as evidence that they have assumed the possibility of representation as such. It strikes me as significant that such exchanges are pedagogical – that these definitions of better and worse readings have taken place through the authorisation of 'the teacher' as the subject presumed to know. Postmodernism here, as a way of teaching, involves the enforcement of ways of reading and ways of not reading certain privileged texts.

What is at stake in the determination of postmodern pedagogy and reading as both an imperative and prohibition? First, there is the assumption that to address issues of sexual violence in such texts one must be working with a naïve model of representation. Second, there is an assumption that certain kinds of texts, which experiment with literary form, disallow readings which focus on questions that have traditionally been seen as a matter of 'content'. These two assumptions work together to secure a reading which cannot deal with how violence operates in fictions which experiment with literary form. Such a reading disallows, not only an analysis of representations of violence, but also an analysis of the violence of representation.

This chapter is an attempt, as a feminist, to read these fictions which are designated as postmodern, against the tradition of postmodern literary criticism. I will do so by thinking through how sexual difference is narrated in the meta-fictions of Robert Coover, and then effaced as a form of difference by the postmodern re-reading of this writing. I will argue that such differences do not simply operate at the level of representation (though they do operate at that level), but also as a mode of enunciation in which the postmodern reader, through the non-recognition of violence, becomes implicated. My concern is theoretical, political and also personal: ways of reading literary texts also involve performative utterances ('I do', 'you should do') that can be sedimented into communities of ideal ('sophisticated') and failed readers. Ways of reading and not reading become ways of teaching and not teaching and ways of living and not living.

Reading postmodernism

In order to move from an analysis of postmodernism as a generic term for writing to postmodernism as a way of reading, I want firstly to consider Jean-François Lyotard's appendix to *The Postmodern Condition*. Here, Lyotard considers the role and function of aesthetics and seems to qualify some of the arguments that formed the basis of the report on knowledge which I discussed in my introduction. In the opening stages of the appendix, Lyotard addresses the demand for realism and unity. He writes:

The demands I began by citing are not all equivalent. They can even be contradictory. Some are made in the name of postmodernism, others in order to combat it. It is not necessarily the same thing to formulate a demand for some referent (and objective reality), for some sense (and credible transcendence), for an addressee (and audience), or an addresser (and subjective expressiveness) or for some communicational consensus (and a general code of exchanges, such as the genre of historical discourse). But in the diverse invitations to suspend artistic experimentation, there is an identical call for order, a desire for unity, for identity, for security, or popularity. (Lyotard 1989: 73)

Here, an opposition is constructed between the desire for artistic experimentation and the desire for unity. As a result, Lyotard interprets the urge to liquidate the heritage of the avant-garde as, 'an irrefutable sign of this common disposition' (Lyotard 1989: 73). Any writers or artists who refuse to endorse this retreat by questioning the rules of plastic and narrative arts, 'are destined to have little credibility in the eyes of those concerned with "reality" and "identity"; they have no guarantee of an audience' (Lyotard 1989: 75).

Lyotard's argument about how the demand for realism constructs aesthetic experimentation as dangerous engenders a different narrative of (post)modernism. At one level, he argues that the technological or performative criteria of the modern – in which usefulness becomes the primary measure of value – involves the reduction of art to capital. Such a reduction prevents forms of artistic experimentation which do not support the accumulation of capital. But at another level, the refusal of a concept of the real beyond the demands of capital enables transformation in the form of the expansion of commodity objects into art. To this extent, the performative criteria may function to expand and transform conceptions of aesthetic value.

Lyotard's argument within the report on knowledge, that the modern relies on forms of determinism and totality, is complicated by the suggestion that the modern may in itself suspend the real, if only for the cynical demands of capital. This suspension comes from the need to break down a concept of an objective reality which is beyond the production of new rules for games. The process of suspension is reflected in the avant-garde, where the regeneration of plastic and narrative arts takes place through a questioning of the rules of aesthetics. Such questioning leads to a conceptualisation which awaits an object, and participates in a generalised sense of social disintegration, in the lack of totality which would give meaning (and beauty) to objects. As a result, Lyotard argues that a suspicion of realism is implicit in the performative and technological criterion of the modern. The modern becomes the unpresentable, that which can be conceived but which lacks an object for its presentation – the sublime sentiment.

Lyotard then performs a complex shift which seems to qualify the bulk of his report on knowledge. He writes, 'A work can become modern only if it is first postmodern. Postmodernism thus understood is not modernism at its end but in the nascent state, and this state is constant' (Lyotard 1989: 79). Modernism is a withdrawal from the real which 'allows the unpresentable to be put forward only as the missing contents' (Lyotard 1989: 81), while postmodernism, 'would be that which, in the modern, puts forward the unpresentable in presentation itself' (Lyotard 1989: 81). Lyotard ends with a celebration of the postmodern potential inherent in the modern's tragic withdrawal from the real: 'The answer is: Let us wage war on totality: let us be witness to the unpresentable; let us activate the differences and save the honour of the name' (Lyotard 1989: 82).

What are the implications of Lyotard's complication of the modern and postmodern as discrete categories? One of the most obvious details about this appendix is the maintenance of a hierarchical model, despite the complication of the chronological narrative – modern to post-modern. But rather than the hierarchy being sustained by the division modern/postmodern, *it becomes sustained by the division realism/(post)mo-dern*. While Lyotard may argue that a suspension of the real is implicit to the modern and to the literary avant-garde, he does this through a contrast to a school of realism. So, although Lyotard recognises that the demands for realism are differential, even contradictory, the evaluative demand of his own argument leads to a final gesture of totalisation: 'there is an *identical* call for order, a desire for unity, for identity, for security, or popularity' (Lyotard 1989: 73, emphasis mine). Ironically, Lyotard's argument about realism's relation to identity relies on identity thinking: it makes claims about realism as *being identical*, which leads to a final reduction of realism to terror.

Following this totalisation and negation of realism, the text makes the corresponding gesture of assuming that the suspension of the real is a positive event (however much an event that is always to come) in aesthetics. Hence his final polemic: 'Let us wage war on totality: let us be witness to the unpresentable' (Lyotard 1989: 82). This narrative of (post)modernism as a suspension of the real fixes the aesthetic value of realism, and through this, of (post)modernism itself. The narrative of realism to (post)modernism, which is a narrative characterised by assumptions of progress and hierarchy, sustains itself only by refusing to complicate the category of realism and to investigate the specificity of contradictions that invest generic differences.

Much contemporary literary theory also constructs a progressive shift from realism through modernism and on to postmodernism. Such a narrative of progress depends on an assumption that realism is necessarily a tool of the dominant culture. This assumption is evident, for example, in Catherine Belsey's influential theory of 'classical realism', where any ambiguities in a narrative are artificially and aesthetically resolved and the reader passively interpellated into the dominant ideology and subject position (Belsey 1980: 67–70).[1] The assumption that realism is inherently conservative is especially evident in Alison Lee's *Realism and Power: Postmodern British Fiction*. Lee defines realism as a formula for the literal transcription of reality into art whose conservatism is determined by the pretence to normality and neutrality (Lee 1990: ix, 11, 27). Lee compares realist narratives to the subversive techniques of postmodern fiction. Such fiction 'plays (seriously) with the structures of authority' and radically de-doxifies the very conventions of realism and common sense (Lee 1990: xii). Postmodernism is privileged precisely through the reduction of realism to a transcription of the real.

What is at stake in this model of reading which is organised through such an interpretation of realism? Firstly, one has to consider the extent to which these arguments presuppose the 'success' of realism, either in the form of the passive interpellation of the reader into a dominant subject position, or in the transmission of common sense from text to reader. Such a model of reading is no model of reading at all: it assumes that the realist text does not need to be read or, indeed, that it is already read. Secondly, this model of reading assumes that the realist text *can* successfully resolve the contradictions it opens out in the form of a symbolic closure (in which 'the real' is maintained as the cohesion or even destiny of the text itself). As such, these readings of post-modernism against realism exercise the very concept of realism that they critique: they assume the possibility that the 'real' can be secured in the text. Finally, such a reading of realism assumes that the politics of a text is reducible to genre: that the politics of a text is determined by its formal properties. It is this final issue that I want to explore further.

How does the critical classification of literary texts as postmodern assume that politics is reducible to literary form? Readings of 'post-modern fictions' have focused on 'experiments' in conventional narrative form as signs of the subversion of authorising narratives in general (both literary and social). These experiments are read as complicating the reading process and hence undermining the ideological control of realism. Take the definition of postmodern fiction offered by John Mepham:

This fiction has often emphasised the decentering or disintegration of the subject, the effort of fiction to defeat rather than to endorse the reader's will to interpretative synthesis, the reality of contradictions, not to be worked out or resolved in a monological discourse, the plurality of discourses and of worlds. Instead of the fragment from which we draw forth all human life, postmodernist fiction postulates a plurality of discursive contexts or frames within which even the seemingly most reliable and stable unities take on a shifting and disturbingly plural aspect. (Mepham 1991: 145)

Here, the desirability of the postmodern is set up through an implicit contrast with a fiction which *does* resolve contradictions and draw a totality from fragments. The hierarchy which places a monological and unitary realism beneath a pluralistic and fragmentary postmodernism, establishes the political value of postmodernism as inherent to its displacement of realism. This scheme of value differentiation relies, not simply on an implicit theory of what constitutes realism, but also on a theory of how fiction produces or subverts a sense of 'the real', according to whether or not it participates in the ideological conception of a unit and a totality. The hierarchy that produces postmodernism as the space of an anti-real, works to identify these fictions with a set of values by erasing (at least temporarily) the contingency of literary form. Here, postmodernism as a way of reading assumes that 'realism' has fixed the subject in place, in order then to read the fictions it designates as postmodern as the *over-coming* of the generic limits of realism (as the over-coming of identity, fixity, transparency, closure, and so on).

The use of postmodernism as a frame that reads for signs of a subversion of narrative conventions (understood as the ideology of realism) has a specific set of implications for the status of meta-fiction, which Hutcheon defines as a manifestation of postmodernism (Hutcheon 1985: xiii). Hutcheon draws attention to the way that 'post-modern meta-fiction' works to make readers aware of both its production and reception as a cultural product, as a fiction which is about itself, and the process of its own construction (Hutcheon 1985: xiii, 1). Patricia Waugh approaches meta-fiction as, 'writing which consistently displays its conventionality, which explicitly and overtly lays bare its conditions of artifice, and which thereby explores the problematic relationship between art and fiction' (Waugh 1984: 4). Waugh elaborates on this point as follows:

Any text that draws the reader's attention to its process of construction by frustrating his or her conventional expectations of meaning and closure problematises more or less explicitly the ways in which narrative codes – whether literary or 'social' – artificially construct apparently 'real' and imaginary worlds in the terms of the particular ideologies while presenting these as transparently 'natural' and 'eternal'. (Waugh 1984: 22)

What interests me here is the status of the 'particular'. The project of meta-fiction, while dependent on particular ideologies, is presented as concerned with the general function of the ideological in the reproduction of the literary and the social. In this way, the politics of the meta-fictional 'laying bare' of the ideological is abstracted from any particular ideology, becoming reducible to the form those ideologies take. This theory of meta-fiction may be open to complication precisely by re-tracing the role and effect of specific or particular ideological regimes, and how those regimes may differentially determine the realm of reader identifications. In other words, reading strategies which construct post-modern meta-fiction by assuming that meta-fictions over-come the possibility of representation as such, cannot deal with the role of particular representations within the narratives and how they may affect practices of identification.

Indeed, I think the question of how meta-fiction resists implication in structures of identification (naïve or otherwise) needs to be rethought. Hutcheon argues, for example, that meta-fiction's:

central paradox for readers is that, while being made aware of the linguistic and fictive nature of what is being read, and thereby distanced from any unself-conscious identification on the level of character or plot, readers of meta-fiction are at the same time mindful of their active role in reading, in participating in making the text mean. (Hutcheon 1985: xii)

A problem here may be an overly hasty equation between meta-fiction's self-reflexivity (and its consequent suspension of the real) and the distancing of the reader from any 'unself-conscious' identification. This implies that 'unself-conscious' identifications are dependent on the extent to which a text represses its fictional status. It may also presuppose that such identifications function as a singular investment in the 'real'. Indeed, Raymond Federman makes the even stronger claim that self-conscious fictions make identifications within the reading process *impossible* (Federman 1981: 14). But I think identifications are more complex than this. As I argued in chapter 4, subjectivity itself is a complex process of identification and dis-identification entailing phantasmatic acts of (mis)recognition in the daily meetings with others. If we understand reading as an enactment of subjectivity (a production of the reader as subject), then the processes of identification do not depend simply on the coherence of the text (as image, illusion, or real) but rest precisely on the complex investment of the reader in the process of self-making. So although meta-fictional texts may lay bare their fictionality, it does *not* follow that they necessarily distance the reader from identifications. The inscription of meta-fictional texts as postmodern has neglected the specificity of identifications that such text may elicit, precisely by assuming that identification as such is rendered impossible by the formal and self-reflexive properties of the texts themselves.

The way which postmodernism as a mode of literary criticism can exclude the question of the particularity of representations and the eliciting of reader identifications, is evident in the criticism on Robert Coover's meta-fictional narratives. Brian McHale in *Postmodernist Fiction* discusses the story 'Quenby and Ola, Swede and Carl' by first representing it as 'a story of illicit sex and murderous revenge' (McHale 1987: 107). But what follows is an immediate qualification, 'or not, as the case may be' (McHale 1987: 107). The story seems to be *about* such themes as illicit sex, but that about-ness is automatically negated by the formal properties of the text itself, with its realisation of multiple and contradictory possibilities. McHale elaborates: 'self-erasing narratives of the kind I have been discussing violate linear sequentiality by realising two mutually exclusive lines of narrative development at the same time' (McHale 1987: 108). Here, the significance of the story is read as being located in its formal experimentations, its disobeying of the rules of (realist) narrative. This formal disobedience cancels out the role of 'content' or representation: what the story is about is translated by a representation of its form. While this is certainly a simple strategy of reading, one that does not complicate the text by troubling it with questions about its specific ideological investments, it is also one that produces and frames the text in a certain way, deciding what constitutes its meaning in advance. The question of sexual difference which appears in McHale's original (and cancelled out) description (this story of illicit sex) is excluded from the frame of a postmodern strategy of reading by being placed on the side of a metaphysical content (the content of realism) – on the side of what is automatically negated by the form of the text itself.

Postmodernism as a way of reading hence reduces politics to literary form at the same time as it places issues such as sexual difference on the side of content. While many of the meta-fictions which are read as postmodern are fascinated with sexual difference and sexuality, especially within the context of life in middle-class white American suburbia, they are read as precisely not being 'about' such differences. Such a way of reading against realism (which fixes realism in place in order to situate postmodernism as the over-coming of realism) cannot deal with how differences and identifications may be partially fixed through formal experimentation. It also does not consider how sexual differences may operate beyond 'representation': for example, how such differences may be determined at the level of enunciation. Postmodern fictions, rather than suspending or transcending such differences, may re-constitute those differences differently, through the very experimentations with literary form. The question of how that re-constitution may take place is hence worthy of further consideration.

Narrating sex and the politics of form

In this section, I will closely examine three of Robert Coover's most 'experimental' stories, concentrating on how the experiments with form are dependent in certain ways on the maintenance of gendering effects at the level of enunciation. We can return here to Felman's re-thinking of the Freudian question, 'what does a woman want?', as occupying a gendered relation of address, whereby authors are sexed according to their differential relation to the enigma of woman-as-text. I will read Coover's stories against the 'postmodern grain' by examining how their textual strategies make sexual difference critical, in the very production of a masculine mode of enunciation where 'woman' becomes an enigma within the narrative trajectory. My readings will also raise more general issues regarding the status of meta-fictionality in relation to post-modernism.

Meta-fiction is most often understood, as I have already suggested, as an extreme form of self-reflexivity within literary texts. Coover's story 'The Magic Poker' certainly displays this formal characteristic. The first person narrator, named only as 'I', self-consciously is involved in writing and producing a fictional world. The story begins as follows:

I wander the island, inventing it. I make a sun for it, and trees – pines and birch and dogwood and firs – and cause the water to lap the pebbles of its abandoned shores. This, and more: I deposit shadows and dampness, spin webs, and scatter ruins. Yes: ruins. A mansion and guest cabins and boat houses and docks. Terraces, too, and bath houses and even an observation tower. All gutted and window-busted and autographed and shat upon. I impose a hot midday silence, a profound and heavy stillness. But anything can happen. (Coover 1970: 20)

Here the narrator's 'I' is repeated in the form of an agency. The narrator is inventing rather than describing, an active and determining force, rather than a passive voice for presenting the reader with an already mapped out 'real'. This suggestion of narrative agency is linked in the final sentence with the opening out of multiple possibilities: 'But any-thing can happen.' The fictional space is unconstrained by any represen-tational demand. The 'I' here, as an inventive 'I', appears unsexed, unlocated and disembodied. In the various small extracts that follow, the passage of the 'I' invents and re-invents bizarre plot twists and developments that wildly contradict each other. The shifts in narrative follow the passage of an 'I' whose appearances and disappearances call into question the stability of the fictional 'real'.

This story of an inventing narrator inscribes a certain pleasure of and in the text. The 'I' of the narrator 'arranges', 'rots', 'tatters', 'infests', 'tears', 'guts', 'smashes', 'shits', 'rusts', 'kicks' and 'unhinges', but then comments, 'Really, there's nothing to it. In fact, it's a pleasure' (Coover 1970: 22). This pleasure of creation is at once a space of desire in which the 'I' articulates the longing for an agency of self which is highly physical, a self that does things as it inscribes things, a self that literally knocks things into shape. If the inventing 'I' is here the subject of desire (for the rendering present of the self in others) then its inscriptions and travels bear the passage of desire, at once desiring and desire's effect. In this way the meta-fictional passage of the 'I' may enact an ideology of individualism, in which the self is unconstrained by the other (or by others), in a phantasy of the self as originary, determining and transformative.[2]

Already my reading of the 'I' inscribed by Coover's text as a subject which desires self-presence is complicated by the text which troubles the identification of the 'I' as inventor. For when the narrator returns to the characters she or he has invented (the girls, the caretaker's son and the tall man), an uncertainty emerges: 'But the caretaker's son? To tell the truth, I sometimes wonder if it was not he who invented me' (Coover 1970: 27). This confusion over who (or what) is inventing, brings the reader's attention to the discursive status of the 'I' as itself an effect, no longer commanding the text, but structured by an anxiety over loss and passivity. Indeed, towards the end of the story an extract begins 'I am disappearing', confusing real and fictional maps and geography with a loss of certainty over the integrity of what is being invented (Coover 1970: 40). The momentary reversals from self-confidence to anxiety nevertheless sustain the 'I' as the centre of a phenomenological exploration of the passage of writing into fiction (the 'I' still speaks of its own disappearance, cancelling itself out only through a repetition).

Asking the question of the gendering effects of this 'I' may enable us to examine the ideological implications of this desirous but anxious passage from subject to object and back again. The 'I' invents two male and two female characters, but it is the latter two that seem central to the plot dynamics of the story: 'The girl in gold pants? yes. The other one, Karen? also. In fact, they are sisters. I have brought two sisters to this invented island, and shall, in time, send them home again' (Coover 1970:25). Here, the action of the story becomes defined in terms of making the two sisters appear and disappear from its frame.

Their appearance is centred around the various mythologies the text employs to contextualise its narratives. The numerous 'Once upon a times' introduce fairy tales of deserted islands, princesses and magic pokers, as well as contemporary stories of romance and of corruption, all of which seem to work as tales of transformation and desire. The magic poker, however, is self-consciously named within the text as a symbol, as something 'archetypal and even maybe beautiful, a blend of eros and wisdom, sex and sensibility, music and myth' (Coover 1970: 30). By self-consciously naming the symbolic function of the poker, the text refuses to enable the poker to *have* a symbolic meaning, drawing our attention to the way in which the meanings attached to objects are acquired through phantasy and myth. Indeed, the transformations of the story itself (does the girl in the gold pants turn the poker into a prince when she kisses him, or is it just a dirty old object?) which are not resolved into one plot option, centre around the myth of the poker and the desires of the characters to realise its meanings.

These various (and often contradictory) myths are certainly made up of gendered assumptions. For example, one section begins, ' "Call it woman's intuition", she says with a light laugh. He appraises her fineboned features, her delicate hands, her soft maidenly breasts under the ruffled blouse, her firm haunches gleaming golden over the shadowed grass' (Coover 1970: 31). This passage relies upon a conventional image of woman as spectacle.

However, could it be argued that the 'truth' of this image of femininity is called into question given the narrative's contradictory and self-reflexive nature? Do the contradictory inscriptions of 'woman' open the way for seeing this story as destabilising gendered assumptions? But the homology that has appeared in these questions (between the destabilisation of truth and the destabilisation of sexual identity) is itself open to being complicated by asking the question of sexual difference, not simply at the level of representation (where the contradictions and ambivalence of the narrative suggest it can both repeat or destabilise gendered assumptions), but also as a mode of enunciation. Such an approach would involve asking the question of whether the narrative voice is itself gendered, and the implications of this gendered modality for the representations of sexual difference which saturate the text.

A later passage may suggest that the gendering of the narrative as masculine takes place through the stabilisation of woman as the scene for the crossings of male desire. This passage begins:

At times, I forget that this arrangement is my own invention. I begin to think of the island as somehow real, its objects solid and intractable, its condition of ruin not so much an aesthetic design as an historical denouement. I find myself peering into blue teakettles, batting at spiderwebs, and contemplating a greenish-gray growth on the side of a stone parapet. I wonder if others might wander here without my knowing it; I wonder if I might die and the teakettle remain. 'I have brought two sisters to this invented island,' I say. This is no extravagance. It is indeed I who burdens them with curiosity and history, appetite and rhetoric. If they have names and griefs, I have provided them. 'In fact,' I add, 'without me they'd have no cunts.' This is not . . . meant to alarm, merely to make a truth manifest – yet I am myself somewhat alarmed. It is one thing to discover the shag of hair between my buttocks, quite another to find myself tugging the tight gold pants off Karen's sister. Or perhaps it is the same thing, yet troubling in either case. Where does the illusion come from, this sensation of 'hardness' in a blue kettle or an iron poker, golden haunches or a green piano? (Coover 1970: 33–4)

The first and perhaps most noticeable characteristic of this passage is its self-consciousness about its own status as fiction: the way it troubles the notion of a simple narrative trajectory towards a proper and closed ending, and its reflexive attention to the illusionism that renders objects substantive and perceptible within writing. However, this reflective narrative voice, while troubling, also performs a very specific gendering effect. The object of invention is here the female character, whom the narrative voice has created as a substantiation of femininity. The placing of the direct sexual utterance within quotation marks, 'without me they'd have no cunts', personalises the address, as a relation between speakers, rendering women, and women's sexuality, a term in an exchange. The suggestion that woman as a sexual being originates through the narrative address is disassociated from trouble or alarm (it is not meant to provoke), but is represented (ironically) as a manifestation of truth. The truth of his narrating woman is here the truth that woman does not pre-exist his narrative, but is made substantial through its travels.

The narrative 'I' is italicised and 'alarmed' at the point of declaring this 'truth'. And it is here, in the play of personal pronouns, that the implication of 'I' in a structural relation of masculinity becomes evident, not necessarily at the literal level of plot, but certainly as a mode of enunciation. The difference or division between the male character and the narrator shifts into an identity ('It is one thing to discover the shag of hair between *my* buttocks'). The shift in personal pronouns connects the male character and the narrator and so embodies the narrator as male. That embodiment and enclosure of the 'I' in an expression of a male identity (from two to one, both subject and object in his discourse) leads to a certain fulfilment of a narrative desire ('quite another to find *myself* tugging the tight gold pants off Karen's sister'). Here, the non-identity of the male narrator and the female character organises the plot in terms of his desire for penetration, where the woman becomes knowable in the form of an event. The agency of the 'I' that seems autonomous from any representational demand is structured around the repetition of woman as a plot vehicle for the formation of masculine identity. The announcement of the possession of the woman takes place through a shift from a division to an identification between the male character and narrator.

The masculine mode of enunciation implicit to the identification forged between the male character and narrator complicates the supposed inherent radical-ness of this meta-fictional form, precisely by drawing our attention to the ways in which self-reflexivity may participate in a masculinist (and liberal) discourse as the freedom to create (or give substance to) woman. The integrity of the male 'I' is enabled as a meeting of the morphology of the male character with the grammar of the narrator, a meeting which sexualises and embodies the 'I' as a subject whose desire for woman sustains the interpretative potential of the text itself. Such a reading of the way in which the linguistic 'I' is determined and embodied as a structure of masculinity remains, of course, a speculative and tentative one. Reading for the gendering effects of the narrative's self-reflexivity is necessarily an inscription of that text's instability – the way in which the identifications it elicits are both already there and are not fully determined (to assume that identification is over-come would be to negate this constitutive instability).

Another story from the collection, 'The Babysitter', also uses the technique of multiple and contradictory plot sequences and includes acts and phantasies of sexual violence against women. As many critics have observed, the story does not choose or privilege any particular sequence (for example, McHale 1987). The contradictory possibilities lead only to an absurd conclusion: ' "What can I say, Dolly?" the host says with a sigh, twisting the butter strands of her ripped girdle between his fingers. "Your children are murdered, your husband gone, a corpse in your bathroom and your house is wrecked. I'm sorry" ' (Coover 1970: 239). The alternative plot sequences present the perspectives (and phantasies) of the varying characters (as well as the fictional narratives on TV) over the timespan of an apparently single night and an apparently single event: the babysitting of a suburban middle-class couple's children.

But despite the variations and difference of the perspectives offered in the plot sequences, a primary point of continuity is the sexual desire for the babysitter expressed by her boyfriend and his male friend, and the father of the children. She is certainly the focal point of the plot and its contradictions, as the title suggests. The narrative shifts from depicting her gestures and actions during the night (such as taking a bath) to the phantasies about her body expressed by the male characters. All are plotting to enter the house and sexually advance upon her, either in the form of rape or seduction. The following passages may enable us to contrast these double plottings:

'Stop it!' she screams. 'Please stop!' She's on her hands and knees, trying to get up, but they're too strong for her. Mark holds her head down. 'Now, baby, we're gonna teach you how to be a nice girl,' he says coldly, and nods at Jack. When she's doubled over like that, her skirt rides up her thighs to the leg bands of her panties. 'C'mon, man, go! This baby's cold! She needs your touch!' (Coover 1970: 225)

Probably some damn kid over there right now. Wrestling around on the couch in front of his TV. Maybe he should drop back to the house. Just to check. None of that stuff, she was there to do a job! Park the car a couple of doors down, slip in the front door before she knows it. He sees the disarray of clothing, the young thighs exposed to flickering television light, hears his baby crying. 'Hey, what's going on here! Get outa here, son, before I call the police!' Of course, they haven't really being doing anything. They probably don't even know how. He stares benignly down upon the girl, her skirt rumpled loosely around her thighs. Flushed, frightened, yet excited she stares back at him. He smiles. His finger touches her knee, approaches the hem. Another couple arrives. Filling up here with people. He wouldn't be missed. Just slip out, stop back casually to pick up something or other he forgot, never mind what. He remembers the other time they had this babysitter, she took a bath in their house. She had a date afterwards, and she'd just come from cheerleading practice or something. Aspirin maybe. Just drop quietly and casually into the bathroom to pick up some aspirin. 'Oh, excuse me, dear! I only . . .!' She gazes back at him, astonished, yet strangely moved. Her soft wet breasts rise and fall in the water, and her tummy looks pale and ripply. He recalls that her pubic hairs, left in the tub, were brown. Light brown. (Coover 1970: 215)

An important difference between these two extracts is that the first represents itself as a real event and the second as a phantasy. This difference, however, refuses to sustain itself across the text, with reality and phantasy unable to be separated, such that it becomes impossible to discern what does and does not happen. But despite the inability of the plot to manifest itself in narrative as a series of events, the text still elicits varying identifications. For however unstable and contradictory the 'real' maybe within the textual frame, there is still a centring on the question of the outlines of the babysitter's body, as the body of woman whose shapes elicits the desire for both penetration and interpretation (in the form of a violence). The use of such plot techniques which supposedly cancel out the representational role of narrative hence functions to enable the violence to be *repeated*. That violence is repeated again and again, as phantasy, fiction or impossible event, and forms the imaginative trajectory of the narrative itself. Indeed, rape becomes narratable in this text precisely because it involves the contradiction and splintering of what is already a masculine desire to find and penetrate the enigma of woman herself.

Even the narrative of the TV programme involves the identification of woman as the face behind the mask, sought after by the spy/interpreter: 'The assailant's down, yes! the spy's on top of him, pinning him, a terrific thrashing about, the spy rips off the assailant's mask: *a woman*' (Coover 1970: 224). The male search for the truth, as a search for 'he', returns us to the unveiled face of woman who, as signifier, is italicised, distinguished from the plain type of the body of the text. This phantasy of an arrival at the naked face of woman repeats the acts of rape and seduction which strip and violate her body. So even if rape is not secured as an event in narrative, it is sustained as a trajectory of desire and phantasy, which positions the reader as a participant in the violence done to woman-as-text. Given this, a postmodern reading of this text would perpetuate a further violence precisely in so far as it does not recognise the violence in which it is already participating.

The use of contradiction as a narrative device also has specific gendered implications in the story, 'Quenby and Ola, Swede and Carl'. Again, it is impossible to discern exactly what does and does not happen within the frame of this story, in the uncertainty over what exchanges take place between these characters – although, here, it is more difficult to follow which character's perspectives are being followed by the narrative trajectory. The following passage returns us to the question of woman:

The old springs crush and grate like crashing limbs, exhausted trees, rocks tumbling into the bay, like the lake wind rattling through dry branches and pine needles. She is hot, wet, rich, softly spread. Needful. 'Oh yes!' she whispers. (Coover 1970: 151)

Here, the narrative shifts from addressing nature to addressing woman, in the structure of a phantasy of woman's sexuality *as nature*. This slippage is repeated throughout the text. A later extract, which begins 'She is an obscure teasing shape', ends with two words 'You follow' (Coover 1979: 152–3). This 'you' is ambiguous. Could it represent a contractual projection of the reader by the narrative perspective ('you', as reader, following the image of woman written into the narrative), or does 'you' offer the perspective of one of the male characters, Carl or Swede, or could it be an undifferentiated 'you', the 'you' who simply desires and discerns the image? Despite the ambiguity, and whether functioning as assertion, desire or demand, 'you follow' metonymically conveys the narrative itself as following the trajectory of woman's imaging, pursuing woman as object of desire, that obscure and teasing shape that is *almost* discernible. In this way the narrative announces itself as following a masculine trajectory of pursuit and mastery, however much that trajectory fails and falters in the impossibility of finding itself in a single shape and sequence.

The way in which the 'you' solicits a structure of masculine identification is evident in the juxtaposition with a later extract: 'Her hips jammed against the gunwales, your wet bodies sliding together, shivering, astonished, your lips meeting – you wonder at your madness, what an island can do to a man, what an island girl can do' (Coover 1970: 154). Here, the 'you' quite clearly indicates the position of a male subject who speaks his desire for woman in the form of a madness and a meeting by projecting the event of that desire onto the figure of woman (something *done* to man, what a girl can *do*). The 'you' becomes included within a structure of address (and transference) which attributes sexual desire as something done by woman to man, so designating woman as demanding her own violation by the travels and crossings of the text itself. The dispersal of 'you' throughout the text, and its opening out as a site and signifier within narrative, enables the reader to become the 'you' by occupying this gendered structure of identification (where woman provides the contours of the masculine subject through the very transference of sexual desire onto her figure).

The invitation of the reader to adopt the 'you' and its implicit gendered modality is not cancelled out by later developments in the story where 'you' becomes more closely identified with the perspective of the male characters in the stories of illicit sexual desire between Carl, Quenby, Swede and Ola. For the ambiguity that lodges itself as determinate of the place of 'you' enables the collapse of narrative into the phantasies and desire of the male characters, such that the reader is invited to participate in those phantasies as a mode of interpretation (what is the shape of this woman? what is the shape of this text?).

Speaking of how such meta-fictional stories elicit identifications is to challenge the postmodern way of reading which assumes identification itself is transcended by the use of formal experimentation. By not assuming that identification is over-come *or* fully determined, my reading has opened the texts to different possibilities of interpretation. Differences such as sexual difference matter in these texts: but how they matter remains subject to the yet-to-be-determined nature of reading.

Phantasies of over-coming

In this section, I will discuss how the distribution and fluidity of personal pronouns in Coover's meta-fiction enacts phantasies of over-coming gendered and generic limits as an aspect of a masculine mode of enunciation.[3] However, this discussion of over-coming as a function of narrative is not reducible to these narratives. Rather, as I discussed in section one, what is at issue is how these narratives are always subject to a re-narrativisation through the event of being read *as* postmodern. Postmodern readers have read such stories precisely as an over-coming of the generic limits of realism (Mepham 1991; McHale 1987). In so far as they do this, postmodernism constructs itself as an over-coming of realism (= meta-fictionality as symptom of what postmodernism already is). My reading of Coover's stories will suggest that this narrative of over-coming is, in fact, a phantasy which grants 'postmodern subjects' the fluidity to be anywhere at anytime. A feminist reader hence reads – and tells different stories about – these narratives of over-coming, as the coming-over of the masculine subject into the empty space of the other.

What must be at stake here is an account of how sexual difference becomes privileged as the difference in such (re-)narrativisations (at work within and beyond the literary) as well as how that difference becomes effaced through the very drama of over-coming. What is the link between the privileging and effacement? What different stories are tellable about this story? We must return, here, to the meta-fictions themselves in order to tell a different story about the stories that have been read as signalling postmodernism's coming-into-being as an over-coming.

In the opening prologue to *Pricksongs and Descantes* the shifts in narrative entail a shift in personal pronouns. The story opens up with, 'the hard truth: *to be Jack become the Giant*' (Coover 1970: 13, emphasis added). That truth is the trajectory of a male narrative as a fully determined place of being – what one is determines what one becomes. This story of the determinism implicit to fairy-tale mythology (genre) begins then *as* a story of gender, and of the entrapment of masculinity and femininity within the demands of genre: 'he' knows that 'the Ogre in him wouldn't drop away and leave her free' (Coover 1970: 13). The opening passages also narrate a story of family and paternity inscribed within genre: 'And so he was afraid. For her. For himself. Because he'd given her her view of the world, in fragments of course, not really thinking it all out, she listening, he telling, and because of her gaiety and his love, his cowardly lonely love, he'd left out the terror' (Coover 1970: 14). Here, the story of father and daughter is a story of his speech and her silence, his construction of fragments that conceal from her the 'hardness' of masculine truth. The relation of address inscribed by the genre parallels the representations of gender – the innocent girl learns only what the knowledgeable father tells her. She is vulnerable, a potential victim of the maleness of his narrative: 'He'd pretended to her that there were no monsters, no wolves or witches, but yes, god-damn it, there were, there were' (Coover 1970: 15).

The following two sections shift from this phallic 'he', entailing a complication in 'his' language and discourse. The second section is a first-person narrative, and it is written without punctuation – as a sentence that goes on and on. It is written from the perspective of the grandmother who takes on the persona of the Granny awaiting her goodies from Little Red Riding Hood. Her 'I' is defiant and aggressive. However, this defiance and aggression does not inscribe her as a subject with agency. For the humour and coarseness of her language introduces the sexual pun of the title, 'death-cunt-and-prick-songs', but as '*his* songs' (Coover 1970: 16). This leads to a conflation between the male writer of the text and the male character – a conflation that takes place through the association of woman with death. But this conflation also involves a critical distanciation: the pun rewrites the proper title (*Descantes and Pricksongs*) so creating a division, as well as identification, between the male character in the text and any notion of its author. The apparently feminine 'I' of the Grandmother enables, then, a link and a gap between the male subject in the text, and the male subject of the text. Indeed, the 'I' does not take the form of an inventor, but is caught within the travels of its own ungrammatical text, as the text of sexual puns and sexual aggression. By introducing 'his song' about 'death-cunt-and-prick-songs' the Grandmother's 'I' re-confirms the masculine joke at the expense of the woman becoming the subject of the text: 'his song' rewriting the title of the text into an aggressive sexual pun.

The third section of the story shifts finally to a 'she'. Her narrative begins through a recognition of change, as a form of suspension, abandonment and orphanage (loss of the father) (Coover 1970: 17). But it is also a discovery, an opening of a door. This open door functions, of course, as a trope firmly established within fairy-tale genres. Here, the open door inscribes a passage beyond the confinement of the paternal stories, and 'the old woman's witless terrors', although 'she' remains aware of the mythic and conventional nature of her own narrative (such as the basket she clutches) as a 'big production' or 'an elaborate game'. The final passage of the story narrates her opening a door:

Inside, she felt the immediate oppression of the scene behind her drop off her shoulders like a red cloak. All that remained of it was the sullen beat of the lumberman's axe, and she was able to still even that finally, by closing the door firmly behind her and closing the hatch. (Coover 1970: 19)

Here, opening the door metonymically suggests a passage beyond the confinement of the mythic, which is at once the confinement of the truth of gender, the phallic 'he' and the Grandmother's 'I' that converted the narrative into an aggressive sexual pun. The shift towards the 'she' in the final passage may work then to narrativise an over-coming, where the 'oppression of the scene' of gender and genre disappear through the beyondness of the 'she' itself, who opens a passage beyond the door of phallic mythology.

This narration of an act of over-coming of gendered and generic limits is paralleled at the level of enunciation through the shifting of personal pronouns. That is, the fluidity of personal pronouns in this opening story (from 'he' to 'I' to 'she') inscribes a phantasy of overcoming the structure of masculinity, and the truth of determinism it inscribes as its law. To read the fluidity of personal pronouns as a phantasy of over-coming is not necessarily to critique this text – or to celebrate it. But it does pose the question of gender as a relation of address. For it could be argued that although this story, at the level of representation, calls into question the gendering function of myth, it may do so by keeping in place a narrative trajectory which is sustained by the desire to become 'she', as the story of the passage of his desire.

This enunciated phantasy of becoming woman can be associated with the general postmodern appropriation of woman as a figure for other-ness discussed in chapter 3. Indeed, it is interesting to consider how the arrival at the singularity of 'she' by the narrative trajectory may work to homogenise the figure of woman, and obliterate the division and difference that may be located within her name. Laura E. Donaldson examines the production of woman within postmodern culture, arguing that woman is taken on through the use of an exchange abstraction, which marks 'she' with homogeneity (Donaldson 1992: 126). It is important, if we are to avoid assuming that sexual difference is the only difference that matters, that we re-consider what is at stake in this narrative in terms of the violence of representation. On the one hand, you have the privileging of sexual difference such that gender and genre become conflatable. Indeed, here gender becomes inscribed metaphori-cally: the crisis of plotting is figured *through* the crisis of sexual differ-ence. But on the other hand, through the phantasy of over-coming, gender ceases to matter – we get beyond 'he' and 'she' as forms of constraint. What I want to argue, and this returns us to my reading of philosophical as well as literary narratives, is that the privileging and effacement of gender are mutually constitutive: it is precisely through the ontologising of gender *that the over-coming of forms of being ('to be Jack become the Giant') can be expressed through the over-coming of the 'he'*.

The phantasy of over-coming sexual identification is also evident in 'The Marker', one of the 'Seven Exemplary Fictions'. The story begins with the male character, Jason, watching his wife get ready for bed. The narrative follows his gaze, such that the reader participates in the voyeuristic appraisal:

Nude now, she moves lightly about the room, folding a sweater into a drawer, hanging up Jason's jacket which he has tossed on the bed, picking up a comb from the floor where it had fallen from the chest of drawers. She moves neither pretentiously or shyly. Whatever meaning might exist in her motion exists within the motion itself and not in her deliberations. (Coover 1970: 88)

The following of her movements entails an act of interpretation which assigns her with a meaning. 'She' becomes inscribed as the very gesture of her body. She returns his look in the form of a smile, 'in subtle recognition perhaps of the pleasure he finds in her' (Coover 1970: 89). The exchange of looks inhabits, then, a structure of (hetero)sexual recognition (where man and woman find pleasure in each other's difference). This structure is interrupted when the light suddenly is turned off: 'The image of his wife, as he has just seen her, fades slowly', leaving an image on his eyes, of 'an abstract Beauty that contains somehow his wife's ravaging smile and musical eyes' (Coover 1970: 89). Her eyes are inscribed on his as an image, devoid of sight and agency.

But the loss of light leaves Jason disorientated and unable to find his wife. When he does find her he feels a momentary loss of desire, but regains it in 'the anxiety and its riddles' and penetrates her, 'with an almost brutal wish to swallow, for a moment reason and its inadequacies, and to let passion, noble or not, have its way', despite her dryness and strange smell (Coover 1970: 90). He is interrupted by the policemen, who turn the light on to reveal him having sex with a three-week-dead corpse:

Jason looks down and finds that it is indeed his wife beneath him, but that she is rotting. Her eyes are open, but glazed over, staring up at him, without meaning, but bulging as though in terror of him. The flesh on her face is yellowish and drawn back towards her ears. Her mouth is open in a strangely cruel smile and Jason can see that her gums have dried and pulled back from her teeth. Her lips are black and her blonde hair, now long and tangled, is splayed out over the pillow like a urinal mop spread out to dry. There is a fuzzy stuff like mold around the nipples of her shrunken breasts. Jason tries desperately to get free from her body, but finds to his deepest horror that he is stuck! (Coover 1970: 90–1)

The image of woman converts from beauty to horror, leading to a shift in the narrative from an identification to a dis-identification with woman as object of desire (abjection). Significantly, the breakdown in a prescribed structure of sexual recognition (male voyeurism) leads to a narrativisation of chaos through the association of woman and death. The dead woman comes to figure in this way the loss or failure of sexual identification (Jason loses his ordering book marker in the event). But this narrative trajectory, where the loss of sexual identification is figured through an association of woman and death, can be problematised. The phantasy of a loss of sexual orientation is complicated by the repetition of a conventional identification of woman's sexuality with death and decay, signifying the deterioration of the proper (masculine) boundaries of the body. The phantasy of loss hence does not so much enact the failure of sexual recognition, but constitutes a mode of its operation: that is, a way in which the (hetero)sexual recognition implicit to gender relations repeats itself. Indeed, the narrative whereby woman's image fades and reappears as death and entrapment, leading to chaos and disorder, does not simply disrupt sexual identification. The narrative of a disordering of sexual identifications operates through rendering woman the centre of a male crisis in identity, which entails a re-ordering of sexual identifications. 'She' becomes the vehicle of his crisis – visible only within the terms of a narrative trajectory of the ordering and disordering of the realms of masculine subjectivity. The narrativisation of the overcoming of the determining limits of a gendered gaze is hence undone by the very gendered modality of the phantasy itself, which secures the space of the masculine subject as indeterminate and trans-formative.

This suggestion that the identification of the male subject proceeds through a phantasy and narrative of its own transformative passage, is also evident in 'The Scene from Winter', which begins by drawing attention to the visibility of the word 'MEN' on a weathered sign (Coover 1970: 170). The narrative focuses on the image of a man who is represented as familiar, 'much like someone we have seen before', leading to a complex and detailed portrait of his face (Coover 1970: 71). This man is 'utterly alone, in a vast, white desolation', taking the form of a singular and discrete figure. The man then proceeds to relieve himself, and does so by inscribing a (forgotten) word on the snow with his urine, a performance which is filled with an increasingly hysterical and violent laughter. The final passage reads:

For a brief but stunning moment, we suddenly see the man's hysterical face again, as though in a memory, a sudden terrorizing recollection that drives a cold and unwanted terror through us – but we gradually perceive that it is not the man at all, no, it is only the face of the white rabbit, nothing more, its wide-nostriled nose quivering, its rodent eyes cloudy, its mouth split in a sardonic grin. As we slip back, we discover that it is between the jaws of the lean-bodied dog. (Coover 1970: 174)

The meanings of this story are multiple and contradictory. A post-modern reading may focus on how the story problematises the illusion of a discrete subjectivity by narrating the way in which the discernible subject becomes unfamiliar, diffused and dis-placed through the shift-ings of gaze and perspective. But, perhaps alongside this reading, it is interesting to consider the trajectory of the text as itself an inscription of a phantasy about the category of 'MEN' it capitalises. For the two faces, one de-limited by gender as representation (in the form of a portrait), and the other existing only as a passage of transformation, do not simply cancel each other out. The vision of the transforming face could be seen as inscribing a phantasy of over-coming the masculine, of moving beyond gender in a succession of animalistic images. It is a phantasy of man becoming other, of losing the signifier 'he', in a dizzy space of *self-transformation* where the self is beyond limitation and constraint from structures of interpretation (such as the gendered portrait). In this sense, the phantasy of over-coming or becoming other is inscribed within the masculine as part of its own power to address itself as a subject in the form of a narrative which loses the signifier 'he'.

The following extract from 'The Sentient Lens', entitled 'The Milkmaid of Samaneigo', also deals with the question of transformation and fluidity, but in relation to the inscription of woman. The narrator begins with the contractual 'we' (including the reader within the narrative trajectory) and describes the moment of realisation that a milkmaid is approaching before she arrives, for 'we do not now see her' (Coover 1970: 174). There is, 'an unspoken but well understood' prologue to her arrival, which cannot be derived from the details of the setting, as if there is, 'a precise structure of predetermined images' (Coover 1970: 175). The arrival of woman onto the scene of the text, as a form of waiting and expectancy, positions her as the absent centre to the narrative. The narrator writes of our shared awareness, detailing her figure, but without her being there *as figure*. The narrative follows her movement and passage towards us: 'as she walks, her skirt flutters and twists as though caught by some breeze, though there is none' (Coover 1970: 176). But immediately there is an interruption, actualised as if in the present, 'Her – but the man, this one with the tattered hat and bulging eye, he stands and – no, no! the maid, *the maid*!' (Coover 1970: 176). The exclamatory narrative voice makes present a sexual threat, as a threat to the subject of the narrative.

But then the narrative returns to the maid (the eddies of dust swirling about her feet, her hands and her nose). In this way, the narrative adopts the gaze of the male character it has introduced as a sexual threat. The narrative 'eye' shifts to the pitcher she carries, which strikes the narrator with its resemblance to white eggs. Those eggs suddenly transform into chicks and sows, tumbling and flustering around the maid until she is surrounded and glorified by sows, chicks and cattle. The narrative again shifts to a sexual threat depicting, 'a tall lad, dark and fineboned with flashing brown eyes and bold mouth' who struggles towards her: and then, suddenly, the pitcher, and the eggs and the tall lad and sows, chicks and cattle are all gone (Coover 1970: 177). But she is helped from the shock of her loss by a dark bearded man with a bulging eye. We are left, finally with the pitcher: firstly stable, then bursting into fragments.

The shifts of this bizarre narrative could be read as shifts from the woman as absent centre (who becomes the subject of the text by the rendering present of sexual threats, from both the male characters, and the voyeurism of the narrative trajectory) to the bursting of limitations and conventions in the expansions and fragmentation of an object – the pitcher. This constant dialectic between woman as image or figure and fragmentation and dispersal serves to shift the narrative finally from the weight of a 'she' to an object world devoid of subjects, made up of tiny fragments. In this way the narrative does not simply complicate the representation of subjectivity, but fantastically narrates its over-coming, in the metonymic explosion of plot itself into a fragmented object. Woman, as an image structuring the development of plot, is herself over-come in this imaginary fragmentation: as an over-coming of the sexual threat of the feminine itself to the disordering realm of the narrative trajectory.

What is fascinating in all the stories I have discussed is the way in which it is impossible to fully decide upon the meanings and politics of the various identifications elicited in the narrative trajectories. The various stories I have told about these stories (the phantasy of an over-coming of gender limits as inhabiting a masculine mode of enunciation) are themselves open to complication. It seems to me that the implications of the fluidity of personal and sexual pronouns evident in these stories of transformation are deeply ambivalent. I would argue that this ambivalence takes the form of a dependence upon (or an openness to) different kinds of critical or interpretative frames used in the event of reading. Within a postmodern mode of literary criticism, which has tended to efface the question of sexual difference, I would argue that the emphasis on fluidity functions as a mode of denial, and as such serves to implicitly protect a masculine mode of enunciation (self-reflexivity as liberation from generic and gendered limits). But in the case of a feminist reading, which draws out the implication of these narratives in sexual identification as a form of violence, an emphasis on fluidity could open out the potential for a re-inscription of gender otherwise. Here, sexual difference is not ontologised as the very quality of difference, only then to be effaced through a phantasy of over-coming. This different reading of the meta-fictions privileged by postmodernism as a symptom of its own over-coming of realism, may then return to postmodernism as a different reading of its own coming-into-being.

7 Screens

Is postmodernism on screen? Can postmodernism be screened? Such questions demand their own negation. Postmodernism is not a series of images that may exist on the screen as such ('look, there's postmodernism!'). Indeed, I would even suggest that there is nothing that is screenable *about* postmodernism: postmodernism does not have a nature that lends itself to the screen (postmodernism is not a scene that can be transported from one screen to another). Rather, thinking of postmodernism in relation to the screen requires that we analyse what film theory does when it names films as postmodern: what does it look for? How does it see? In other words, my consideration of postmodernism *and* the screen will not assume that we can find postmodernism *on* the screen. Rather, it will involve an analysis of films which have been theoretically framed as postmodern, that is, as transgressing the modes of classical cinema through the implosion of the image. In this chapter, I will analyse 'postmodernism' as a theoretical frame which looks for signs of transgression in the forms of identification available in classical cinema. I ask: what is at stake for feminism in the seeing of postmodernism on the screen?

Seeing postmodernism

Despite my opening comments, it must be noted that there is comparatively little film theory that operates through designating films as postmodern. The introduction to the volume of the British film studies journal *Screen* (1987) dedicated to postmodernism hence opens by attempting to explain the relative absence of the term 'postmodernism' in film studies. In relation to literary studies, there has been a proliferation of books and articles that describe 'postmodern literature' and install that term as generic. Although there have been some attempts to do this in film studies (Denzin 1988; Sharrett 1988), the term 'postmodern film' remains relatively absent from film studies (although, given the constructions of postmodernism that are already in place, we might assume that we know how such films would look). If we take such a relative absence as given, you might ask, then why end this book with a chapter which takes the question of screening postmodernism as a point of departure? Partly, my concern is to introduce to the debate on postmodernism the question of the technical and visible limits of 'screening'. In the previous chapter, I concerned myself with post-modernism as a way of reading (rather than a way of writing). Here, I want to think through how postmodernism might operate as a way of seeing (what is on the screen), a way of seeing that is determinate in the constitution of postmodernism as an object (however unstable).

But why is the term 'postmodernism' relatively ignored within film studies? The editors of the 1987 volume of *Screen*, argue that film studies has ignored postmodernism, because postmodernism ignores the specificity of film. That is, postmodernism moves across generic boundaries in such a way that it cannot address the specificity of the cinematic apparatus. They write, 'after the sort of cinematically specific textual analyses which still dominate the material submitted to *Screen*, the ease with which postmodern theory leaps from medium to medium is not a little worrying in its audacity' (Hayward and Kerr 1987: 4). Postmodernism, through transgressing the law of genre, comes to threaten the project of *Screen* itself which begins and ends with the specificity of the cinematic apparatus. As Stephen Heath suggests, the concept of the cinematic apparatus moves us from what can be defined as a history of the technology of the cinema, towards a history of the cinema-machine that can include, 'its developments, adaptations, trans-formations, realignments, the practices it derives, holding together the instrumental and the symbolic, the technological and the ideological' (Heath 1981: 227). The concept of the cinematic apparatus is over-determined by the reading of film through psychoanalysis. Jean-Louis Baudry's outline of the problematic whereby the cinema becomes a machine with a certain arrangement or disposition is influenced by Freud's notion of 'the psychical apparatus', specifying a series of relations between spaces, operations and temporalities (Baudry 1992: 304). The project of *Screen* can hence be understood as bound up with this history of the cinematic-psychical-machine. Postmodernism is alien to the screen as it has no respect for this history – or so it seems.

To some extent then, I think the relative absence of the term 'post-modernism' in film studies can be explained by the dominance of a particular theoretical framework derived from a reading of psychoana-lysis. Indeed, the narrative offered by Hayward and Kerr to explain the absence sets up an opposition between psychoanalytical film theory and postmodern cultural theory. At the same time, while the dominance of psychoanalysis has meant the relative absence of 'postmodernism' as a generic term, that dominance *may also define the terms under which postmodernism can come into existence within film studies.* Both psycho-analytical film theory and postmodernism have, after all, become visible under the sign of 'transgression'. Psychoanalytical film theorists have constructed a model of classical cinema or classical realism as inherently conservative: as bound to reproduce the dominance and mastery of the subject (see especially, Metz 1982; Mulvey 1989). This model privileges avant-garde filmic strategies as providing the means for transgressing such a subject. Theories of postmodernism easily inhabit such a model: the primary theory is precisely a theory of realism, and a theory of the avant-garde as transgressive easily slides into a theory of postmodernism as transgressive. As I emphasised in chapter 6, this slippage is clear in Lyotard's discussion of aesthetics in *The Postmodern Condition.* In order to theorise how postmodernism is constructed as a way of seeing, we need then to consider how psychoanalytical film theory already sees the classical cinematic text.

A psychoanalytical theory of classical cinema is bound up with a theory of the relation between the subject and the field of vision. In Christian Metz's *Psychoanalysis and Cinema: The Imaginary Signifier,* for example, spectator identification with the screen is discussed through the use of an analogy with the Lacanian mirror stage. He argues that the dynamic of the mirror stage (the child's misrecognition of itself as I, the imaginary identification with its imago) is, 'undoubtedly reactivated by the play of that *other mirror,* the camera screen, in this respect a veritable physical substitute, a prosthesis for our primarily dislocated limbs' (Metz 1982: 4). The screen is *like the mirror.* Metz elaborates:

what *makes possible* the spectator's absence from the screen – or rather the intelligible unfolding of the film despite that absence – is the fact that the spectator has already known the experience of the mirror (of the true mirror), and is thus able to constitute a world of objects without having first to recognise himself within it. (Metz 1982: 46)

The spectator is already in the symbolic and, through watching the film, re-enacts the drama of its primary and imaginary identification with itself as image, an identification which provides the self with the illusions of unity and agency. The cinema becomes inscribed as a scene for this re-enactment – positioning the spectator as all-perceiving, looking at the other on the screen, yet unlooked at. The spectator's gaze is not returned and so returns only to itself (Metz 1982: 48). In this way, Metz argues that the spectator's eye (and ear) constitutes the cinematic signifier (Metz 1982: 48). The self-identification of the spectator with 'his' own look involves, for Metz, a primary identification with the camera, 'which has looked before him at what he is now looking at and whose stationing (= framing) determines the vanishing point' (Metz 1982: 49). Alongside this primary identification there are secondary ones available to the spectator through the complex relay of looking within the filmic diegesis (Metz 1982: 56). The spectator who looks at the characters looking (through the primary look of the camera) constitutes the absence of the filmic object and her or his own presence before and beyond the screen.

Metz's theory of classical cinema is also a theory of realism (classical realism). As is clear in Colin MacCabe's work, this theoretical approach has significant links to theories of classical realism in literature. MacCabe argues that the theory of the classic realist text translates into film in the following way:

The narrative prose achieves its position of dominance because it is in the position of knowledge and this function of knowledge is taken up in the cinema by the narration of events. Through the knowledge we gain from the narrative we can split the discourses of the various characters from their situation and compare what is said in these discourses with what has been revealed to us through narration. The camera *shows us what happens* – it tells the truth against which we can measure the discourses. (MacCabe 1985: 37, emphasis mine)

This process whereby the camera transparently presents the spectator with 'the truth' – or at least appears to do so – provides a supremacy of point of view with which the spectator identifies, a process which removes any threatening other in a perpetual re-enactment of a textual and political mastery. Within classical realism, the camera 'shows': it reveals the world to the spectator. The pleasure of classical realism is precisely its elimination of contradiction and otherness, its enabling of an automatic identification between spectator and text (MacCabe 1985: 68). A theory of classical cinema hence makes a fundamental link between voyeurism and realism: the world is made available to the spectator's gaze through the transparency of the screen. The mastery of the text constitutes the mastery of the look.

Consequently, MacCabe argues that the breaking of the imaginary relation between text and spectator is necessary for a politicised and critical film practice (MacCabe 1985: 73). The classical realist film is *bound* to be conservative, and *can* only be transgressed through the use of alternative screening strategies. MacCabe's theory produces a hierarchy in which the meaning and 'politics' of classical realism is already determined, leaving little room for a multiplicity of interpretations (even though there may be *moments* of subversion, MacCabe argues that such film texts *by definition* cannot be *strategically* subversive) (MacCabe 1985: 47–8).

The model of classical cinema exercised here easily slides into a theory of postmodernism. Postmodern film has become a category precisely through this language of transgression: for example, postmodern films have been named as those which threaten linear time (the boundary between past and present is severed), linear narrative (the loss of unity), and the mastery of the all-perceiving look (Denzin 1988; Sharrett 1988). Such a theory of postmodernism as transgression is bound up with an attention to 'the image'. As Jean Baudrillard puts it, 'the image has taken over and imposed its own immanent, ephemeral logic; an immoral without depth, beyond good and evil, beyond truth and falsity; a logic of the extermination of its own referent; a logic of the implosion of meaning' (Baudrillard 1987: 23). Here, postmodern cinema is inscribed as the transgression of the opposition between surface and depth: the image has taken over and has 'exterminated' the referent.

The over-determination of 'postmodern film theory' by the model of classical cinema suggests that postmodernism constructs itself, in Mac-Cabe's terms, as a *strategic subversion* – a subversion through the detachment and play of the image. The problems of this model of subversion are multiple. In the first instance, such a model is overly deterministic: it suggests that the political function of cinema is already decided by the nature of the filmic text. It also suggests that classical cinema *can only* reproduce the mastery of the subject. Through such a reductionism, this model of classical cinema implicitly positions (post)modernism as *inherently* radical, that is, as radical due to the form in which it is embedded. Postmodernism is here already seen before being seen: a sight which fixes postmodernism into a certain image which it is bound to reproduce (= implosion of the image).

But how would Metz's and MacCabe's approach constitute postmodernism as a way of seeing? We can return here, to the use of the analogy between screen and mirror in Metz's work. One problem with taking the film/spectator relation as a perpetual re-staging of the mirror stage within the context of the symbolic, is that it narrativises that relation in terms which are always already in place. Jacqueline Rose points out some of the limitations of Metz's approach, arguing:

By confining the concept of the imaginary within the debate about realism, Metz makes the spectator's position in the cinema (the fantasy of the all perceiving subject) a mirror-image of the error underpinning an idealist ontology of film (cinema as a ceaseless and gradually perfected appropriation of reality). (Rose 1985: 173)

The delusion of the spectator is made dependent on the ontology of specific filmic processes, while cinema itself becomes merely a machine for the reproduction of imaginary identity. Metz's theoretical approach not only presupposes a specific teleology for filmic production (the perfecting of the transparent surface which returns the spectator's look to itself), but also presupposes a teleology of the subject, in the sense that the subject is assumed to be deluded by the phantasy of identity (again, the mastery of an unreturned look). Both teleologies exclude the possibility of film eliciting other affective, desirous and contradictory or ambivalent responses within the spectator. Rose's approach, in contrast, asks what specific identifications are at stake within film, rather than assuming that identification simply inscribes a teleology of text-into-ego (Rose 1985: 176). Her argument coincides with my approach to literary meta-fiction outlined in chapter 6. I suggested, there, that identifications involve multiple investments and complex processes of subject formation that cannot simply be transcended through the problematising of realism at the level of form or aesthetics.

Furthermore, what is problematic in Metz's and MacCabe's approach is not simply the equation of realism with the masterful look – an equation which opens the way for a theory of (post)modernism as a transgression of this look – but also the very assumption that such a masterful look is possible in the first place. As Joan Copjec has pointed out, the model of spectatorship in film theory has tended to rely on an over-reading of Lacan's mirror stage (Copjec 1994: 18). Elsewhere, in Lacan's work, there is an elaboration of a psychoanalytical approach to the gaze which is fundamentally irreducible to the point from which the subject sees: the eye. The split between the eye and the gaze is made evident in the following formulation: '*You never look at me from the place in which I see you*' (Lacan 1991: 103). However, the gaze which finds the subject does not constitute the subject as already-seen. Rather, the gaze loses the subject in its irreducibility to the eye which sees. The phantasy that one can see oneself seeing oneself is a manifestation, therefore, of the transcendental Cartesian subject. The gaze which returns to the subject – from more than 'the one' of sight – does not constitute the mastery of the subject, but its vanishing or loss:

From the moment that this gaze appears, the subject tries to adapt himself to it, he becomes that punctiform object, the point of vanishing being with which the subject confuses its own failure. That is why it is, more that any other object, misunderstood (*méconnu*), and it is perhaps for this reason, too, that the subject manages, fortunately, to symbolise his own vanishing and punctiform bar (*trait*) in the illusion of the consciousness of *seeing oneself see oneself*, in which the gaze is elided. (Lacan 1991: 83)

Following Lacan, we can see that the assumption of the masterful gaze within film theory involves an elision of the gaze: it does not deal with how the spectator's eye already *fails to see* (the gaze is returned, but only to abolish the place from which the film is seen). This elision of the gaze has significant consequences for how postmodernism is seen. Postmodernism is seen precisely as the undoing of ways of seeing which are identified with realism (the mastery of the spectator's look confirmed on the transparency of the screen). But if that model of seeing involves an elision which operates at the level of phantasy – postmodernism seeing itself seeing itself – then postmodernism can see itself only by suspending the difficulty and loss that *already* inflects the gaze, including the gaze of classical cinema. *To identify the sight of postmodernism as transgression is hence not to be looking at all.* It is through the event of *not seeing*, that postmodernism becomes visible in an ontology of the break ('look, here is where realism is broken').

If postmodernism comes to operate in film studies by not seeing – by equating classical cinema with the masterful gaze – then what are the implications of this 'not seeing' for feminist theories of spectatorship? The use of psychoanalysis within feminist film theory has led a theory of classical cinema as bound up with a male gaze. Laura Mulvey's germinal article, 'Visual Pleasure and Narrative Cinema', opens out the debate by elaborating on the sexing of cinematic relations within a psychoanalytic model. She argues that:

in a world ordered by sexual imbalance, pleasure in looking has been split between active/male and passive/female. The determining male gaze projects its fantasy onto the female figure, which is styled accordingly. In their traditional exhibitionist role women are simultaneously looked at and displayed, with their appearance coded for strong visual and erotic impact so that they can be said to connote *to-be-looked-at-ness*. (Mulvey 1989: 19)

Mulvey examines the representation of woman as an image that frustrates the story line within classical cinema (holding it in place by undressing her figure), as well as the representation of a heroic or active male subject (Mulvey 1989: 19, 20). This leaves the male spectator in both a direct scopophilic contact with the female form (as an erotic object at a distance), as well as in a narcissistic identification with the male subject on the screen (Mulvey 1989: 20). The male experience of scopophilia and narcissism is not simply a question of his pleasure: for Mulvey, woman also provokes the anxiety of the threat of castration, of the lack she conceals and affirms as fetish (Mulvey 1989: 21). Mulvey's argument that classical cinema involves a primary narcissism and scopophilia for the male spectator leads her to conclude that feminist cinema must disrupt or transgress the system of looking that such cinema inscribes. Her project hence entails outlining a feminist avant-garde filmic practice. Indeed, she argues that women, 'cannot view the decline of the traditional film form with anything much more than a sentimental regret' (Mulvey 1989: 26).

One of the central problems with Mulvey's approach is, in fact, symptomatic of the problems that have already been linked to the employment of this psychoanalytic model within film theory generally – a tendency to represent the effects of specific cinematic techniques as intrinsic or already determined. Indeed, the terms of Mulvey's argument lead her to conclude that women can only gain pleasure from classical cinema either by taking the position of the transvestite (identifying with the active male figure) or through a primary masochism. Mulvey assumes that the classical cinematic text fixes the gaze as male, in order then to theorise that feminist cinema must involve the unfixing of that gaze. In contrast, what is required is an analysis of how the gaze itself is not fully determined or fixed, but is already splintered. Such an approach is evident in Jackie Stacey's work, where there is an account of the spectator as a subject-in-process, not fixed by the text to a predetermined gender identification, but emerging through a complex interlocking of desires and identifications (Stacey 1990: 370). In other words, how the gendered spectator looks, identifies and desires is always *yet to be determined*. Such an approach may open out the possibility that both realism and (post)modernism could be seen otherwise.

As Tania Modleski suggests, Mulvey's theory presents us with a picture of classical cinema which is too monolithic. Modleski calls instead for an analysis of 'weak points' and contradictions in classical narratives (Modleski 1990: 66). Indeed, other feminists have rejected the assumption that a feminist politics has an 'objective alliance' (Mulvey 1989: 112) to avant-garde and postmodern filmic practices – which in itself implies that all realist film is necessarily anti-feminist or, at least, is inevitably bound to repeat the specularisation of femininity. For example, Alexandra Juhasz has called for a re-reading of feminist documentary film, arguing that the anti-realist aesthetic of psychoanalytic feminism has excluded an analysis of contradictions within such genres (Juhasz 1994: 176). The contingent and complicated relation of form and politics must return to trouble this psychoanalytic narrative, dividing the singularity of its terms from the effects of specific filmic practices. If we can no longer equate classical cinema with the reproduction of the masterful male gaze, then the relation between the cinematic text and the spectator's look is open rather than closed. The absence of an inherent relation between classical cinema and a male gaze, suggests also the absence of an inherent relation between (post)modern cinematic techniques and a female or, more accurately, feminist gaze.

But while there has been a substantial amount of feminist work on how 'classical cinema' exceeds the narratives offered by psychoanalytical film theory, there has been less attention given to *how alternative filmic practices may exceed the model of transgression privileged in these narratives.* The following sections of this chapter will displace the hierarchy realism/ (post)modern implicit to some psychoanalytical film theory by a closer look at particular films that have been designated as postmodern. I will ask: how has postmodernism seen these films or been seen in these films? How else can these films by seen? The assumption that any generic breaks with classical realism constitute transgression as such, means that postmodernism, as a way of looking, may only look for signs of transgression. As a result, seeing a film as postmodern (as transgressing the look of classical cinema) may over-look other aspects of such filmic texts.

My analysis focuses on how films that have been inscribed as transgressive and postmodern are implicated in the forms of sexual violence which they supposedly have over-come, in the very event of their 'overcoming' of classical cinema. Sexual violence is often discussed in relation to classical cinema and pornography. Stephen Heath brings the two together by arguing that, 'At the same time today that pornography has become one of the most commercially viable sectors of film-making, the Hollywood feature film, cinema, has involved itself increasingly in a violence of the body in film: the body cut, sawn, rent, dismembered' (Heath 1981: 185). I will argue that it is also important for feminism to consider sexual violence in films which have been designated as postmodern. Indeed, postmodernism may involve *not seeing* the violence which takes place, precisely by seeing such films purely in terms of transgression.

Sex and violence in David Lynch's *Blue Velvet*

Alice Jardine argues in *Gynesis* that recent postmodern narratives include an increasing depiction of violence against women, and against 'woman' as a figure of difference (Jardine 1985: 243–4). To this extent, we could read *Blue Velvet* (David Lynch, 1986) as the re-narrativisation of postmodernism on the screen. The first screening of *Blue Velvet* on British television began with a warning about the level of violence shown in this film. Given the level of violence, especially sexual violence, displayed in *Blue Velvet*, the authors of *Women Viewing Violence* announce that they decided it would be ethically questionable to include this film in their research into how women respond to violence on film and television (Schlesinger *et al.* 1992: 20). In terms of distribution and reception, the significance of violence in *Blue Velvet* seems clear.

However, in the criticism on *Blue Velvet*, violence has not been foregrounded as structural to the film's meanings and effects. This absence of an attention to sexual violence is achieved through reading the representations of sexual violence as a means by which the film *does something else*, the way in which it involves a postmodern problematising of the 'real', including the 'real' of both sex and violence. In other words, the seeing of the film as postmodern (as transgressing forms of realism) involves *not seeing* the violence that is at stake. This is very clear in Peter Brunette and David Wills's *Screen/Play: Derrida and Film Theory*.[1] They claim that the meaning of *Blue Velvet* cannot be reduced to the acts of violence it depicts. Indeed, Brunette and Wills argue that, despite the violence against women that is depicted in the film, 'the call for a singular reading is not so much a form of oppositional resistance as an abdication of strategic possibilities, at worst a form of critical masochism' (Brunette and Wills 1989: 149). In Brunette and Wills's approach, a critical reading which raises the question of violence against women is implicitly positioned as a 'singular reading' which closes the play of the film itself. Brunette and Wills imply that a reading which admits of the multiple textual possibilities must move beyond the demand for an interrogation of the role of sexual violence within the filmic diegesis. An opposition is constructed here between an open reading (which attends to the film's postmodern character) and a closed (and feminist) reading which foregrounds sexual violence at the level of representation. Brunette and Wills' analysis assumes that the destabilisation of the 'real' of sexual violence through postmodern filmic strategies suspends the effects of sexual violence at the level of enunciation.

Other critical readings of *Blue Velvet* have focused on how this film enacts, at the level of representation, the critique of classical cinema evident in recent film theory. Linda Buntzen, for example, argues that *Blue Velvet*, 'provides a feminist and psychoanalytic film criticism with a rare opportunity to test many of its assumptions', by foregrounding the relations of voyeurism that have been associated with classical cinema (Buntzen 1988: 187–8). Wittenburg and Gooding-Williams discuss how *Blue Velvet*, 'thematises the implications of spectatorship', and provides us with, 'an explicit depiction of the way in which woman is objectified and potentially brutalized in the viewing process' (Wittenburg and Gooding-Williams 1990: 152–4). Both critical readings do attend to the issue of sexual violence, but they also argue that the film, despite representing violence, does not *enunciate* that violence. That is, the film, through various postmodern or self-reflexive tactics, manages to dis-place or over-come the relations of violence it represents (Wittenburg and Gooding-Williams 1990: 154). But this assumption that the style of the film automatically destabilises the material it represents is in itself open to complication, by considering how sexual violence can operate beyond the thematic, within points of filmic enunciation and address. Indeed, such arguments assume that the difference or gap between representation and enunciation is self-evident: that the difference is determined by the text itself (spectators who confuse representation with enunciation hence fail the text). In contrast, I would suggest that the relation between representation and enunciation is unstable.

The narrative of *Blue Velvet* centres on the discovery of a severed ear by the central male character, Jeffrey. This discovery takes him on a trail of intrigue, involving his eye-witnessing of rape, sado-masochism, kidnapping, as well as drug abuse and trafficking. At one level, the narrative repeats the tradition of the thriller in which a heroic male figure seeks to find the truth and to convert a situation of disorder and violence into a scene of order and peace. The opening and closing shots of the film, with their juxtaposing frames of middle-class suburbia dressed in tranquillity (blue skies, white picket fences, roses) ironically conveys this passage of conversion; the loss and discovery of the truth that introduces and ends the witnessing of violence within the diegesis. Jeffrey, as a heroic figure, is indeed positioned as being in search for truth: which is at once the truth of the woman. For his pursuit centres on the dark and seductive figure of Dorothy, whose association with the severed ear is made evident to Jeffrey by the fair and innocent Sandy. These two contrasting figures of woman (polarised as the virgin and the whore) give Jeffrey access to the truth, assisting him on his discovery of the violence behind (and within) the severed ear.

The structural position of Jeffrey within the narrative operates as a mode of enunciation. Through the figuring of Jeffrey's pursuit for truth the spectator follows a trajectory: we witness what he witnesses through the movement of his desire. Indeed, as Jeffrey waits to enter Dorothy's room Sandy comments, 'I don't know if you're a detective or a pervert.' He replies, 'That's for me to know and for you to find out.' The double possibility raised by Sandy's comment becomes a structural relation: Jeffrey's desire to detect entails a perversion, putting him in the place of the pervert who watches the woman undressing (he hides in the wardrobe when Dorothy enters the flat unexpectedly). But this double possibility amounts to his knowledge: through the use of a cliché, Jeffrey deflects Sandy's query into a knowledge to which she is denied access given that she embodies its enigma.

The paradigmatic scene in the film, often cited as that which involves the exposure of the violence and voyeurism sustaining cinematic address, occurs when Jeffrey enters Dorothy's flat and is interrupted on his quest for the (her) truth by her return. The camera shifts from Jeffrey peering through the louvred doors of her wardrobe, to Dorothy undressing. A postmodern way of seeing this scene may point to the transgression of the classical cinematic relation – by drawing the spectator's attention to the frame, the film demonstrates that the woman is an image which is always mediated by the partiality of a gaze (the postmodern gaze as the deferral of the object: the gaze which looks at classical cinema looking at . . .).

However, there are other ways of seeing this scene. For the camera shifts from Jeffrey, and what *he can see* (through the slits in the wardrobe), to a larger frame of what *she is doing*. The juxtaposition of a smaller and larger frame of her undressing expands, for the spectator, the partiality of his mediating vision into a more embracing image of her *as image*. In doing so, the partiality of his vision acts to affirm his hold over her, returning her, as an image which is irreducible to what he sees, to the frame through which he sees. The frame constitutes the organ of his eye – the place from which he sees – such that the possibility of seeing her otherwise is collapsed into the frame itself. We see more than he sees – a larger frame – but that more-ness returns to him even if it does not originate with him, in the form of his ghostly presence behind the screen. The self-reflexive attention to the frame enables then the camera to return again and again to the image of woman (the implosion of the image is here the implosion of the woman). Indeed, the attention to framing which disembodies the male 'eye' (all we can see is his eye through the frame when the cinematic gaze returns to him), involves a fascination with the imaging of woman, rather than its dissolution. She comes to stand for that which can only return to his eye, *even if he cannot see her* (= the detachment of the image from an originary look).

What is enunciated in *Blue Velvet*, however, is not simply a confirmation of the fetishism that sustains the conflation of woman and image. The image remains irreducible to woman. *Blue Velvet* fascinates itself with her white body: the whiteness of the body against which blue and black marks appear as signs of violence, as the threat of violence to the frailty of her white skin. Richard Dyer has argued that whiteness is reproduced within mainstream cinema: techniques of glamour shooting enable the white feminine body to stand out magically, like a fetish, from the dim background (Dyer 1988: 63). In so far as *Blue Velvet* remains fascinated with the framing of the image by the gaze, then that fascination brings into play racialised as well as gendered ideologies of glamour (see also Young 1996: 32–3; Dyer 1997).

The dynamic of looking (detection/voyeurism) is explicitly related to that of violence (perversion, sado-masochism). Jeffrey is heard and discovered by Dorothy inside the wardrobe. Violence is first dramatised as an act perpetrated by Dorothy against Jeffrey: she wields a knife at him (suggesting the threat of castration) and commands him to undress so that she can see and touch his genitals (which the spectator is denied access to; the penis remains structurally and visually absent). She holds the power of the phallus and of the gaze, shouting at Jeffrey, 'don't look at me' and 'don't touch me or I'll kill you'. They are interrupted by a knock on the door. Frank arrives and Jeffrey hides in the wardrobe. The film narrates a second act of violence: as Jeffrey watches, Frank brutally violates Dorothy's body, commanding her to 'spread her legs' and 'show it to me', while refusing her the power of the look, shouting, 'Don't you fucking look at me.' The act of rape does not involve penile penetration, but involves the thrusting of his fist into her (although there is some ambiguity here as to what is actually being depicted): that is, the *simulation* of male 'thrusting' and penetrative movements. The act of violence is witnessed by Jeffrey (again his partial vision works as a framing device, containing its own violence), and through Jeffrey, the spectator. This violence establishes retroactively that the previous act of violence was an inversion of an originary structural and power relation.

The depiction of a sexual violence against the body of woman is graphic, but it is also overtly framed (within the frame of the screen, we have the frame of the wardrobe through which Jeffrey looks). Given this framing, the depiction of violence is ambiguous. There is an element of uncertainty as to whether the rape is 'real' within the context of the filmic diegesis. And yet, at the same time, the act of witnessing the violence becomes re-inscribed as an act of violence. Jeffrey shifts eventually from watching the woman's abuse to hitting her himself, an act for which she masochistically appeals: 'What do you want?', he asks. She replies, 'I want you to hurt me.' The passivity of the woman is represented here in the form of her desire to be violated. The imaging of woman as desiring the violence returns to the look of the witnessing camera to reaffirm its act of violence, its inclusion within a masculine contractual relation which positions woman as an object to be exchanged through violation. The scene of the rape, while destabilised as event through the use of framing and simulation, becomes restabilised as a relation of address which positions woman as a desiring subject of her own violation through the celebration and reification of her image as already violated.

Significantly, Roger Luckhurst's concern with complicating the narrative of *Blue Velvet*, by examining how the narrative always exceeds its framing around Jeffrey's point of view (Luckhurst 1989: 176), leads to the question of Dorothy's pleasure. Luckhurst cites Barbara Creed's analysis of the close-up of Dorothy's mouth when she is being beaten as a way of theorising the film's complication of a sexual identification, its subversion of the regime of pleasure which equates pleasure only with activity and masculinity (Luckhurst 1989: 178). Indeed, Creed argues, 'it *becomes clear* that she enjoys the violence' (Creed 1988: 107, emphasis mine). But these close-up shots of 'female pleasure' can also be read as far from subversive, and as far from 'clear'. The camera here seeks to penetrate the mouth of the woman, to seek access to the depths of her desire, and returns from that search with a truth: the truth of the question 'what does a woman want?' is the language of male violence which in *Blue Velvet* merges her pleasure with his. The arrival at Dorothy's mouth within the filmic diegesis does not, then, necessarily exceed the narrative framing from Jeffrey's point of view (as a figure of masculinity), but may re-inscribe it. Indeed, it is interesting that Creed's and Luckhurst's readings proceed by reframing Dorothy's mouth as a sign of female pleasure: this entails a strategy of reading which closes off her mouth at a certain point, making decisions about how and what the mouth means. The violence of the camera's penetration of Dorothy's body (which fragments and fetishises her body) is repeated here through the use of a postmodern theoretical frame, *which reads for signs of a narrative and sexual transgression within the mouth of woman*. This is an important example of how seeing a film as postmodern can complete rather than disrupt the violence against women narrated in the diegesis (in the form of a doubling).

We can compare this double identification of female pleasure within a relation of violence to a scene in David Lynch's later film *Wild at Heart* (1990). In this scene, Bobby (a villain) is approaching the central female character, Lula, and says to her aggressively:

I sure do like a woman with nice tits like yours who talks tough and looks like she can fuck like a bunny. Can you fuck like that, huh? Do you like it like a bunny? Cause if you do baby, I'll fuck you good like a big old Jack rabbit bunny, jump all around that hole. Bobby Decoe don't come up for air.

The camera moves from Bobby to Lula, and depicts signs of fear and anxiety on her face as she exclaims, 'get out'. He then grabs her asking, 'Is it wet?' A close up shot depicts her struggles as he demands that she say, repeatedly, 'fuck me'. The camera then proceeds to move down her body as his hand moves down her body, pressing her breasts and finally her genitals. The camera shows her hands flinch[2] and her body respond to his touch: and then finally her whisper, 'fuck me'. Here, the sign of female desire is produced and affirmed through a relation of violence, in which the camera and male character violently demand a response from her body. Her return and affirmation of the demand ('fuck me') allows both Bobby and the camera to move away. He says, 'Some day honey I will but I gotta get going', while the camera moves back to show a fuller picture of her body falling apart. The violence of the diegesis and camera movement here structures the depiction of female pleasure, a depiction which returns the camera to the phallus as signifier of a primary, and perpetually repeated, invasion of woman's bodily limits.

The narrative trajectory of this film works primarily through a series of flashbacks to an event in Lula's past which Soldier has witnessed, her mother's killing of her father (the mother's pursuit of Soldier becomes the primary plot vehicle). The flashbacks build up the filmic diegesis in complex ways, shifting from a specific character to scenes of the filmic past, such that the frame works as an 'individuated memory' available to the spectator. The scenes of the past are built around Lula's memories, including her memory of being raped as a 13-year-old girl. But as the rape is represented as having already happened when it confronts the spectator's eye, its enunciation might seem less violent and shocking than the image itself depicts.

This representation of a woman's memory of sexual violence can be contrasted with the story Soldier tells Lula about one of his past sexual encounters, also involving a shift between the present and the past as present. The representation of the past involves an archetypal image of woman as seductress, revealing and swinging her ass for the gaze of the male character and the camera. Soldier tells Lula how he grabbed the woman between the legs. Lula's response to Soldier's story is identical to the woman's response to Soldier's gesture in the past-frame. They both say: 'baby, what a bad boy you are'. This identical response frames Lula within the diegesis of Soldier's story line, including her within its terms. The telling of this story involves a double instance of female desire. Firstly, we have the representation of the desire of the woman from the past. Soldier recalls how the woman, 'spread her legs real wide' and then, through a flashback, the woman says in her own words, 'Take a bite out of my peach.' Secondly, we have the representation of Lula's desire: 'Baby, you better take me back to your hotel. You've got me hotter than George Ashfelt.' Lula's desire is determined through (and as) the story of female desire framed by a male narrative: a doubling that inscribes woman's desire within the terms of that story, while it produces that desire *in her own words*. The identification of the two figures of woman, within and beyond the masculine narrative of possession, through their double desire for the male subject emphasises how woman is made intelligible through the phantasy of speaking in her words, of having reached into the memories and physicality of her interiority. The camera, which perpetuates this phantasy of having reached woman through the reframings of memory, identifies with Soldier, enunciating a masculine desire to capture or hold the image of woman in a frame or act of violation.

Both *Wild at Heart* and *Blue Velvet* enunciate a level of violence which remains irreducible to the figure of woman. So although I have argued that the imaging of woman merges with the event of violence, it is also necessary to consider the violence beyond her image. While *Blue Velvet* depicts Frank's violence against Dorothy's husband and Jeffrey, *Wild at Heart* depicts extreme and graphic forms of racial violence. It is this latter example that may help us to consider the implications of the non-reducible nature of the relation between violence and woman. For *Wild at Heart* begins with a disturbing and brutal scene, involving the murder of a black man by a white man. Sharon Willis, in 'Special Effects: Sexual and Social Difference in *Wild at Heart*', discusses the way in which the racial context of this scene is displaced through its status as spectacle or as a spectacular aestheticisation (Willis 1991: 276). The 'event' of the murder does not become inscribed as a narrative event: the violence overtakes any narrative function in the brutality or shock value of an image. Indeed, Willis argues that the abject body of the murdered black man forces the spectator to look away and hence invites the elision of its racial reference (Willis 1991: 277). Willis's analysis of this scene extends to the way in which racial difference and violence become displaced onto a primary sexual difference through the relying of looks which position the mother as guilty of the murder: 'Sexual difference, and specifically, the mother's sexuality, becomes the site of a displacement, a displacement that the film repeats at key moments, as it uses culture's eroticization of racial difference to privilege a strictly sexual reading of power relations' (Willis 1991: 280). I would also argue that the violence committed against the body of the woman is enabled by the elision or displacement of racial difference from the scene of the text. It is this elision that enables the 'whiteness' of the woman to become invisible: she becomes see-able as 'the woman'. The merging of 'the woman' and violence at the level of phantasy proceeds by introducing and displacing a primary racial violence and difference onto her figure (here, the figure of the mother). So the racial violence beyond the image of the woman is made invisible by the blurring of woman with violence (a blurring which relies on the invisibility of whiteness). Willis discusses the way in which the critical concern with the film as postmodern (as an ironic celebration of the play and spectacle of the image) has meant a failure to attend to the enunciation of racial violence (Willis 1991: 275). Making the racial violence implicit to this scene visible, would be to refuse critically both the sexist and racist regimes upon which the aestheticised phantasy of inhabiting and violating the figure of the (white) woman rests.

One of the final scenes of *Blue Velvet*, which some theorists have cited as an example of its destabilisation of classical cinema's misogyny, involves the representation of Dorothy's body as abject. Here, Jeffrey and Sandy find Dorothy naked on his porch. Her body is battered and bruised. Wittenburg and Gooding-Williams argue that the sight of Dorothy's bruised body is unpleasurable for the spectator – interfering then with the dominant cinematic pleasure of the look (Wittenburg and Gooding-Williams 1990: 154). However, the reappearance of Dorothy's body as bruised, while departing from her presentation as erotic object, does not necessarily depart from the voyeurism of the narrative trajectory, which seeks to penetrate her enigma, however self-consciously. For her body invites the response of sympathy and paternalism from Jeffrey. He covers her naked body with his touch: he holds her. The spectator is invited to identify with Jeffrey's gesture, to treat the violated body of the bruised white woman as an object to be held and protected. Moreover, the camera's lingering on the battered body may not simply disrupt the regime of pleasure in looking. The witnessing of the bruises restores to the centre of the text the body of woman in violation, the desire to see her body's bruises inscribing *a fascination with the marks and signs of male presence on her body*. This body does not force the gaze of the spectator to be deflected (as with the abjection of the black male body in *Wild at Heart*), but instead invites the spectator to both witness and protect her body as an image and vessel. The look of the camera invites then, not simply the masculinity inscribed in a protective gaze, but also a relation of address where violence against the white woman is repeated by being witnessed on the text of her body. By foregrounding the signs of violence on her body, the imaging of the white woman appears to merge with the event of that violence.

Indeed, by deflecting the spectator's attention from violence as a material event, through various postmodern framings and simulations, *Blue Velvet* seems to repeat that violence, positioning women as always already violated in inscriptions of filmic writing. The enunciation of masculinity as a relation of violence is here enabled rather than interrupted by these postmodern filmic strategies. The ambivalence determined by the use of postmodern and parodic strategies can be read as expanding the vision of masculinity through a perpetual *reframing* of the imaging of woman (as implosion of her image), and the repeating or *restaging* of violence against her body.[3]

Narrating rape in Peter Greenaway's *Baby of Macon*

Peter Greenaway's *Baby of Macon* (1993) has certainly been controversial, and it is perhaps symptomatic of postmodernism and the screen that this controversy has centred around a representation of sexual violence. The film's ending portrays graphically and horrifically the gang rape of a female character. It is important for me to note at the beginning of my analysis that it was due to the way in which the ending of this film angered and disturbed me that I developed an interest in investigating patterns of sexual violence in 'alternative' films.

It is the representation of the rape that shaped the media's response to the film. Derek Malcom, for example, comments:

The odious ritual rape, during which the number of men taking part are meticulously counted one by one in what looks like a deliberate attempt to engage our emotions uneasily, may well be too difficult for many to take. Yet this elaborately staged and copiously detailed study of duplicity, greed and hypocrisy fails not so much on any moral count but because it is technically deficient. (Malcom 1993)

Malcom's response forms an interesting contrast to Quentin Crisp's, who argues:

The film has already fallen foul of the famous British squeamishness and anti-intellectualism. Be warned: there is gore, there are ideas. Greenaway has always been punctilious in presenting his horrors. He shows us the odour of existence but doesn't rub our nose in it. Here, the rape, though rightly shocking, is heard, but hardly seen. (Crisp 1993)

In both examples, the critics concentrate on the shocking nature of the film's representation of rape from a moral and technical point of view. Both argue that the rape is not open to objection on moral grounds, although the former argues that the rape is objectionable for reasons of technical deficiency. By limiting possible objections to the rape to the grounds of either morality or technique, the question of the politics of this representation is elided. The potential effect of this scene becomes an issue of whether spectators are shocked (and in this sense duped by the reality effect) or whether they have joined the intellectual contract by acknowledging the rape as technique or as an elaborate staging.

The issues raised by the media's reception of the film are compounded in interesting ways by some of the 'defences' of the film made by Peter Greenaway in his article 'Deceiving is Believing' (Greenaway 1993). Here, Greenaway draws attention to deception as the dominant and contractual relation of the cinema. He argues that death and copulation are the 'two unsustainable dupes of the cinema' always only produced as an illusion before the screen, never having really happened behind it. He then elaborates on this statement as follows:

The *Baby of Macon* makes many representations of these cinematic fictions and then pushes them to the edge. The film, with grim neutrality, steadily builds and draws you into the central contentious, deeply disturbing scenes and the camera does not let you get away. There are no edits to let you off the hook – you've come this far so you must watch or hide. Yet we know, we say we know, that this is all still representation, simulation, fakery. We say we know all these things, and the shrill cry of distaste appears to be evidence that we do not. It seems that when a space is claimed for a representation of cause-and-effect violence in order to demonstrate and examine it with some degree of passionate detachment, out come the responsibility filters that say you must keep these supersensitive verities sentimentalised, deodorised, side-stepped, turned into a joke to make them viewable. Is this some sort of hypocrisy? (Greenaway 1993)

According to Greenaway, then, *Baby of Macon* represents the cinematic fictions of death and sex as the limit of narrative (and indeed, the ending brings death and sex together in a graphically violent way: the female character's rape leads to her death). The disturbing nature of these representations traps the spectator in front of the screen, forcing her or him to confront the violence of the image *as an image*. To resist those representations would be to be deceived – it would be to mistake the theatrical illusion for the real thing. Greenaway's reading of *Baby of Macon* announces its postmodern character (its concern with the structures of deception and illusionism in cinematic address) in terms of a filmic refusal of the possibility of political judgement (whereby such judgement constitutes an over-investment in the 'real'). The critique of a model of reference (the film is fake, after all) shifts into an argument that cinema is severed from any *connection* to what is beyond the screen. Postmodernism becomes inscribed here as an internalised, self-effacing and self-contained world of the hyper-image, a space where violence can be explored aesthetically on its own terms.[4] But, as I have suggested elsewhere in this book, judgements are not only possible, but necessary: they are necessary precisely in the absence of 'the real' to ground them. Judgements do not have to confuse representations for the real thing, but may question the very ontology which sustains this distinction.

The film is set in the seventeenth century, and involves the performing of a play before an audience. A double narrative emerges. Firstly, the narrative of the actors working in the play (including shots 'behind the scenes') and secondly the narrative within the play (which can be basically characterised as the exploitation of a 'miracle child' by his sister and then the church). This second narrative takes up a large part of the filmic diegesis, with the audience itself forming part of the dramatic action of the film. Through the construction of space within the film as theatrical (as already staged, as illusion or artifice) the film draws attention to its own framing devices as filmic discourse, that is, to its own technological (re)production of space. The viewer is constantly interrupted by being made aware that the flow of narrative witnessed by the camera is in fact framed as a play text (for example, when one of the characters suddenly announces, 'I could play the part of the father better', the deficiency of the performance is highlighted). This self-reflexive attention to the performance of theatrical and cinematic address (which involves an emphasis on both the spectacle and sounds of theatre) within the film also makes explicit the dialogic and interactive relation between spectator/audience/actor and text in the negotiation of meanings. In doing so, it may serve to problematise any simple identification of the spectator with the text (MacCabe 1985:68).

What Greenaway refers to as the unedited camera shot – the sweeping movement of the camera with limited editing within some scenes – may also complicate, at one level, the suturing effect of classical cinema. Following Stephen Heath, Kaja Silverman's analysis of suture stresses the importance of the cut. The cut fragments the filmic narrative into partial and incomplete moments, and in doing so, moves the narrative forward, acting upon the viewer only through the constant intimation of something which has not yet been fully seen, understood or revealed (Silverman 1983: 205). The relative absence of cutting at certain strategic points in *Baby of Macon*, while it does not fully negate the role of suspense within the narrative, entraps the spectator in the prolonging of a gaze. It is almost as if the use of long shots *embodies* the 'eye' of the camera, so that, moving around the set, the constraints of its own physicality delimit and perpetually reframe its vision (and in this sense the limited mobility of the camera's 'eye' makes it more difficult for the spectator to adopt it). The sweeping shots may disturb the viewing process by elongating and reframing cinematic space.

But despite the varying technical and stylistic ways *Baby of Macon* draws attention to its status as framing device and troubles the association of the spectator and camera's 'eye', it still opens out specific identifications through the gendering of the narrative function (the relation between the two frames). The film opens with the beginning of the play, in which the sweeping shot of the camera follows the audience from behind and onto the stage. As the camera shot arrives at the stage the play's plot is announced: an 'old' and 'ugly' woman is giving birth to a child. The camera focuses on the body of the woman giving birth, as the audience chants expectantly, 'It is coming', and a female actor/character exclaims, 'praise the Lord that the body of the woman can be so fruitful'. The play text begins then with the mystery and enigma of motherhood. But the arrival (or appearance) of the baby and the miracle of his birth deflects the narrative's attention from the mother. The baby is exchanged between women, with pronouncements of the miracle and beauty of his birth:

Are we really born like this?
Is the child really hers?
Or did we find it?
He is so beautiful.

The mother's face is covered, conveying her absence in the collective desire for, and affirmation of, the boy child that begins the narrative of his exploitation as an object to be exchanged, as a miracle birth. In this way, the exchange of the child that structures the narrative trajectory is enabled at the expense of the mother, whose absence from the scene of the text represents its centring on a masculine separation from her. Indeed, this scene is immediately followed by the entrance of the father onto the stage. His entrance turns the stage into a spectacle of women (lined in a row before the audience): he tries out the women's breasts to see which woman is the most suitable to feed the son. His speech involves the phrase, 'This one's too sweet . . . this one's too . . .' What follows is a 'debauched' parade of women, fondled and consumed by the figure of the father. While this is highlighted as performance (another actor whispers he could do it better) it still produces a positive identification with the play audience as both an erotic and comic spectacle: reframing this event as a contract between text and audience that turns the woman's body, not only into a spectacle for the voyeur, but also into a joke made possible by the terms of its exposure.

The plot's centring on the boy child as a miracle that has come from the veiled woman involves the production of a figure of woman as villain: a figure that, importantly, cuts across the borders between play text and the filmic diegesis, opening and closing a gap between them. The child's sister within the play text emerges as a villain through her exploitation of the child. She uses the child to 'complement her ambition', by giving him a voice and turning him into a saint (and a commodity). Following her introduction into the play text as a villain, the camera retreats to a sweeping shot of the whole stage/audience, and then cuts to a 'behind the stage' scene to which we, as spectators, have a privileged access (detaching us from the audience of the play in a more definite way). The actress is repeating and mimicking her lines, 'I want to be rich', ironically distancing herself from her character. A male actor, who watches her revised performance of these lines, interrupts abruptly, 'You wanted this part so badly . . . You'd have paid them.' She replies, 'Who are you . . . a spear carrier?' Here, the actress is constructed in a parallel way to her character: she is a woman-villain who uses her sex to further herself, who is ambitious and greedy, and who doesn't give men the power and authority they demand. This doubling in her representations both separates the play text and filmic diegesis (as two things) and yet reconnects them in the same moment, blurring the persona of woman-as-villain as something that transfers or *translates* across the frame. The parallel fictions merge to render woman a signifier that exceeds the theatrical and filmic frame, effectively and ironically enabling the reification of the image of woman in an ontology of her spectacle (that is, not despite, but *through* her framing as performer).

Indeed, the central conflict within the play text/filmic diegesis is between this woman and the male church, which becomes inscribed in semi-archetypal terms as a conflict between femininity (superstition, emotion, the body) and masculinity (scepticism, rationality, science). This conflict emerges as a struggle over the interpretation (as exploitation) of the boy child. The sister claims the child as hers, pronouncing a 'virgin birth', a claim which is denounced by the bishop and his son as heretical. The conflict settles on the issue of her virginity, and the sister claims, 'examine me and I will shame you . . . are you frightened to learn the truth, the child deserves more than your contemptuous scepticism'. Her claim leads to an examination of her genitals by other characters in order to prove or disprove the existence of her virginity. The examination becomes a joke – an effeminate prince is tricked by the placing of a sheep's head in front of her genitals – leading to laughter both on and off the stage. Here, woman's genitals, and the existence of the hymen, become the centre of the plot and the stage, as an 'object' which is associated with the gendered struggle of interpretation as well as the production of a joke. This relation of address whereby woman's genitals become the vehicle of both plot, humour and audience identification, inscribes women's sexuality as a means through which the narrative is sustained. While the filmic audience is dis-placed from this scene of laughter (if we laugh, then we laugh as much at the laughter as at the joke: our access to this joke is mediated by the laughter of the play audience), the filmic spectator is nevertheless invited to adopt the position of participant. For the frame or division between play and filmic text is here blurred by the excesses of laughter which bring the characters, actors and play audience together in the form of a collectively affirmed joke directed against the woman.

The way in which 'woman-as-villain' translates across the frame within *Baby of Macon* is most violently evident in the final scenes of the film. The sister is to be executed for killing the child (taking him away from the church) but the play text names a problem: virgins cannot be hung. The narrative resolves itself through rape: take the woman by force so she can be 'rightfully punished'. The camera shows men grabbing straws in anticipation, as the sister screams, 'You cannot hang me. You cannot touch me.' The camera, at a distance, shows a veiled bed being rolled over: she is thrown onto it. A line of men queue, distracted, waiting their turn. What follows is a graphically violent scene made all the more 'real' by a 'playful' narrative twist. The sister, when thrown back into the bed, becomes the actress, shown by the camera to be no longer in the part of the character as she is unseen by the play's audience. One man enters and the character screams while the actress laughs at his prick. There is a division: the gang rape is a performance from which the film spectator will be spared. But that division is immediately lost as the actress says, 'All right, no need to act any more. The audience can't see you are acting.' The performance of rape is sustained *behind the screen*. She screams, 'You bastards, you can't. Let go of me.' The male actor holding her down replies, 'You wanted this role so badly. You ought to see it through . . . Imagine an audience of 300. And nobody knows you aren't acting'.

Within the split of the filmic diegesis (within and beyond the play text) the rape hence re-unites the frames, both as performance (what is part of the narrative of the play) and as 'real' (what is part of the acting of the play within the filmic narrative). The rape exceeds the boundaries between performance and real within the larger frame of the filmic diegesis, which certainly makes it *appear* more real than if the split within the diegesis hadn't already overtly delimited a level of performance. The rape punishes the woman who translates across the split and the frame within the double text of the film. For indeed, the blood on his prick becomes readable as a potential signifier of the actress's and just not the character's virginity, identifying the outer limit of the filmic diegesis with the play text. So while at one level, the rape is destabilised as an event which loses a secure place within the con-text of the diegesis, it is also restabilised as an event that blurs the double filmic frame into one. The acting of the rape as that which really happened to the actress who acts in the play does not in this way simply point to the deferring of the real of rape along an endless chain of simulation. Rather, it secures rape as a violence against, or punishment of, a woman whose 'real' exceeds the division of frames within the diegesis – violently installing itself as the truth beyond the frame.

Within this context, the filming of the rape scene invites the spectator to identify the violence through a doubling and merging of play and filmic frames. The 'shocking' nature of this scene does not necessarily constitute the spectator as 'duped', but is held in place by the repetition of violence across the frames. Rape becomes re-inscribed as the limit of representation, to be tested and repeated. Rape is installed as an act, a violence, which positions 'woman' as a vehicle for holding the frame in place. *In this way sexual violence against woman is aestheticised as the play of narrative against itself.*

The way in which rape is used within the filmic diegesis involves its aestheticisation, its conversion into a limit of narrative. The fascination with numbers also emphasises the significance of male penetration[5] within the filmic representation of what constitutes the meanings and effects of rape. These two details (aestheticisation and the focus on acts of penetration as events) suggest that the narrativisation of rape repeats the act of violence represented against the woman-as-villain. My analysis of how rape becomes aestheticised within *Baby of Macon* connects with Rajeswari Sunder Rajan's argument, in *Real and Imagined Women: Gender, Culture and Post-Colonialism*, where she discusses Terry Eagleton's reading of *The Rape of Clarissa* (Rajan 1993: 74). Here, Eagleton suggests that rape functions as the unpresentable, because the 'real' of the woman's body marks the outer limits of language. As Rajan argues, 'Such narrative theory fetishizes rape as a limit of narrative, to be tested over and over' (Rajan 1993: 74). Likewise, *Baby of Macon* fetishises rape by taking it up as an event that blurs textual frames and the limit of filmic narrative, converting rape from the unpresentable (the gap between frames) to the over-represented (the event that re-connects frames). The violence of the act as specifically a violence against woman is lost by being translated into a metaphor of the text and its limits.

In this chapter, I have examined films that have been named and designated as postmodern. What is at stake in my analysis, is not whether these films *are* postmodern, but rather how the event of being *seen as* postmodern involves *not seeing* the role of sexual violence. Indeed, the not-seeing of that violence becomes constitutive of post-modernism in relation to the screen. For that violence is not seen, precisely because of the way in which postmodernism is already seen through the assumption of transgression, through the equation between postmodernism and the transgressive look (the look that does not perform a violence against the body of the woman given its distance from the classical look – the look that looks only at classical cinema looking).

I have offered a different way of seeing such films. Rather than assuming that violence is on the side of classical representation which is automatically transgressed, I have examined how such violence becomes repeated and enunciated (as a re-visioning of masculinity) through these supposedly transgressive filmic techniques (with particular reference to the role of framing in the implosion of the image). The argument that assumes postmodernism is about the violence of classical cinema and does not enunciate that violence is hence problematic on two counts. Firstly, it assumes that classical cinema is reducible to the violence of both voyeurism and realism. Secondly, it assumes that representation and the enunciation of violence can be clearly separated such that postmodernism's over-coming of the violence of representation is an over-coming of violence *per se*. The difference of such a feminist way of seeing is, I would argue, one that matters.

However, to challenge this narrative should not lead us to equate postmodernism with the violence which it sees itself as having over-come. On the contrary, my re-seeing of films seen as postmodern is an attempt to open our field of vision. While postmodernism may not constitute the over-coming of the violence of and in screening, neither is it reducible to it. The question becomes: *how to see postmodernism seeing itself differently.* It is from here, that we may catch a different sight.

Conclusion: Events that move us

I have read enough conclusions about the impossibility of making conclusions to want, in some sense, to make one. In concluding, in coming to an end, I want to return. I want to return to the question of the status of the anecdote that I raised in my opening comments in chapter 6. I want to return to the status of the events that have been named as such in my narrative. Such events are events that have moved me, that have compelled me to write. But what is the relation between the movement of the event – the impossible meeting of work and life – and the movement initiated by the event – where, within my narrative, it no longer stays still? What are the implications of this movement for my argument, for the very question of differences that matter?

Differences matter, this much is clear. I have argued that the differences between postmodernism and feminism are ones that matter. But, as I acknowledged in my introduction, postmodernism does not simply exist as such, but is constructed through the very discourses which write, read and see its existence. So, I have been cautious. I have entered texts very closely. I have moved about in them. Each text has been engaged with in its difference or particularity. Despite the closeness of the difference within, I have still kept a critical distance: I have moved from the (difference) 'within' to the (difference) 'between'. The claims I have made hence move from proximity to distance: I have made judgements by getting closer to the texts, and then leaping away. Of course, there is inevitably violence in the event of reading and in the necessity of making judgements. How to be less violent is a question that has energised my engagement with postmodernism as a feminist.

But here, now, is it not time to go further? Is it not the time to leave the particularity of each reading and take the risk of an even more general claim? Let me now take that risk. Perhaps it is the very question, 'which differences matter here?', which is the site of difference between the feminist positions that I have articulated and the postmodern texts that I have read. Such a question may in itself constitute a point of difference from postmodernism: in so far as postmodernism becomes constructed as a theory of 'difference', then it is predicated on the abstraction of difference from the particular realm of bodily matters. The question, 'which differences matter here?', is a pragmatic question: it recognises that differences cannot be subsumed into each other, but are constituted through relations of force and antagonism.

The difference between feminism and postmodernism then may be determined by the very force of the question, 'which differences matter here?' In other words, the difference between feminism and post-modernism may reside in their different relation to 'difference'. It could be argued that 'postmodernism' is constructed through the reification of 'difference' as such (so that postmodernism is read as being on the side of the difference which is excluded by identity thinking or by classical realism). It is the pragmatic question, 'which differences?', that inter-rupts the designation of 'difference' as a pure category. Which differ-ences matter here? Or, which differences make a difference to one's social identity? Such questions may constitute the specificity of a femin-ist practice – placing it beyond the opposition between modern (struc-ture) and postmodern (difference) – in the very demand that we analyse differences in relation to the structuring of social relations. They also open out the possibility that some differences might matter more than others: the process whereby some differences come to matter involves the implication of differences in relations of power.

This question, 'which differences matter here?', hence demands that we refuse any attempt to forge a philosophy of difference, whereby various categories of difference (race, gender, class and sexuality) are assumed to have a relation of homology. The conflation of regimes of difference is deeply problematic. It prevents any articulation of *contra-dictions* between regimes of difference in the form of antagonistic relations of power. This is surely 'difference' as an onto-theological exclusion of the violence of differences. If postmodernism constructs itself through the value of difference, or the over-coming of identity and structuration, then postmodernism is predicated on the refusal or erasure of differences that matter. To go even further, I would argue that the writing of a philosophy of difference involves a universalism: a speaking from the place of (for example) the white, masculine subject, who re-incorporates difference as a sign of its own fractured and multiple coming-into-being. So here, in *Differences That Matter*, it is not a question of femininity *as* difference, the subaltern woman *as* differ-ence, woman *as* an image of difference. Indeed, I have located a violence in how postmodernism constructs itself through taking up figures of difference in theoretical, literary and filmic texts. 'Which differences matter here?', is a question that I have addressed to postmodernism, a 'speaking back' which constitutes the agonistics of my own narrative, and renders impossible any slippage from one difference to an-other. The impossibility of such a slippage may here demand a general judgement on what postmodernism is doing and not doing by 'siding' with difference.

But to make the question, 'which differences matter?', *the* site of differentiation between feminism and postmodernism is too neat a summation of what my readings have themselves been doing. What is left out in such a reading of my readings? It is the very repetition of this question, 'which differences matter here?', that unsettles me, that commands me to return to the middle, to somewhere in the middle where 'I' got stuck inside the text. Is it this very question, which has framed my argument and the ethics of my reading, one which also suggests its limits? Differences within, differences between. Within feminism, which differences? Of course, at times, I have spoken of the differences within, of post-coloniality as a context in which such questions must already be framed, but is that enough? Is there something else at stake?

So, I must return to the event, the event that functioned as an illustrative example in chapter 4. I remember first writing this chapter as part of my doctoral thesis in 1993. I was working on the question of subjectivity. I needed an example, something to hang my argument on. I remember looking around the room. An object perhaps? Some-Thing to trigger a memory? And then, I remembered this event. I don't know why it came to my mind. I hadn't thought about it for a long time. I remembered the two policemen in the car. It was the perfect example. It all seemed to fit.

So it wasn't simply that the event compelled me to write. The event did not drive me (it was not a 'coming out'): the event came to life after the writing had taken place. The status of the event suggests the limits of the auto-biographical: the writing of the self within criticism is always mediated, always framed by the demands of making an argument. It does not follow that such events aren't moving: that they do not involve movement. The event, precisely by bringing 'the life' into play in the work, comes to life: it cannot be constrained by its status as an exemplary moment (the anecdote).

Events that move us, move away from us. They don't stay in the place where we give them life as signifiers. One can only begin an ending by complicating the supposed discreteness of such events. True, I have written of it as such. But it is the act of remembering, an act which is both critical, affirmative and selective, that places boundaries and edges around the story, giving it its seeming internal coherence. This rhetorical gesture, in which memory plays a crucial part, is not exhaustive. My story entails its own elisions, its own figurations, its own forgettings. It also entails re-writing.

Indeed, since 1993, I keep writing and speaking about this event. In fact, it has become a compulsion: it keeps cropping up everywhere.[1] In repeating itself, it has moved. Why does this make a difference? We must return, yet again, to the event. In it, I analysed the shift in identifications as constitutive of both the fixation and instability of the subject. In the shift of the policemen's address from, 'are you an Aboriginal?' to 'it's just a sun tan, isn't it?', I read a shift from a racialised discourse of otherness (the Aboriginal as outside belonging) to a sexualised discourse (where I was a recipient of a wink and a smile). The shift was enabled by my disavowal of Aboriginality and desire for inclusion within the white neighbourhood. But what has this left out? Where have I gone astray?

A narrative which shifts from race to sex? Immediately, the gesture of the narrative becomes problematic. It has been an argument of this book that differences such as race and sex are mutually constitutive, that they do not work in isolation from each other. The original query about racial origin does not abolish the implication of the original gaze in a sexual regime that found or finds the subject walking the street. The hailing and address of the policeman was surely then an address to an Aboriginal woman. As theorists such as Jan Pettman in *Living in the Margins* have argued, the Aboriginal woman is always sexualised in White Australian colonial narratives (Pettman 1992: 27). So if the original address (are you an Aboriginal?) positioned my colour as a stain, as a sign of a natural criminality determined by the fact of my skin, then how does this criminalisation of colour link with the gendering of the address? It may suggest that the black woman is defined in terms of the physicality of her skin, as a stain which confirms her over-sexed being, her threat to the proper social and sexual order of the domes-ticated suburb. She is constructed in this sense as a social and sexual danger.

It is only through a recognition of the antagonism between relations of address that we can make explicit the positioning of Black women; the *explicit* confrontation shifted my attention from race *to* gender and hence elided the 'Black woman' as a site of contradiction and ambivalence. Is it precisely through rendering visible the *collision* between race and gender, that 'the Black woman' herself (myself) can become visible?

But, again, I must hesitate, with questions that undermine the 'fit'. How to do justice to the Black woman, who has been reclaimed from this story of disavowal and repudiation? Does this reclaiming of the Black woman lose sight of the *particularity* of her various inscriptions even as its renders visible her impossibility as a discrete identity? Returning once more to this event, we can see that the invisibility of the Black woman in the original encounter ('are you an Aboriginal?' to 'it's a sun tan, isn't it?') constitutes a form of ambivalence in which the linear narrative (race to gender) begins to break apart. It is here that I thought I saw her (myself) struggling to get out – in the staging of a collision. But the gesture of taking the 'Black woman' as a figure for what is elided in the narrative of race to gender remains just that – a gesture. It relies on a *figuration*.

This figuring of the Black woman as a sign of an ambivalence which destabilises the encounter is problematic precisely because of what it cannot speak of. That is, it cannot speak of the divisions and antagonisms within the signifier, 'the Black woman'. We need to ask: which black woman? There are many possibilities that are at play – either explicitly or implicitly – in the narrative: Aboriginal woman, Asian woman, mixed-race woman. How to speak of their difference? The slippage from Aboriginal to a generalised category of Blackness conceals the history of racism towards Aboriginal peoples, not just from White Australia, but also from Asian immigrants. How to speak of the difference of the Aboriginal woman, even if she is only present in this narrative in the form of a misrecognition? But then, this misrecognition led to a second misrecognition – it shifted the address to that of the (sun-tanned) white woman. Between these images the cultural and historical particularity of my racial identification (however much bound up – biographically – in phantasy) was left out. This elision of an identification that is neither Aboriginal woman nor white woman is an elision that my own narrative kept in place. By focusing on the antagonism that is covered over by the signifier 'Black women', I am forced into naming myself – a naming which is temporary and partial: mixed-race; English mother, Pakistani father; hybrid woman.[2] Inevitably this identification has the structure of a misrecognition and does not resolve the traumatic *lack of belonging* which is constitutive of the relation of address.

Furthermore, the signifier 'black woman' is also divided in terms of class. It was through my self-identification as middle-class rather than working-class that I was able to renegotiate my position within the encounter. If I had been *already positioned* as working class or indeed as Aboriginal, such movement within the event would not have been possible. In this sense, when and how one can move, when and how the negotiation of naming and identity is up for grabs, brings into play differences that are already constituted and that function precisely as mechanisms of social exclusion.

So my concern in this conclusion with auto-biographical modes of criticism has been to locate myself in the text: a locatedness which does not weigh the text down (this is where I am), but opens it out (this is where I am not yet). Such a locatedness opens out the difficulty of representation: how to speak of oneself, as either a presence or absence, without assuming that one can speak *for others*, who are already absent. As a mixed-race woman, who emigrated from England to Australia, but has returned to England, I feel that I cannot speak for either white women, or for South Asian women in England or Australia or, really, for any particular or clearly demarcated group of women at all. But my inability to speak on behalf of any group of women is not an *exception* of biography or place, but a trace of a dynamic that troubles the very intersection of race and gender in structures of identification. It is this *symptomatic nature of the failure of my own personal address* that my final entry into auto-biography has attempted to explore.

So, the event keeps returning us to a different place. It is a returning that does not return. What difference might this difference make? The instability of this event – made possible through the impossible meeting of work and life – leads me to my self-identification as a Black feminist. It is not an identification that can fix me in place, though it has precise effects. It is also a dis-identification from the place in which I began to speak of 'the event', where the event found existence only as an object of theoretical discourse. It is the movement of the event – of the difficult trajectory of the self in the text – or the self as the text – that forces me to come once more to the difference within: *the difference that matters within feminism.* It is a difference that requires an ethics of closer reading: a closer reading, not only of the authorising texts of postmodernism, but also of the authorising texts of feminism itself.

Writing about differences that matter within feminism suggests the need to suspend any final judgement on where we are or where we should be. We must admit to the differences that we cannot name – as well as those we cannot not name. My concern with differences that matter, and with the possibility of a more dialogical relation between feminism and postmodernism (precisely through a recognition that a dialogue has not taken place), leads me to claim what difference this book might make, and what difference it cannot make. It leads me to recognise that even the event of claiming some differences, is to refuse to admit to others. It also leads me to acknowledge that any phantasy of the 'we' of feminism is a refusal of some differences, differences that are exercised in the phantastic biographies of subjects who are always on the move, but who aren't moving freely.

Of course, some of the differences that are refused in any demarcation of a community (that phantastic 'we') might matter more than others. Differentiating between such differences is a political as well as theoretical task. It is not a pure but a contingent act: an act which recognises the embodied and embedded nature of the differences that come to matter, even those that cannot be named as such. But the marking out of communities is not made impossible by the differences which are not yet named: rather, such communities may come alive through the possibility of such differences. The Black feminist community, for example, may recognise the differences that haunt the category, 'the Black woman', at the same time as the re-figuring of 'the Black woman' (precisely not as a figure *of* difference) may work to defy and disrupt normalised categories of gender and race in ways which may surprise us. The political gesture of establishing an oppositional community is here one that both makes a difference, and is made possible by differences.

Judgements must be made about such differences, about whether and how they might matter, but such judgements are temporary, fragile, even mad. An ethical reading must admit that the differences that matter between us or within us are never simply in the present as such, but open up a radically uncertain future. The deferral of justice is here the condition of possibility for the judgements I have made about postmodernism and its narratives of difference. And yet, perhaps, it is through an ethics of closer readings, of judgements which must fail the texts in question, that we might trace how the differences that matter between us, matter in some places more than others. As I sentence this book to its (inevitably premature) death, I can only draw attention to this 'us' as the impossible and yet necessary community of feminism itself.

Notes

INTRODUCTION: SPEAKING BACK

1 It should be noted that this problem of containment through the use of naming within theory is not unique to 'postmodernism'. For example, some theorists have been critical of the use of 'post-colonial' in recent Australian theories to designate all writings that deal critically with imperial discourses: a usage which blurs the difference between writings by white Australians and Aboriginal peoples, and implies a homogeneity that simply does not exist between how groups and even nations deal with 'de-colonisation' (McClintock 1994: 254–6). Any term or name can be used to contain, and to negate the operation of power differences between different elements. However, the term 'postmodernism', because it is used to designate so many different (and contradictory) phenomena, is particularly slippery and problematic in this respect.

2 Throughout, I will discuss different layers of violence in relation to the uses of postmodernism – the violence at work in the act of naming diverse texts as postmodern, the violent at stake in the taking up of figures of difference (chapters 6 and 7), and the violence at work in the very non-recognition of social violence as a form of constraint (chapters 3 and 4). In such uses of violence, I am concerned with violence at the level of signification. Indeed, I would argue that violence suggests a complex and over-determined relation between the symbolic and material. Violence implies a relation of force, but also a relation of harm. Colonialism involves material violence (the forceful acquisition of land and people), and discursive violence (for example, the violence of taking land through naming it). The material and discursive violence is inseparable and irreducible. I hence use the term, 'violence', in relation to postmodernism, to make clear the enormity of what is at stake – how postmodernism appropriates others through naming is both a relation of force and of harm: it has harmful effects, and it is a taking-over through the force of the name.

3 I am indebted to Celia Lury for this point.

1 RIGHTS

1 See my consideration of how the relation between phallus and penis comes to be determined in chapter 4, section one.

2 Likewise, we can see how the absence of a deconstructive awareness of the iterability of the sign may be structural to pragmatic approaches. This is made evident by Derrida's reading of Austin in *Limited Inc.* (Derrida 1988a). But we could expand the terms of Derrida's analysis to include the philosophies of pragmatists such as Rorty, whose model of philosophy as conversation, and idealisation of linguistic communities, certainly negates the operation of difference, opaqueness and otherness within linguistic exchanges. The failure to deal with such differences leads to a model of language which excludes the operations of power dynamics (see Rorty 1982).

3 I will take up the ethical implications of this re-thinking of rights in chapter 2.

4 Thanks to Imogen Tyler for since sharing with me her exciting work on pregnant embodiment.

2 ETHICS

1 Hence the naïveté of his solution to power inequality: give the public free access to the memory and databanks (Lyotard 1989: 67). This fails to recognise that even if access is legalised formally, it will still be constrained by the differential, asymmetrical relation of subjects to power and knowledge.

2 Indeed, I have found that Gilligan is often alluded to without being addressed, especially in feminist theories influenced by postmodernism – where Gilligan is taken as an example of an essentialist feminism, one that assumes the transparency of experience and the foundational nature of gender difference. I think this forecloses the debate prematurely.

3 See chapter 5 for a discussion of the figuring of 'the woman reader'.

4 I use the term 'collective' here deliberately. Collectivity does not necessarily essentialise 'the group' as the basis of struggle, but rather concerns the formation of temporary and strategic alliances which involve decisions about how power operates to produce patterns of distribution. A collective politics stands in contrast to the political models that have been associated with postmodernism by theorists such as Paul Patton. He argues that a postmodern politics is a politics of 'piecemeal resistance' (Patton 1988: 94–5). Patton constructs a false opposition between a modern politics of 'the total' and a postmodern politics of 'the local'.

3 WOMAN

1 Given this, I wonder about the politics of the argument that man becoming woman relies on woman becoming woman in the first place. Does this reinstate woman as having the 'burden' of responsibility for social change? Does woman here simply exist in order to enable man's becoming? Is there a proper subject implicated then in becoming woman? These questions are posed to open another aspect of the debate about the ordering of becomings (there is an order to this account of becoming, not simply woman becoming woman *then* man becoming woman, but also becoming woman *then* becoming animal *then* becoming imperceptible). The implication of this latter ordering is taken up later.

2 In contrast, in *Limited Inc. a b c*, the question of reference is not reduced to models of literal reference. In this text Derrida suggests that the referent inhabits the text (Derrida 1988a: 137). Here, the difference between signifier, signified and referent is maintained as part of the structure of the text, but the referent is conceived as being contained by that structure, having the function of a trace. As I have shown, the textual construction of 'reference' within *Spurs* contradicts this model, by conflating the possibility of reference with the questions of essentialism and fetishism. As such, the conceptualisation of woman within *Spurs* needs to be dis-placed through an alternative under-standing of referentiality, which may be derived from Derrida's other decon-structive writings or, perhaps more interestingly, from the multifold history of feminist theorising on the relation between woman and women.

3 So, although we can agree with Rosi Braidotti's point that there is no direct relation between the sexualisation of the other as feminine, and either the discursivity, or the historical presence of real-life women (Braidotti 1989: 89), we can still conceive that relation in other terms. There may be no direct passage from one to another but this does not negate that they carry traces of each other and effect and destabilise the constitution of the other in a way which is complex and over-determined.

4 I was very amused by a comment in the margins of my copy of *Spurs* at this point (which I borrowed from a friend of mine). She had written, 'Bet it didn't give him varicose veins!' While this is, at one level, mere quip, and at another, misses the point about the non-availability of the literal, biological body, I think it also really *gets the point*. It is all very well to see 'woman' as a signifier which is detached from any referential link to bodies, but this neglects the extent to which the signification of 'woman' can be traced at the level of embodiment. The body may not be a material given (where varicose veins would serve only to confirm woman-liness), but the materialisation of bodies involves limits and constraints to the signification of sexual difference, and to the lived experience of 'having' a body (the body which speaks). In this sense, 'woman' is not a signifier which is detached from the constraints of embodied experience, but is implicated in those experiences in complex and over-determined ways. See the last section of this chapter for an extension of this point.

4 SUBJECTS

1 The ambiguity of such a question which forms the title of a book is instructive (Cadava, Connor and Nancy 1991). The 'who' evokes a subject as the question itself assumes its passing. We could ask ourselves, does the narrative of the passing by of the subject itself constitute a writing of a form of subjectivity? Such an argument is put forward in chapter 3 in my critique of becoming indiscernible as the writing of a privileged subjectivity.

2 Returning to my reading of *Spurs: Nietzsche's Styles* in chapter 3, it could be pointed out that the dialogue between Nietzsche and Derrida is mediated by the absent presence of Lacan. In *The Post Card: From Socrates to Freud and Beyond*, Derrida's critique of Lacan's alleged phallogocentrism centres on the question of Femininity and its association with Truth. He writes: 'Femininity

is the Truth (of) castration, is the best figure of castration, because in the logic of the signifier it has always already been castrated' (Derrida 1987: 442). In *Spurs* the deconstruction of woman displaces the fact of her castration as truth or non-truth – indeed, 'castration, here again, does not take place' (Derrida 1979: 97). Given this supplementary and submerged dialogue, it is interesting to reconsider how the structure of exchange on the question of woman takes place through *a triad of male masters*, who ask the question *of* her rather than *to* her.

3 To describe this as a shift in Butler's work may be unjust. *Bodies That Matter* could be better theorised as an attempt to explain why *Gender Trouble* does not support a voluntaristic model of social change. However, this reading of *Gender Trouble* is not, properly speaking, either inside or outside the text, but may constitute its limits. This can be read in terms of Butler's 'defensiveness' against this potential reading. That is, Butler recognises the charge of voluntarism (if I am performed, I can unperform my self) and in attempting to explain it away, renders that charge the condition of possibility for her engagement.

5 AUTHORSHIP

1 The sex of the reader can also function as a guarantee within feminist literary approaches. Although I find Annette Kolodny's article 'A Map for Rereading' sophisticated and illuminating, she nevertheless seems to rely on the crucial nature of the sex of the interpreter as already in place *given* the difference of male and female symbolic universes (Kolodny 1989: 158).

2 This returns us to the way in which *Spurs* re-produced a masculine mode of enunciation in the event of taking up a relation to woman-as-enigma. The determination of a scene of interpretation in which woman becomes figured as an enigma will be investigated in chapters 6 and 7, where I will analyse both literary and film texts.

3 Butler reads the crossing or passage of the 'I' differently. She suggests that the exchange of the 'I' opens out its radical potentiality for being claimed, and that by giving up the 'I' (in the form of authorship), Cather enables the event of taking it back, of reclaiming it. Butler elaborates, 'she stages the laying of the claim to authorial rights by transferring them to one who represents the law, a transfer that, in its redoubling, is a kind of fraud, one that facilitates the claim to the text that she only appears to give away' (Butler 1993: 148). I agree that the exchange of the 'I' functions a radical crossing that may demonstrate that the 'I' is open to re-inscription, to being claimed. At the same time, I think Butler under-estimates the importance of the way in which the 'I' cannot be claimed outright by Cather, due to the history of its determination as masculine (the logic of law and property). The mediation of the 'I' by male narrators is here a structural process which distances the reader from the figuration of the woman writer, precisely in her dis-placement in a masculine enunciative frame. But the impossibility of male ownership of the 'I' (the impossibility, that is, of eliminating its transportability) means that the woman writer can reappear to interrupt its travels, as in the forming of a 'W' by the snake.

6 (META)FICTIONS

1 However, Belsey does not use the term postmodernism, preferring 'interrogative' text. Belsey more recently qualifies some of the arguments concerning classical realism (and the distinction between declarative, imperative and interrogative texts) by suggesting 'it now seems to me that this classification may have been excessively formalistic, implying that texts can unilaterally determine their reception by the reader' (Belsey 1988: 407).

2 I am reminded here of David Bennett's argument in 'Wrapping up Postmodernism: The Subject of Consumption Versus the Subject of Cognition'. He discusses the way in which the modernist ideal of the subject's autonomy (the subject as self-creator) may be perpetuated in self-reflexive discourse (Bennett 1988: 249). The 'I' in 'The Magic Poker' may embody in this way a phantasy of creation which escapes the determining constraints or limits of narrative itself.

3 I have already examined the way in which some theoretical constructions of postmodernism deny the structural and determining role of gender limitations on the production of knowledge and subjectivity. It may be interesting to read this section of my chapter alongside such arguments, as a fictional enactment of a postmodern phantasy of over-coming gender (and becoming woman) although, of course, the specificity of any fictional inscription cannot be neglected.

7 SCREENS

1 This text works as application of deconstruction to film theory and connects with my argument in chapter 3, where I discussed Derrida's *Spurs: Nietzsche's Styles* as a postmodern inscription of woman as catachresis. Brunette and Wills specifically deal with the concept of woman in relation to violence, suggesting 'One might ask whether the hymen, as site of potential, and perhaps structural and institutional, violence performed on real women in the real world, was not being overlooked or obscured in the appropriation of the term for deconstruction' (Brunette and Wills 1989: 95). But they then conclude that it would be an act of violence against the text to reduce its figurative duplicities and ambiguities to the merely referential. Should we not instead be alerted to 'the violence that reduces the hymen to a single sense (that of woman), for it is the violence of a clash or resolution of differences, the very opposition that the hymen in question here deconstructs' (Brunette and Wills 1989: 95–6). Here, the problematic of violence as a structural relation is effaced through an argument about the absence of a referent. The way in which violence may work as a modality of enunciation is negated by the assumption that violence installs the 'real' (of woman). See chapter 3, section two, for a critique of the postmodern inscription of woman according to the issue of referentiality.

2 The close-up of Lula's hands flinching is repeated in the various sex scenes between her and her lover Soldier. These scenes are filmed with music and erotic colours, and involve close-ups of a number of sexual positions. Lula's hands are depicted as flinching at the climactic moment, as a sign of female sexual pleasure, synchronised with sounds of orgasm. This obsessive detailing

of female pleasure during sex does not expand to include male pleasure, and works as an attempt to identify, though imaging, woman as subject with the event of male penetration. Indeed, after one sexual encounter Lula exclaims, 'Sometimes Soldier when we're making love you just take me right over that rainbow. You are so aware of what goes on with me. I mean you pay attention. And I swear baby you've got the sweetest cock. Its like your talking to me when your inside. Its like its got a little voice all of its own.' So although woman is here represented as actively sexual, that activity is situated on the side of the phallus, always returning to it as a signifier of desire. Woman's sexuality is presented as active only in so far as it functions a vehicle for the self-presentation of the phallus as the centre of desire. In more concrete terms, women as subjects are only represented as actively sexual in relation to the masculine desire for penetration (a representation which is both sexist and heterosexist).

3 One could think of parody here as working at the outer level of dominant representations, enabling their repetition through the confirmation of a perpetual difference: the difference of the representation to itself is of course already in place (as re-presentation). This is not to deny that parodic narratives can have an alternative or counter-hegemonic role: rather, it is to argue that the parodic is always an element in the restaging of dominant phantasies, and can enable their expansion through the use of self-reflexivity (a space in which the dominant can re-articulate its difference to itself, and in so doing, strengthen its hold on the other).

4 I am reminded of Baudrillard's description of cinema in *The Evil Demon of Images*. He writes, 'There is a kind of primal pleasure, of anthropological joy in images, a kind of brute fascination unencumbered by aesthetic, moral, social, or political judgements' (Baudrillard 1987: 28).

5 As Catherine MacKinnon argues, the focus on the event or act of penetration within (legal) discourses on rape reflects the way in which understandings of rape are delimited by a masculine set of experiential limits, rendering women's experiences invisible (MacKinnon 1987: 87).

CONCLUSION: EVENTS THAT MOVE US

1 I have discussed the event in relation to auto-biography, psychoanalysis and even, most recently, discourses of sun-tanning! See Ahmed 1996b, 1997, 1998.

2 Of course, the category of mixed-raceness is deeply problematic precisely in so far as it implies the possibility of a pure racial identity. See Ahmed 1997 for a further discussion of the question of 'mixed-raceness'.

References

Abrams, M. H. 1953, *The Mirror and the Lamp: Romantic Theory and the Critical Tradition*, Oxford: Oxford University Press.

Ahmed, Sara 1995, 'Deconstruction and Law's Other: Towards a Feminist Theory of Embodied Legal Rights', *Social and Legal Studies*, 4: 55–73.

1996a, 'Beyond Humanism and Postmodernism: Theorising a Feminist Practice', *Hypatia*, 11, 2: 71–93.

1996b, 'Identifications, Gender and Racial Difference: Moving Beyond the Limits of Psychoanalytical Accounts of Subjectivity', in *Representations of Gender, Democracy and Identity Politics in Relation to South Asia*, Renuka Sharma (ed.), Delhi: Indian Book Centre, pp. 359–86.

1997, ' "It's a sun tan, isn't it?": Auto-biography as an Identificatory Practice', in *Black British Feminism*, Heidi Mirza (ed.), London: Routledge, pp. 153–67.

1998, 'Tanning the Body: Skin, Colour and Gender', *New Formations*, 34.

Althusser, Louis 1971, *Lenin and Philosophy and Other Essays*, London: New Left Books.

Arac, Jonathon (ed.) 1986, *Postmodernism and Politics*, Manchester: Manchester University Press.

Arnault, Lynne S. 1990, 'The Radical Future of a Classical Moral Theory', in *Gender/Body/Knowledge: Feminist Reconstructions of Being and Knowing*, Alison M. Jaggar and Susan Bordo (eds.), New Brunswick: Rutgers University Press, pp. 188–206.

Assiter, Alison 1996, *Enlightened Women: Modernist Feminism in a Postmodern Age*, London: Routledge.

Balsamo, Anne 1995, 'Forms of Technological Embodiment: Reading the Body in Contemporary Culture', in *Cyberspace/Cyberbodies/Cyberpunk: Culture of Technological Embodiment*, Mike Featherstone and Roger Burrows (eds.), London: Sage, pp. 215–38.

Barthes, Roland 1990, 'The Death of the Author', in *Image Music Text*, London: Fontana Paperbacks, pp. 142–9.

Baudrillard, Jean 1987, *The Evil Demon of Images*, Sydney: Power Institute.

1990, *Seduction*, Basingstoke: Macmillan.

Baudry, Jean-Louis 1992, 'Ideological Effects of the Basic Cinematic Apparatus', in *Film Theory and Criticism*, Gerald Mast, Marshall Cohen and Leo Braudy (eds.), Oxford: Oxford University Press, pp. 302–13.

Bauman, Zygmunt 1993, *Postmodern Ethics*, Oxford: Blackwell.

Belsey, Catherine 1980, *Critical Practice*, London: Methuen.

1988, 'Literature, History, Politics', in *Modern Criticism and Theory*, David Lodge (ed.), London: Longman, pp. 400–10.

Benhabib, Seyla 1987, 'The Generalised and the Concrete Other: The Kohlberg-Gilligan Controversy and Feminist Theory', in *Feminism as Critique*, Seyla Benhabib and Drucilla Cornell (eds.), Cambridge: Polity Press, pp. 77–96.

1992, *Situating the Self: Gender, Community and Postmodernism in Contemporary Ethics*, Cambridge: Polity Press.

Bennett, David 1988, 'Wrapping up Postmodernism: The Subject of Consumption Versus the Subject of Cognition', *Textual Practice*, 1–2: 243–61.

Bhabha, Homi 1994, *The Location of Culture*, London: Routledge.

Bordo, Susan 1993, *Unbearable Weight: Feminism, Western Culture and the Body*, Berkeley: University of California Press.

Braidotti, Rosi 1989, 'The Politics of Ontological Difference', in *Between Feminism and Psychoanalysis*, Teresa Brennan (ed.), London: Routledge, pp. 89–105.

1991, *Patterns of Dissonance: A Study of Women in Contemporary Philosophy*, Cambridge: Polity Press.

1994a, 'Towards a New Nomadism: Feminist Deleuzian Tracks; or Metaphysics and Metabolism', in *Gilles Deleuze and the Theatre of Philosophy*, Constantin V. Boundas and Dorothea Olkowski (eds.), London: Routledge, pp. 157–86.

1994b, *Nomadic Subjects: Embodiment and Sexual Difference in Contemporary Feminist Theory*, New York: Columbia University Press.

Brunette, Peter and David Wills 1989, *Screen/Play: Derrida and Film Theory*, Princeton, NJ: Princeton University Press.

Buntzen, Linda 1988, ' "Don't look at me". Woman's Body, Woman's Voice in *Blue Velvet*', *Western Humanities Review*, 42, 3: 187–203.

Burgin, Victor 1986, *The End of Art Theory: Criticism and Postmodernity*, Basingstoke: Macmillan.

Burke, Sean 1992, *The Death and Return of the Author*, Edinburgh: Edinburgh University Press.

Butler, Judith 1990, *Gender Trouble: Feminism and the Subversion of Identity*, London: Routledge.

1993, *Bodies That Matter: On the Discursive Limits of 'Sex'*, London: Routledge.

Cadava, Eduardo, Peter Connor and Jean-Luc Nancy (eds.) 1991, *Who Comes After the Subject?*, London: Routledge.

Carter, Angela 1987, *Fireworks*, London: Virago Press.

Carty, Anthony 1990, 'Introduction: Post-Modern Law', in *Post-Modern Law: Enlightenment, Revolution and the Death of Man*, Anthony Carty (ed.), Edinburgh: Edinburgh University Press, pp. 1–39.

Cather, Willa 1991, *My Antonia*, London: Virago Press.

Connor, Steven 1989, *Postmodernist Culture: An Introduction to Theories of the Contemporary*, Oxford: Basil Blackwell.

Coover, Robert 1970, *Pricksongs and Descantes*, New York: New American Library.

Copjec, Joan 1994, *Read my Desire: Lacan Against the Historicists*, Cambridge, Mass.: MIT Press.

Cornell, Drucilla 1992, 'The Philosophy of the Limit: Systems Theory and Feminist Legal Reforms', in *Deconstruction and the Possibility of Justice*, Drucilla Cornell, Michel Rosenfeld and David Gray Carlson (eds.), London: Routledge, pp. 68–91.

1993, *Transformations: Recollective Imagination and Sexual Difference*, London: Routledge.

Creed, Barbara 1988, 'A Journey Through *Blue Velvet*: Film, Fantasy and the Female Spectator', *New Formations*, 6: 97–117.

Crisp, Quentin 1993, Review of *Baby of Macon*, *The Independent*, 19 September.

Critchley, Simon 1991, *The Ethics of Deconstruction*, London: Routledge.

Culler, Jonathan 1982, *On Deconstruction*. Ithaca: Cornell University Press.

de Lauretis, Teresa 1990, 'Upping the Anti (sic) in Feminist Theory', in *Conflicts in Feminism*, Marianne Hirsch and Evelyn Fox Keller (eds.), London: Routledge, pp. 255–70.

Deleuze, Gilles and Félix Guattari 1992, *A Thousand Plateaus: Capitalism and Schizophrenia*, London: Athlone Press.

Denzin, Norman 1988, '*Blue Velvet*: Postmodern Contradictions', *Theory, Culture and Society*, 5, 2–3: 461–73.

Derrida, Jacques 1976, *Of Grammatology*, Baltimore: Johns Hopkins University Press.

1979, *Spurs: Nietzsche's Styles*, Chicago: University of Chicago Press.

1984, 'My Chances/*Mes Chances*: A Rendezvous with some Epicurean Stereophonies', in *Taking Chances: Derrida, Psychoanalysis and Literature*, Joseph Smith and William Kerrigan (eds.), Baltimore: Johns Hopkins University Press, pp. 1–32.

1987, *The Post Card: From Socrates to Freud and Beyond*, Chicago: University of Chicago Press.

1988a, *Limited Inc. abc*. Gerald Graff (ed.), Evanston: Northwestern University Press.

1988b, *The Ear of the Other: Otobiography, Transference, Translation*, Peggy Kamuf (ed.), Lincoln: University of Nebraska Press.

1991, 'At the very moment in this work here I am', in *Re-Reading Levinas*, Simon Critchley (ed.), London: Athlone Press, pp. 11–50.

1992, 'Force of Law: The "Mystical Foundation of Authority"', in *Deconstruction and the Possibility of Justice*, Drucilla Cornell, Michel Rosenfeld and David Gray Carlson (eds.), London: Routledge, pp. 3–67.

Derrida, Jacques and Christie V. McDonald 1982, 'Choreographies', *Diacritics*, 12: 66–76.

Diprose, Rosalyn 1994, *The Bodies of Women: Ethics, Embodiment and Sexual Difference*, London: Routledge.

Doel, Marcus 1995, 'Bodies without Organs: Schizoanalysis and Deconstruction', in *Mapping the Subject: Geographies of Cultural Transformation*, Steve Pile and Nigel Thrift (eds.), London: Routledge, pp. 226–40.

Donaldson, Laura E. 1992, *Decolonizing Feminisms: Race, Gender and Empire Building*, London: Routledge.

Douzinas, Costas and Ronnie Warrington 1991, *Postmodern Jurisprudence; The Law of Text in the Text of Law*, London: Routledge.

1994, 'Antigone's Law: A Genealogy of Jurisprudence', in *Politics, Postmodernity and Critical Legal Studies: The Legality of the Contingent*, Costas Douzinas, Peter Goodrich and Yifat Hachamovitich (eds.), London: Routledge, pp. 187–225.

Dworkin, Ronald 1975, 'Hard Cases', *Harvard Law Review*, 88: 1057–69.

Dyer, Richard 1988, 'White', *Screen*, 24, 4: 44–64.

1997, *White*, London: Routledge.

Eagleton, Terry 1990, *The Ideology of the Aesthetic*, Oxford: Basil Blackwell.

Ebert, Teresa 1996, *Ludic Feminism and After: Postmodernism, Desire and Labour in Late Capitalism*, Michigan: University of Michigan Press.

Eisenstein, Zillah 1988, *The Female Body and the Law*, Berkeley: University of California Press.

Federman, Raymond (ed.) 1981, *Surfiction: Fiction Now and Tomorrow*, Chicago: Swallow Press.

Felman, Shoshana 1987, *Jacques Lacan and the Adventures of Insight: Psychoanalysis in Contemporary Culture*, Cambridge, Mass.: Harvard University Press.

1992, 'Education and Crisis, or the Vicissitudes of Teaching', in *Testimony: Crisis of Witnessing in Literature, Psychoanalysis and History*, Shoshana Felman and Dori Laub (eds.), London: Routledge, pp. 1–56.

1993, *What Does a Woman Want? Reading and Sexual Difference*, Baltimore: Johns Hopkins University Press.

Felman, Shoshana and Dori Laub 1992, 'Foreword', in *Testimony: Crisis of Witnessing in Literature, Psychoanalysis and History*, Shoshana Felman and Dori Laub (eds.), London: Routledge, pp. xiii –xx.

Ferguson, Margaret and Jennifer Wicke (eds.) 1994, *Feminism and Postmodernism*, Durham: Duke University Press.

Flax, Jane 1990, *Thinking Fragments: Psychoanalysis, Feminism and Postmodernism in the Contemporary West*, Berkeley: University of California Press.

1992, 'The End of Innocence', in *Feminists Theorise the Political*, Judith Butler and Joan W. Scott (eds.), London: Routledge, pp. 445–63.

Foster, Hal 1984, '(Post)modern Polemics', *New German Critique*, 33: 67–79.

Foucault, Michel 1980, 'What is an Author?', in *Textual Strategies: Perspectives in Post-Structuralist Criticism*, Josue V. Harari (ed.), London: Methuen, pp. 141–60.

Fraser, Nancy 1989, *Unruly Practices: Power, Discourse and Gender in Contemporary Social Theory*, Cambridge: Polity Press.

Friedman, Susan Stanford 1988, 'Women's Auto-biographical Selves: Theory and Practice', in *The Private Self: Theory and Practice of Women's Autobiography*, Shari Benstock (ed.), Chapel Hill: University of North Carolina Press, pp. 34–62.

Fuss, Diana 1990, *Essentially Speaking; Feminism, Nature and Difference*, London: Routledge.

Gagnier, Regina 1990, 'Feminist Postmodernism: The End of Feminism or the Ends of Theory', in *Theoretical Perspectives on Sexual Difference*, Deborah L. Rhode (ed.), New Haven: Yale University Press, pp. 21–33.

Gallop, Jane 1982, *Feminism and Psychoanalysis: The Daughter's Seduction*, London: Macmillan.

Gardiner, Judith Kegan 1982, 'On Female Identity and Writing by Women', in *Writing and Sexual Difference*, Elizabeth Abel (ed.), Sussex: Harvester, pp. 177–92.

Gatens, Moira 1991, 'Feminism, Philosophy and Riddles Without Answers', in *A Reader in Feminist Knowledge*, Sneja Gunew (ed.), London: Routledge, pp. 181–200.

Gelder, Ken 1991, 'Aboriginal Narrative and Property', *Meanjin*, 50: 2, 353–65.

Gilligan, Carol 1982, *In a Different Voice: Psychological Theory and Women's Development*, Cambridge, Mass.: Harvard University Press.

Greenaway, Peter 1993, 'Deceiving is Believing', *The Guardian*, 16 September.

Grimshaw, Jean 1988, 'Autonomy and Identity in Feminist Thinking', in *Feminist Perspectives in Philosophy*, Morwenna Griffiths and Margaret Whitford (eds.), Bloomington: Indiana University Press, pp. 90–108.

Grosz, Elizabeth 1994a, 'A Thousand Tiny Sexes: Feminism and Rhizomatics', in *Gilles Deleuze and the Theatre of Philosophy*, Constantin V. Boundas and Dorothea Olkowski (eds.), London: Routledge, pp. 187–212.

1994b, *Volatile Bodies: Towards a Corporeal Feminism*, Sydney: Allen and Unwin.

Gubar, Susan 1989, ' "The Blank Page" and Issues in Female Creativity', in *The New Feminist Criticism: Essays on Women, Literature and Theory*, Elaine Showalter (ed.), London: Virago Press, pp. 292–314.

Haraway, Donna 1991, *Simians, Cyborgs, and Women*, London: Free Association Books.

Hayward, Phillip and Paul Kerr 1987, 'Introduction', *Screen*, 2: 2–10.

Heath, Stephen 1981, *Questions of Cinema*, London: Macmillan Press.

Hekman, Susan J. 1990, *Gender and Knowledge: Elements of a Postmodern Feminism*, Cambridge: Polity Press.

hooks, bell 1989, *Talking Back: Thinking Feminist, Thinking Black*, London: Sheba Feminist Publishers.

Hutcheon, Linda 1985, *Narcissistic Narrative: The Meta-fictional Paradox*, London: Methuen.

1989, *The Politics of Postmodernism*, London: Routledge.

Hutchins, Graham and Christopher Munnion 1995, 'Hilary should stick to the US, says Beijing', *The Daily Telegraph*, 8 September.

Irigaray, Luce 1985, *The Sex which is not One*, Ithaca: Cornell University Press.

Jacobus, Mary 1986, *Reading Woman*, London: Methuen.

Jameson, Fredric 1986, 'Postmodernism, or the Cultural Contradictions of Late Capitalism', *New Left Review*, 146: 53–92.

Jardine, Alice 1985, *Gynesis: Configurations of Women and Modernity*, Ithaca: Cornell University Press.

1993, 'The Demise of Experience: Fiction as Stranger than Truth', in *Postmodernism: A Reader*, Thomas Docherty (ed.), New York: Harvester Wheatsheaf, pp. 433–42.

Johnson, Angela 1995, 'Beijing Diary', *The Guardian*, 5 September.

Johnson, Barbara 1987, *A World of Difference*, Baltimore: Johns Hopkins University Press.

Juhasz, Alexandra 1994, '"They said we were trying to show reality – all I want to show is my video" – The Politics of the Realist, Feminist Documentary', *Screen* 35, 2: 171–90.

Kamuf, Peggy 1980, 'Writing like a Woman', in *Women and Language in Literature and Society*, Sally McConnell-Ginet, Ruth Borker and Nelly Ferman (eds.), New York: Praeger, pp. 284–99.

1988, *Signature Pieces: On the Institution of Authorship*, Ithaca: Cornell University Press.

Kintz, Linda 1989, 'In-different Criticism: "The Deconstructive Parole"', in *The Thinking Muse: Feminism and Modern French Philosophy*, Jeffner Allen and Iris Marion Young (eds.), Bloomington: Indiana University Press, pp. 113–36.

Kolodny, Annette 1989, 'A Map for Rereading: Gender and the Interpretation of Literary Texts' in *The New Feminist Criticism: Essays on Women, Literature and Theory*, Elaine Showalter (ed.), London: Virago Press, pp. 144–67.

Kroker, Arthur and David Cook 1988, *The Postmodern Scene: Excremental Culture and Hyper-Aesthetics*, New York: St. Martin's Press.

Kroker, Arthur and Marilouise Kroker 1988, 'Theses on the Disappearing Body in the Hyper-Modern Condition', in *Body Invaders: Sexuality and the Postmodern Condition*, Arthur Kroker and Marilouise Kroker (eds.), Basingstoke: Macmillan, pp. 20–34

Lacan, Jacques 1977, *Ecrits: A Selection*, London: Tavistock Publications.

1988, *The Seminar of Jacques Lacan: Book II The Ego in Freud's Theory and in the Technique of Psychoanalysis*, Cambridge: Cambridge University Press.

1990, *Feminine Sexuality: Jacques Lacan and the Ecole Freudienne*, Juliet Mitchell and Jacqueline Rose (eds.), Basingstoke: Macmillan.

1991, *The Four Fundamental Concepts of Psychoanalysis*, Harmondsworth: Penguin.

1993, *The Psychoses: The Seminar of Jacques Lacan Book 3 1955–56*, Jacques-Alain Miller (ed.), London: Routledge.

Laclau, Ernesto and Chantal Mouffe 1985, *Hegemony and Socialist Strategy: Towards a Radical Democratic Politics*, London: Verso.

Laplanche, Jean and Jean-Bertrand Pontolis 1986, 'Fantasy and the Origins of Sexuality', in *Formations of Fantasy*, Victor Burgin, James Donald and Cora Kaplan (eds.), London: Methuen, pp. 2–27.

Lash, Scott 1990, *The Sociology of Postmodernism*, London: Routledge.

Lee, Alison 1990, *Realism and Power: Postmodern British Fiction*, London: Routledge.

Legal Action for Women 1992, 'The Child Support Act', unpublished paper.

Levinas, Emmanuel 1979, *Totality and Infinity: An Essay on Exteriority*, The Hague: M. Nijhoff Publishers.

1987, *Time and its Other*, Pittsburgh, PA: Duquesne University Press.

1991, *Otherwise than Being or Beyond Essence*, Dordrecht: Kluwer Academic Publishers.

Lorde, Audre 1980, *Sister Outsider*, Freedom, Calif.: The Crossing Press.

Luckhurst, Roger 1989, 'Shut(ting) the fuck up: Narrating *Blue Velvet* in the Postmodern Frame', *Bête-Noire*, 8–9: 170–82.

Lyotard, Jean-François 1988, *The Differend: Phrases in Dispute*, Manchester: Manchester University Press.

   1989, *The Postmodern Condition: A Report on Knowledge*, Manchester: Manchester University Press.

MacCabe, Colin 1985, *Theoretical Essays: Film, Linguistics, Literature*, Manchester: Manchester University Press.

MacKinnon, Catherine A. 1987, *Feminism Unmodified: Discourses on Life and Law*, Cambridge, Mass.: Harvard University Press.

   1992, 'Privacy v. Equality: Beyond Roe v. Wade', in *Ethics: A Feminist Reader*, Elizabeth Fraser, Jennifer Hornsby and Sabina Lovibond (eds.), Oxford: Blackwell, pp. 351–63.

Malcom, Derek 1993, Review of *Baby of Macon*, *The Guardian*, 16 September.

McClintock, Anne 1994, 'The Angel of Progress: Pitfalls of the Term "Post-Colonialism"', in *Colonial Discourse/Postcolonial Theory*, Francis Barker, Peter Hulme and Margaret Iverson (eds.), Manchester: Manchester University Press, pp. 253–66.

   1995, *Imperial Leather: Race, Gender and Sexuality in the Colonial Context*, London: Routledge.

McGowan, John 1991, *Postmodernism and its Critics*, Ithaca: Cornell University Press.

McHale, Brian 1987, *Postmodernist Fiction*, London: Methuen.

Mepham, John 1991, 'Narratives of Postmodernism', in *Postmodernism and Contemporary Fiction*, Edmund Smyth (ed.), London: Batsford, pp. 138–55.

Metz, Christian 1982, *Psychoanalysis and Cinema: The Imaginary Signifier*, Basingstoke: Macmillan.

Miller, Nancy K. 1989, 'Changing the Subject', in *Coming to Terms: Feminism, Theory, Politics*, Elizabeth Weed (ed.), London: Routledge, pp. 3–16.

Minda, Gary 1995, *Postmodern Legal Movements: Law and Jurisprudence at the Century's End*, New York: New York University Press.

Modleski, Tania 1990, 'Hitchcock, Feminism and the Patriarchal Unconscious', in *Issues in Feminist Film Criticism*. Patricia Evans (ed.), Bloomington: Indiana University Press, pp. 58–75.

Mohanty, Chandra 1991, 'Under Western Eyes: Feminist Scholarship and Colonial Discourses', in *Third World Women and the Politics of Feminism*, Chandra Talpade Mohanty, Ann Russo and Lourdes Torres (eds.), Bloomington: Indiana University Press, pp. 51–80.

Moore, S. 1995, 'It's time for all good women to be party poopers', *The Guardian*, 24 August.

Morgan, Sally 1995, *My Place*, London: Virago Press.

Morris, Meaghan 1988, *The Pirate's Fiancée: Feminism, Reading, Postmodernism*, London: Verso.

Mulvey, Laura 1989, *Visual and Other Pleasures*, Basingstoke: Macmillan.

Nancy, Jean-Luc and Philippe Lacoue-Labarthe 1992, *The Title of the Letter: A Reading of Lacan*, Albany: State University of New York Press.

Norris, Christopher 1990, *What's Wrong with Postmodernism*, Hemel Hempstead: Harvester Wheatsheaf.

1993, 'Old Themes for New Times: Postmodernism, Theory and Cultural Politics', in *Principled Positions: Postmodernism and the Rediscovery of Value*, Judith Squires (ed.), London: Lawrence and Wishart, pp. 151–88.

Owens, Craig 1985, 'The Discourse of Others: Feminists and Postmodernism', in *Postmodern Culture*, Hal Foster (ed.), Sydney: Pluto Press, pp. 57–82.

Patton, Paul 1988, 'Giving up the Ghost: Post-Modernism and Anti-Nihilism', in *It's a Sin: Essays on Postmodernism, Politics and Culture*, Lawrence Grossberg, Tony Fory, Ann Curthay and Paul Patton (eds.), Sydney: Power Publications, pp. 88–95.

Petchesky, Rosalind Pollack 1990, *Abortion and Woman's Choice: The State, Sexuality and Reproductive Freedom*, Boston: North Eastern University Press.

Pettman, Jan 1992, *Living in the Margins: Racism, Sexism and Feminism in Australia*, St Leonards, NSW: Allen and Unwin.

Poovey, Mary 1992, 'The Abortion Question and the Death of Man', in *Feminists Theorize the Political*, Judith Butler and Joan W. Scott (eds.), London: Routledge, pp. 239–56.

Poster, Mark 1995, 'Postmodern Virtualities', in *Cyberspace/Cyberbodies/Cyberpunk: Culture of Technological Embodiment*, Mike Featherstone and Roger Burrows (eds.), London: Sage, pp. 79–96.

Probyn, Elspeth 1996, *Outside Belongings*, New York: Routledge.

Rajan, Rajeswari Sunder 1993, *Real and Imagined Women: Gender, Culture and Post-Colonialism*, London: Routledge.

Rights of Women Bulletin, Spring 1993.

Robinson, Sally 1990, 'Deconstructive Discourse and Sexual Politics: The Feminine and/in Masculine Self-Representation', *Cultural Critique*, 13: 203–27.

Robinson, Stephen 1995, 'Mrs Clinton urged not to visit China', *The Daily Telegraph*, 18 August.

Rodaway, Paul 1995, 'Exploring the Subject in Hyper-Reality', in *Mapping the Subject: Geographies of Cultural Transformation*, Steve Pile and Nigel Thrift (eds.), London: Routledge, pp. 241–66.

Rorty, Richard 1982, *Consequences of Pragmatism*, Sussex: Harvester Press.

Rose, Jacqueline 1985, 'The Cinematic Apparatus: Problems in Current Theory', in *The Cinematic Apparatus*, Teresa de Lauretis and Stephen Heath (eds.), Basingstoke: Macmillan, pp. 172–86.

Ryan, Michael 1989, *Politics and Culture: Working Hypothesis for a Post-Revolutionary Society*, Basingstoke: Macmillan Press.

Schlesinger, Phillip, R. Emerson Dobash, Russell P. Dobash and C. Kay Weaver 1992, *Women Viewing Violence*, London: BFI Publishing.

Schor, Naomi 1989, 'Dreaming Dissymmetry: Barthes, Foucault and Sexual Difference', in *Coming to Terms: Feminism, Theory, Politics*, Elizabeth Weed (ed.), London: Routledge, pp. 47–58.

Sharpe, Jenny 1993, *Allegories of Empire: The Figure of Woman in the Colonial Text*, Minneapolis: University of Minnesota Press.

Sharrett, Christopher 1988, 'Postmodern Narrative Cinema', *Canadian Journal of Political and Social Theory*, 12: 1–2.

Showalter, Elaine 1987, 'Critical Cross-Dressing: Male Feminists and the

Woman of the Year', in *Men in Feminism*, Alice Jardine and Paul Smith (eds.), New York: Methuen. pp. 116–33.

1989, 'Feminist Criticism in the Wilderness', in *The New Feminist Criticism: Essays on Women, Literature and Theory*, Elaine Showalter (ed.), London: Virago Press, pp. 243–70.

Silverman, Kaja 1983, *The Subject of Semiotics*, Oxford: Oxford University Press.

Spelman, Elizabeth V. 1990, *Inessential Woman: Problems of Exclusion in Feminist Thought*, London: Woman's Press.

Spivak, Gayatri Chakravorty 1988, 'Can the Subaltern Speak?', in *Marxism and the Interpretation of Culture*, Cary Nelson and Lawrence Grossberg (eds.), Urbana: University of Illinois Press, pp. 271–313.

1989, 'Feminism and Deconstruction Again: Negotiating with Unacknowledged Masculinism', in *Between Feminism and Psychoanalysis*, Teresa Brennan (ed.), London: Routledge, pp. 206–23.

1995, Translator's preface and afterword, *Imaginary Maps*, Mahasweta Devi, New York: Routledge.

Squires, Judith 1993, *Principled Positions: Postmodernism and the Rediscovery of Value*, London: Lawrence and Wishart.

Stacey, Jackie 1990, 'Desperately Seeking Difference', in *Issues in Feminist Film Criticism*, Patricia Evans (ed.), Bloomington: Indiana University Press, pp. 365–79.

Tiffin, Helen 1988, 'Post-Colonialism, Postmodernism and the Re-habilitation of Post-Colonial History', *Journal of Commonwealth Literature*, 18, 1: 169–81.

Turkle, Sherry 1995, *Life on the Screen: Identity in the Age of the Internet*, New York: Simon & Shuster.

Visweswaran, Kamala 1994, *Fictions of Feminist Ethnography*, Minneapolis: University of Minnesota Press.

Waugh, Patricia 1984, *Meta-Fiction: The Theory and Practice Self-Conscious Fiction*, London and New York: Methuen.

1992, *Practising Postmodernism: Reading Modernism*, London: Edward Arnold.

Whitehouse, Ian Paul 1989, 'A Reading of the Postmodern', PhD. dissertation, Cardiff Arts and Social Studies Library, Cardiff University.

Williams, Patricia 1991, *The Alchemy of Race and Rights: Diary of a Law Professor*, Cambridge, Mass.: Harvard University Press.

Willis, Sharon 1991, 'Special Effects: Sexual and Social Difference in *Wild at Heart*', *Camera Obscura*, 25–6: 275–95.

Wittenburg, Judith-Bryant and Robert Gooding-Williams 1990, 'The "Strange World" of *Blue Velvet*: Conventions, Subversions and the Representation of Women', in *Sexual Politics and Popular Culture*, Diane Raymond (ed.), Ohio: Bowling Green State University Popular Press, pp. 149–58.

Wolf, Margery 1992, *A Thrice Told Tale: Feminism, Postmodernism and Ethnographic Responsibility*, Stanford: Stanford University Press.

Young, Iris Marion 1987, 'Impartiality and the Civic Public: Some Implications of Feminist Critiques of Moral and Political Theory', in *Feminism as Critique: Essays on the Politics of Gender in Late-Capitalist Societies*, Seyla Benhabib and Drucilla Cornell (eds.), Cambridge: Polity Press, pp. 56–76.

1990, *Justice and the Politics of Difference*, Princeton, NJ: Princeton University Press.

Young, Lola 1996, *Fear of the Dark: 'Race', Gender and Sexuality*, London: Routledge.

FILMS CITED

Baby of Macon 1993, Director Peter Greenaway.
Blue Velvet 1986, Director David Lynch.
Wild at Heart 1990, Director David Lynch.

Index

5809895R00137

Printed in Great Britain
by Amazon.co.uk, Ltd.,
Marston Gate.